CW00550683

A Long Way Home

A Long Way Home

Mike Walker

WILEY

Published in 2005 by   John Wiley & Sons, Ltd, The Atrium, Southern Gate
Chichester, West Sussex, PO19 8SQ, England
Phone   (+44) 1243 779777

Copyright © 2005   Mike Walker

Email (for orders and customer service enquires): cs-books@wiley.co.uk
Visit our Home Page on www.wiley.co.uk or www.wiley.com

Other Wiley Editorial Offices

John Wiley & Sons, Inc. 111 River Street, Hoboken, NJ 07030, USA

Jossey-Bass, 989 Market Street, San Francisco, CA 94103-1741, USA

Wiley-VCH Verlag GmbH, Pappellaee 3, D-69469 Weinheim, Germany

John Wiley & Sons Australia, Ltd, 33 Park Road, Milton, Queensland, 4064, Australia

John Wiley & Sons (Asia) Pte Ltd, 2 Clementi Loop #02-01, Jin Xing Distripark,
Singapore 129809

John Wiley & Sons Canada Ltd, 22 Worcester Road, Etobicoke, Ontario, Canada, M9W
1L1

Wiley also publishes its books in a variety of electronic formats. Some content that
appears in print may not be available in electronic books.

Library of Congress Cataloging-in-Publication Data

(to follow)

British Library Cataloguing in Publication Data

A catalogue record for this book is available from the British Library
ISBN 0-470-09346-3 (hb)

Typeset in $9\frac{1}{2}$/14pt New Baskerville by Mathematical Composition Setters Ltd, Salisbury,
Wiltshire.
Printed and bound in Great Britain by T.J. International, Padstow, Cornwall.
This book is printed on acid-free paper responsibly manufactured from sustainable
forestry in which at least two trees are planted for each one used for paper production.
10 9 8 7 6 5 4 3 2 1

Contents

Note to Readers

A glossary of eighteenth-century slang can be found on pages 381–398.

The terms used for British currency are now less familiar than they once were. Sterling consisted of pounds, shillings and pence; twelve pence made one shilling and twenty shillings a pound. A farthing was worth a quarter of a penny; two shillings and sixpence was often called a half crown and a guinea was worth a pound and a shilling. Modern equivalents for eighteenth-century values are almost impossible to work out.

In Memory

MICHAEL WALKER

Executed opposite Smart's Buildings, Holborn, London, 18th of December, 1786, for Murder. MICHAEL WALKER, Richard Payne and Robert Cox were members of a young but desperate gang of street-robbers. Cox was not quite fifteen years of age. On the 17th of November, 1786, Mr Robinson was walking with his friend, Mr Hunt, a painter, through Smart's Buildings, Holborn, when the latter, feeling something at his pocket, seized a man's hand. Yet the villain was dextrous enough to convey what he had stolen to an accomplice whom Mr Hunt instantly collared, and a general scuffle ensued. Mr Robinson was dreadfully wounded and was carried home in a mangled condition, with little hope of his recovery. In a short time the malefactors above named were apprehended, and sworn to by both the sufferers.

Mr Robinson soon after died of his wounds. The malefactors were convicted and, unpitied, suffered the sentence of the law. For this purpose a temporary gibbet was erected opposite Smart's Buildings. Payne appeared in a state of stupidity. Cox, the boy, cried bitterly; and when he came within sight of the gallows he screamed, and was in a state of distraction when turned off. Walker was greatly affected at his fate, and held a book in his hand, which some said was a Bible and others a full record of his crimes.[1]

Yet others said it was nothing more than a farrago of lies and inventions.

Openings

'I told him it would be a life in *scenes*.'

James Boswell, *Journals*

Mary

~ JULY 1792

ondon is by any accounting the biggest city in the kingdom. So far as its citizens, now approaching a million, are concerned, it is the richest and greatest city in the world. To be tired of it is to be tired of life. To wander its streets is to see something so complex, so full of vitality and change, of light and dark, kindness and cruelty that it is akin to being within the body of a thing alive in its own right.

If the parks with their walks and ordered gardens are its lungs; if Westminster is its mind, though a mind often in selfish and partial disarray; if the great markets like Smithfield, where the gutters brim with the blood of a thousand slaughtered animals, are its stomach; if its lust runs riot in Haymarket and Drury Lane and its purses empty themselves in the dressmakers, tailors and goldsmiths of Ludgate Hill; if the Thames, an artery almost choked now with the rich fat of trade, runs with its sluggish, avaricious lifeblood; if its hospitals like St George's or the London cut into its body with dirty steel and kill or cure pretty much by chance; if Bedlam clamps iron bands around the heads of its madness, then the vast organ of undiscriminating pain and punishment that is Newgate Prison is its dark, secret heart. It beats at the very centre of daily life with a visible urgency, informing every citizen that if once it should stop working, the city will be consumed by a seething, maggoty mass of riot, revolution, anarchy, crime and horror.

It draws the curious, the concerned and the connoisseur of last moments too, now that they've moved the gallows from Tyburn Field to the prison yard. No more progresses of the condemned along

Oxford Street inflaming the lower sort, who might all too easily repay the compliment, as they did only a dozen years ago, burning Newgate for Lord George Gordon and his lost Catholic cause; not that the crowds had any particular opinion on the religious issue but they do love a riot, the London mob, a bit of a song and dance.

When the old prison was rebuilt, the deadly tree was replanted within its walls on the principle that if the spectacle did drive the audience to sedition, they were handy for the law courts next door at the Bailey. It was also easier to charge and seat spectators. For where there is money to be made, then the Londoner is there to make it, and what more enticing than a pretty neck in a noose or a fine young cavalier of the highways expiring in a moment both private and yet so satisfyingly public? As Mr Gay richly puts it in his *Beggar's Opera*: 'If any wench Venus's girdle wear, though she be never so ugly; lilies and roses will quickly appear and her face look wondrous smugly. Beneath the left ear, so fit but a cord (a rope so charming a zone is) a youth in a cart has the air of a Lord and we cry: There dies an Adonis!'

Always a good show at the King's Head Inn, as the flash mob call Newgate, and on this last day of June 1792 it promises to be something terrific! Adventure, heroism, a convict maid, desperate villains, a voyage, a thrilling trial and a hanging certain to come: who could want for more? Certainly not the crowd gathering in the yard outside the office of magistrate Nicholas Bond, who will today take depositions and give direction for the future entertainment of the audience.

And what an audience – hundreds of 'em, seething with impatience under the low, boiling clouds of a heavy summer day. There are many of the respectable sort, ladies and gents and tradesmen too; there are adam-tilers and dips on the lookout for loose pockets; young bucks, their aggressive cropped hair sending the message 'Stand clear, cully or I'll thump you like Mendoza!'; writers from the journals and newspapers – sad, broken-down fellows, stained with ink and hunched after years of ill-paid, ill-lit hackery; apprentices, snuck out of work because they've heard the tales of the pretty girl and her convict gang and consider the sight worth a beating; lechers, eager to press themselves against females brazen enough to wear the new fashion in clinging skirts that leave so very little to the imagination; anglers sitting on the high walls around, lowering their hooks on thin twine to snatch wipes and hats; the gingerbread man pushing through with his tray full of Banbury cakes: 'Only the cakes from May to July, Cully, you wants the ginger, come back in August and don't ask my why, or I'll black your eye!' There are hot rolls for a penny, mackerel for a shilling at this time of day, 'but come back later, Jerry, and you can have em for half that.' The town and his wife and the whole flash mob are waiting for the doors to open.

Open they do and the mob surges through – but in a thoroughly decorous and British way, none of your French practices here, except in the fashions, of course. Down the corridor they flow and into the magistrate's office where they settle out like water in a trough, finding their level and filling every crevice of the dark, wooden-panelled chamber. It is, like the prison and courts at the Bailey, expressly made to evoke the highest and sternest qualities of the law; levity is to be left outside, here matters of life and death are to be decided.

The magistrate enters with his various functionaries and seats himself behind his oak desk. The audience falls silent under his professional glance: this, he seems to be saying, is not a circus, it is a business, the business of the law. His severity might also have something to do with the stifling atmosphere in the room: the low clouds are still boiling without, trapping the heat of the last few days and withholding the relief of a storm. Sweat drips from beneath wigs and hats – the roaring boys are glad of their close crops – and thick broadcloth absorbs it and becomes heavier and thicker; powder clots; thin skirts and expensive silk breeches begin to creep up buttocks, stocks are loosened and fans fanned but to little effect.

At last, after arranging his damp papers, Mr Bond calls for the accused to be brought out. They have been waiting for hours. They were brought across from the prison just after dawn. Their comfort is not at question here, only their presence and their fate.

She enters first and a shiver goes through everyone present and they all crane forward because somehow she seems smaller than they imagined; smaller but still with the quality that gleams from someone who is known by everyone in the room and yet knows none of them. It is celebrity, and in this first great age of the press, pencils race over drawing blocks and nibs scratch and splatter in the haste to capture who and what she is, this Mary Bryant.

Thin as well as short, dark haired, in her twenties but looking older, her complexion sallow but, withal, something about her grey eyes, the way she holds herself, the style of her clothes, prison stuff, certainly, but recut and sewn to a degree that shows she cares what she looks like today. Her companions enter behind her but are scarcely noticed: the crowd closes around them, all attention focused upon the small woman who walks calmly to her place and stands waiting with the air of one who has waited an age already and still has the patience to wait some more.

Tipstaffs flash and a few heads are bruised as the four remaining prisoners are propelled through the closely packed bodies into their places around the woman. Mr Bond looks up at them, quizzically, as his clerk delivers the bare facts of the matter: That Mary Bryant, James Martin, Nathaniel Lilley, John Butcher and William Allen did, with persons now deceased, escape from the colony at Port Jackson, Botany Bay, to which they had been lawfully sentenced. That they should be here examined and if cause is found, should be tried at the Old Bailey for this offence and (unspoken but deafening every ear in the room) that the inevitable and only sentence for such a crime is hanging by the neck.

In the silence after the quiet, professional reading of the words, come questions: where do you escape to from Botany Bay? Surely the place is the far south of the human race, nothing beyond it save ice, nothing around it save sea for thousands of miles? Who were these others not here today – wasn't there a child, two children and a husband to this woman amongst them? And how is it that these five are still alive and standing?

Magistrate Bond asks the questions and the answers, from the woman, are quiet, without drama or fuss, almost as if these were everyday things that anyone might cope with had the circumstances been different.

Yes, sir, she had been taken up by the authorities for a robbery on the highway out of Plymouth. She had been sentenced to death but this was set aside and she was given seven years. She was sent to the hulks at Devonport for three years, during which time she fell pregnant. She was taken up and sent to London where she was put aboard a transport for New South Wales. She survived the journey and once arrived had been lodged with the other women convicts and put to work. She began a liason with one William Bryant, a fisherman and, under the insistence of the governor, the two were married before Bryant's sentence was completed. She had a second child with Bryant and when the colony ran out of food and starvation threatened, she, Bryant and seven others decided to escape. She and Bryant stole a twenty-foot open boat and provisions and, with their companions, sailed more than three thousand miles to East Timor where they gave themselves out to be shipwrecked mariners. She was accepted by the Dutch governor as being what she claimed but drink and loose talk gave their secret away and they were imprisoned in conditions which brought about the death of her husband and her youngest child, Emmanuel. She and her companions were given into the custody of Captain Edwards, who was seeking out the *Bounty* mutineers, and he put them in irons aboard his ship and transported them back to Britain, during which time her daughter Charlotte died and was buried at sea. She freely admits that in all matters relating to the escape her voice was foremost. She says she sincerely repents of her original offence. She says she would rather die than go back to New South Wales. She falls silent.

The room, too, is silent; so much has been said – but so much remains unsaid.

The men are questioned, their stories much the same as hers, confirming not only the facts but also the resolution of this woman: 'She has shown greater courage and resource than any of us, sir.'

This is a crowd with a heart, a crowd that can turn in an instant from bloodlust to sentiment, and this is the flowering of the age of sentiment. A warm feeling suffuses the audience – a collection is suggested, money passes from hand to hand, is gathered in a purse and handed to the prisoners. Mr Bond does not call for order. He considers the matter and thanks the five standing before him, particularly Mrs Bryant. He is not, he says, ready yet to send them for trial; he is not, he forbears from saying, ready yet to send them to the execution chamber at Newgate where they will hang by the neck until they are dead. He is not ready but what can be done? What can mercy do, what can sentiment conspire that will not cause this dark heart of justice to miss a beat?

'Take them away,' he says.

Arthur

There is no sight in the world, he thinks, the equal of mighty ships in line of battle bearing down upon the enemy. Vast pyramids of white sail towering into the blue Mediterranean sky, an intricate web of ropes, sheets and lines, worked by thousands of sailors swarming up ratlines and into the highest tops, edging out along the spars, reefing in and letting out the great billows of canvas, catching every cupful of wind to gain the weather gauge and dictate the action.

Far below on deck, the officers, each with half an eye on the admiral at the rear of the line, are sending up message flags like a firework display at Vauxhall. Each one of them is willing the fleet towards the French, caught between the van of the British line and the coast of Minorca where a small but valiant British garrison are holding out against a French army. Surely soon battle will be joined, just as long as the Frenchies don't turn tail and run for safety. Once more the Royal Navy will prove its value to a grateful nation and prize money will lubricate the inns and whores of Portsmouth.

Flying fish skim in and out of the crystal bow wave thrown up by the *Buckingham*, fourth in line, a sixty-eight gun second-rate commanded by Captain Everitt, a distant cousin of Arthur's mother. That's why he's here on board, his heart thumping at the thought that in a few minutes he'll have chance to show his mettle, to make his reputation in a great victory. And he has a reputation and a way to make, for beyond getting that first step on the rope ladder, there is no more influence in his family; his father is dead, his mother and sister are living an existence of genteel poverty. It is down to the seventeen-year-old youth to make the family fortune and he has every intention of doing just that. Rated able and serving as ship's corporal, his station is under the very eye of Admiral West, commanding the van and second in command to Admiral Byng aboard *Ramilles* at the rear of the line.

In the various messes below, in the days before the action, the talk has all been of the French and their rascally attempts to meddle in His Majesty's North American colonies. Warnings have been issued, Admiral Hawke has sailed with orders to take and hold French ships of war as well as merchantmen as a guarantee of better behaviour in the future, but the Frogs have taken no notice – worse, they have invaded British territory: the strategically vital island of Minorca. The government and the Lords of the Admiralty have decided it is time to give them a bloody nose and Admiral Byng is the man to don the silk drawers and put up his derbies – or is he?

Just yesterday, when news of the French Fleet's position was brought by a fast-running snow, Byng's first move was to dispatch Captain Hervey and the *Phoenix* to see if the fleet could slip past the French and into the harbour at Port Mahon. Now why, the question has shot round *Buckingham* like the spark in a quick match, would he do something like that rather than square up to 'Monsewer Crapeau', yardarm to yardarm and blast away; and how would such a landfall, even if it happened, allow them to relieve the besieged garrison at Port St Phillip? As it turned out, the French sailed faster than expected, and Captain Hervey was able to report that it would be impossible to gain the harbour, so those questions were left begging. But now they are to join battle, it is equally difficult not to wonder at the Admiral's tactics.

The fleets are approaching each other like the two arms of a V. *Defiance, Portland, Lancaster* and *Buckingham* in the van will soon be within cannon shot of the leading French ships and at this speed, dashing through the seas as they are, it will not be much longer before boarding and fighting it out man to man will become a real possibility. And yet the second and third divisions of the fleet, its main strength, are at such extreme range at the open end of the V that they may not be able to inflict damage upon the enemy at all. Nor does there seem to be any plan for the second division to pass through the French Fleet, effectively cutting it in two, so that the rear division can engage at their leisure, turning the battle into a series of ship-to-ship contests in which the British, being British, must inevitably prevail.

Arthur has made a study of naval tactics, as has every enthusiastic young fellow in the British Fleet, and has a bad feeling about today. In the last war, the one over Mr Jenkins's ear, cut off by Papists in Spain, there was a great engagement between the British and the Spanish and French Fleets at Toulon. Lord Hawke and Admiral Anson commanded but so hedged about were they by instructions from their Lordships of the Admiralty that they were hardly able to move a bomb-ketch without getting a letter of authorisation. The battle was a stalemate, neither British commander was able to show the dash and fire that later distinguished their careers and confounded their opponents. The enemy got away on that day – might they get away again today?

The wind is increasing, the sails shiver and draw and the mainmast creaks. *Buckingham* heels slightly, following the line of the three ships in front of her. In the tops, the marines steady themselves and make sure they've removed the ramrods from their musket barrels; below, Arthur can imagine the officers moving hunched along the 'tween deck, checking each gun is aligned, that the balls waiting to be loaded for the second broadside have been chipped smooth of rust and that the slow and quick match is glowing and ready.

Along the sweep of the upper decks everything that can be stowed is stowed, otherwise it is lashed down; hammocks are puddinged along the bulwarks, netting has been strung under the rigging to prevent falling blocks dashing out the brains of those men underneath. Buckets of water and sand stand ready, the crews crouch round the great guns. A lookout high above hails the deck: the admiral is showing the red flag, it is the signal to engage.

The French have seen the signal too and they fire at once, long broadsides rippling down the length of their ships, flashes obscured almost immediately by smoke and followed by a huge roar as tons of metal smash into the wooden walls of the *Buckingham,* sending out a curtain of splinters, vicious shards of wood up to three or four feet long. The balls passing overhead buzz like vast bumblebees; ropes part, lines and blocks fall into the netting, there are screams and shouts and an odd sound, like curtain rods shimmering through the air, and Arthur realises this is the noise of musket balls fired from the French tops. There is a smell like ... like a hundred rotten eggs broken at once. The noise is immense, it seems to suck all the air out of the world as it passes, making his ears pop, and then it's gone.

In the stiff breeze, the smoke clears in moments, showing the French – he can see now, it is the *Sage* – are still there as plain as you like, the gun crews slewing their carriages to follow the target as they reload and then another ripple of fire and the smoke springs up and the whole world is once again filled with crashing and that stink of old eggs.

At last, Admiral West nods and Captain Everitt gives the command: 'Fire as you bear!' Arthur notes down the time. *Buckingham* comes about, closing rapidly on the *Sage* until Arthur can see the muzzles of their guns as huge as ogres' eyes. He jumps as the carronade closest to him fires with an unimaginable noise, then the others along the upper deck follow and they don't seem so loud at all. Perhaps he's getting used to it? It's only when Captain West shouts to him to deliver a note to the first lieutenant below on the gun deck that he realises he's gone virtually deaf.

As he hares off, he hopes his hearing will return but this is a matter of little importance beside the glimpse he gets, through the smoke, of the British ships astern of *Buckingham.* None of them appear to be firing yet. And *Ramilles* has laid aback her maintops and, it being the admiral's ship, the rest of the divisions, those unengaged, are obliged to do likewise, which can only mean they will not come up to the action any time soon. Then the smoke returns and with it the smashing impact of another broadside and he is thrown down the hatchway onto the upper gun deck.

He lands in a pool of blood and brains. Looking up he sees daylight and smoke through a ragged breach in the ship's timbers. One of the great guns is lying on its side, blown clean out of its carriage. The noise down here, even to his muffled hearing, is indescribable; peering about he can hardly see through the smoke but what he can make out reminds him of pictures he's seen of Pandemonium: naked backs straining against intolerable weights, muscles standing out like blades; lightning flickering from port to starboard; faces distorted and sweating, bellowing hoarse-voiced commands and curses. The eggy stink of sulphur from the gunpowder is so strong it coats the insides of his mouth and his throat until he too yells and struggles aft, towards a glimpse of blue and white that might indicate the first lieutenant.

Someone grabs his collar and jerks him back at tremendous speed and the guns go off again, the broadside more ragged but still thunderous, like Jove himself is trapped in the 'tween decks. The black iron bulk of a twenty-four pounder appears from nowhere out of the smoke, recoiling in front of him, truck wheels squealing. It comes to a shuddering stop, straining its ropes to the limit. He hears the hoarse call: 'Two, six, heave,' as the sweating gun crew reload and haul it back into position. Had he not been pulled out of the way, he would have been no more than a smear of blood and gristle under the monster's wheels. He turns to thank his saviour but there is no one there, just the long sweep of the deck, like the throat of Hell itself. He staggers on and delivers the note, noticing it is smeared with blood. Not his own, he prays. The first lieutenant, his face grey and pitted with tiny specks of black powder, acknowledges it and calls out for every gun crew to look alive, they're about to engage a second Frenchie, maybe even a third. A ragged cheer goes up. It's clear nobody is thinking straight down here today.

Arthur is lost, surely the forces are equal, have the French been joined by more ships? The lieutenant has no time for the boy and pushes him back towards the steps. He's knocked down yet again, picks himself up and struggles back up to the main deck, breathing in deeply – even this polluted air is a relief after the horrors below. He notices the masts are still standing, no spars have fallen yet, for all the noise and flying shot, *Buckingham* seems to be suffering little damage. But that is about to change: out of the smoke to port appears a second

French ship, its guns run out and ready to fire. He throws himself flat as once more that huge sound punches the air and all around him the hiss and slither of canister shot tears anyone in its path to rags of flesh and splinters of bone. *Buckingham* returns the broadside, though diminished, since a good quarter of her guns have been silenced by now.

Where is Admiral Byng and the rest of the fleet? Why have they not engaged the enemy? Another storm of shot: along the deck, this time. The French ships are everywhere, the British outnumbered and outgunned. Arthur gets back to the main deck where Admiral West and Captain Everitt stand wonderfully tall and untouched amidst the flying shot and splinters. Their faces, however, tell the story: stern, angry, wondering, like every other man in the van of the British fleet, where is that bugger Byng? Why does he not come up and engage closely?

A broken cable-end whips past the little group. If it had caught anyone, it would have sliced them in half. Captain Everitt sends Arthur to gather enough men to bend it fast. He hurries off through the din and the smoke into a world of flying metal and confusion, shot through by moments of clarity: a marine falling from the rigging almost at attention, his musket clasped to his side; the clang of a ball hitting the ship's bell; a bucket of water from which he scoops up a handful and drinks and finds it the best he's ever drunk; a sailor looking stupidly at the end of his arm where there is no longer a hand; the great golden stern of a French ship suddenly vanishing under a broadside, wood and glass swept away like so much paper in a roaring fire; and blood, everywhere blood in sprays and slicks, painting canvas and staining uniforms, running along the scuppers like water, dripping from the rigging, so much blood, smelling of ink or iron and then, as the day stretches out and the sun glares down, the smell changing to something out of Hell's own butchers that attracts hoards of flies, risen from nowhere, unaffected by the mayhem all around.

Then it stops.

Within five minutes, there is quiet, comparative quiet: men still cry out, one of the pigs squeals from below, officers shout and parties of men hurry off under the carpenter, bosun, sailmaker and surgeon to make good the damage. And for those who have come through it all, there is that moment of sheer amazement, of re-introducing oneself to the world and saying 'Well, after all that, here I am!'.

And where are the French? They have broken off the engagement and are sailing away. They could have closed and caused great damage, even taken many of the British ships in the van. They did not; no one knows why but everyone is grateful. The second and third British divisions are coming up at last; some of them, at least, have been firing but none has been at close quarters with the enemy. On the *Ramilles*, the admiral sends a signal: 'All captains to the flagship.' Perhaps now he will make plain his strategy.

When Admiral West and Captain Everitt return from the conference, they are clearly dissatisfied. Orders are given: make ready to come about and set sail for Gibraltar. Arthur is not alone in his confusion. The whole point of the expedition is to relieve the British garrison; they have, through luck or chance, avoided defeat by the French, surely the thing to do now is proceed to the fort and complete the mission? But it is not to be. Admiral Byng has, so it is whispered by those who were in the long boat and overheard the protests, asked such questions of his captain that the only possible answer has been to agree with his plan to preserve the fleet: in other words, turn tail and run, leaving the marines manning the ramparts to inevitable defeat and surrender.

There is not a man in the fleet – apart from Byng – who does not feel scalding shame at this behaviour. They can hardly look one another in the eye. Never mind what the letter of the Admiralty orders might be, any man of spirit would press on and damn the consequences, make a landfall and relieve his countrymen. For those in the van, who have acquitted themselves with courage and resolution, furious anger is added to the cauldron of their resentment: their sacrifice and effort has all been for nothing. Those in the second and third divisions have not even the comfort of a hard-fought battle: a few long-range broadsides, a hole or two in their sails are all their battle honours. Even the canvas breaking out, white against the blue sky, does not bring its usual exhilaration. It is a deeply wounded fleet that creeps back to Gibraltar and, as long as John Byng remains at its head, the gangrene from the injury will fester and spread.

It is a lesson Arthur takes to heart: the actions of one man can make a vital difference to the conduct and morale of thousands.

The actions of one man can also be laid before him and he will have to answer not only to his own conscience but to the laws of his country. At Gibraltar, Byng is relieved of his command. Men turn their heads away and offer the departing admiral the least honour they can under King's Regulations. He is sent home to face a court martial and the proceedings are followed avidly by all and none more so than Arthur, who writes to his sister of the admiral's downright cowardice.

Further reflections bring Arthur to the consideration that matters are rarely as simple as they appear at first. Orders given by their Lordships of the Admiralty did not allow Byng – who, admittedly, had little inclination to do so in the first place – to go beyond certain bounds and exercise his own ingenuity. The war is unpopular at home. There were to be no adventures, no risks, nothing drawing public attention to the costs in men and machinery. However, there were to be no consequences either and now that there are, one thing is certain: their lordships will not be the ones to pay: the man on the quarterdeck is going to be stuck with the accounting for this meal.

So it turns out. The court martial has no choice but to find Byng guilty of neglect of duty and, under article twelve of King's Regulations, sentence him to death. They recommend mercy. The government, which is employing its agents to ferment a nationwide hue and cry against Byng and for the war with Spain and France, cannot throw down its cards now; there is always a compliant judge or twelve to hand and the sentence is upheld. He will be shot on the quarterdeck of the *Monarch* in Portsmouth harbour. Arthur reads of the execution in the journals:

> '*About noon the admiral walked out of the great cabin onto the quarterdeck, where two files of marines were ready to execute the sentence. He had a*

firm and resolute step, a composed countenance and was resolved to suffer with his face uncovered until his friends told him that his look would intimidate the soldiers and prevent their aiming properly. He submitted to their request, threw his hat on the deck, kneeled upon a cushion, tied one white handkerchief about his eyes and dropped the other as a signal to his executioners. They fired a volley so decisive that five balls passed through his body and he fell down dead in an instant. The time between his walking out of the cabin and being deposited in his coffin, did not exceed three minutes.'

Jamie

~ MAY 1763

ames finds a good position on the wooden seats overlooking the gallows at Tyburn Tree; he's come early because he knows there'll be a crowd: a highwayman is to be turned off and a show like that always fills up the bleachers early. The pie sellers are already out in force and the savoury smell of pork and beef and bacon add to the tang of juniper and point up the crisp morning air like perfume on a beautiful woman. And 'Miss' is certainly here today in all her abundance – a sea of hat-brims and feathers bobbing and flowing around stalls and booths: a glorious, he thinks, effulgence of femininity, enough to make a man quite faint.

But he is here as an observer and looking past the soft swell of cottons and dimities, tabbies and poplin, he sees an apple seller holding up a ripe red fruit with one hand whilst guarding his barrow from thieves with the other. Boys with nothing better to do are rooting and rioting amongst the people, getting under men's feet and women's skirts. A biscuit seller, his early morning basket ringed with candle-holders, the candles used and guttered now, packs up and heads for home, his wares sold long since. A young whore, sitting with her sisters in a cart, peels an orange in an unbroken yellow curl and he just knows he can smell the zest on the wind.

A pigeon flutters overhead, a message canister tied to its leg: it means the condemned have passed through Oxford Street and are on their final furlong. The hangman takes a last puff or two at his pipe and knocks out the dottle against the gallows post, scuffing the still-glowing tobacco worms with the sole of his boot. He doesn't want to burn the old tree down before it has fruited. He tucks the pipe into his hat-band, pulls up his breeches and planting his feet firmly apart, waits for his good customers.

The rising hum of the crowd announces the appearance of the cart; an ordinary hay cart it appears, crowded with the condemned, the coffins and a priest-for-hire praying away as if his fee depended upon it, which it does. The wind is riffling the pages of his prayer book but it makes no difference, he has this stuff by heart and could as well be reciting the office in a hurricano. But it's not Mr Bollocks the crowd has come to see, it's Paul Lewis, alias Captain Lewis, all flashing smiles and dashing silks, snapping pistoleros and snorting horses; so genteel, so slim and, like Jamie, just twenty-two years old. Now it becomes clear why so many young women are here today, waving their handkerchiefs, sighing as if they are the ones about to expire!

It might almost be worth it, Jamie thinks, to be Captain Lewis in that cart, the hero, the cavalier of today, just perfectly the High Toby in white silk coat and breeches set off with a deep blue and silver waistcoat, his shoes shone to a brilliance and his hat, black with silver lace, smartly cocked over hair so neatly curled that he must have sacrificed a good few of his last moments to the barber. The bonds he wears he hardly seems to notice: he shrugs off the cart and straw and the coffins piled longwise next to him. He looks out over the crowd with a serene expression, favouring now one, now another lady with a nod or a smile. There is, Jamie thinks, almost nothing they wouldn't do for him now, these women; there is, to be honest, almost nothing Jamie himself wouldn't do for that calm figure standing at the centre of this storm of sentiment.

What has brought this Adonis to the deadly tree? Buying a copy of *The Last Confession of Captain Lewis* from a vendor he reads that it was not want or cruel circumstance but nature herself that formed his character. Young Paul was the son of a worthy clergyman who was sent to grammar school where he had the ambition to become a fine gentleman. He ran up bills to his tailor to the amount of £150 and unable to pay, ran away, as many a young fellow has, to sea. In this new occupation it appeared he was able to make something of himself, being firstly rated midshipman and not long after passing for lieutenant in the Royal Navy. He served with distinction in the squadron under Admiral Hawke and was present at the Battle of Cancale Bay and the Siege of Guadalupe in the recent wars, where he acted with all the courage and activity the nation expects of its tars.

It was at this moment of achievement that temptation called and was heeded: charged with buying stores for his fellow officers to provision a voyage to India, Lieutenant Lewis collected three guineas from each – but once the yellow boys were in his purse all the old vicious inclinations rose again and he deserted his ship with the money and ran for the land, setting himself up as highwayman in the localities of Newington and Southwark.

His first robbery might have been his last, for he was taken and brought to trial. But so strong an impression had his charm made upon the his new companions around the drinking houses and cellars, that they forswore themselves, saying he had been with them and not on the Heath wielding his pistols. After this he committed a variety of robberies, on one occasion discharging his lock at a gentleman trying to escape, though fortunately the weapon misfired. He was taken, finally, by Mr Pope, a constable who, hearing that Lewis was abroad, rode on to the Heath where he interrupted a robbery and pursued and threw the highwayman from his horse. Despite Lewis then presenting a pistol, Mr Pope struggled with the villain, took the gun from him and apprehended him.

Captain Lewis was brought to trial at the Old Bailey and received sentence of death. It is some measure of his viciousness that when his heartbroken father, the worthy clergyman (it could be a novel, Jamie thinks, or on the stage at Drury Lane) visited his son and gave him twelve guineas for his necessaries, the wretch concealed a coin in his sleeve and, opening his hand, showed the grieving and vulnerable old man that there were only eleven guineas, and thus tricked a thirteenth from his father.

Jamie folds the paper and slips it in his pocket. That business with the father strikes home. He has often enough been called ungrateful and uncaring himself but at least he's never drawn a pistol upon anyone yet and hopes he never will.

The cart stops under the scaffold. The crowd presses forward as if they would enclose the condemned man, absorb him. He takes a step back, the hangman reaches out a hand to steady him and whispers something in his ear. Paul Lewis straightens his back and looks around for the last time and as he does so, something changes. That handsome face, so like Jamie's own, takes on a look of pure and inexpressible anguish. It is as if, for the first time, Paul realises that he lives in a world that exists apart from himself: here he stands, his feet in the dirty straw on the bottom of the cart and there is all London, that smoky old town; there are two boys in the crowd, fighting, not even aware of his fate; there is a young man of his own age sitting high on the bleachers clutching a notebook; there is a girl with a face so beautiful it might break your heart to look at it; and, in just a minute from now, he will not be here and yet all of this will go on without him.

The hangman offers the neck of a brandy bottle and the condemned gulps eagerly. The spirit burns going down, recalling Paul to himself. All he has to do is get through it without disgrace. He speaks his last words. He wrote them himself, rather than hiring one of the hacks who hang around the condemned cell. It seems his grammar school has stood him in good stead at last. 'This dreadful sight will not, I believe, invite any of you to come here by following my example; but rather to be warned by me. I am but twenty-two years of age, a clergyman's son, bred up among gentlemen, and this wounds me the deeper. For to whom much is given, from them, much is required.'

In the crowd a young girl sighs and subsides into the arms of her companions. The hangman steps forward, slips on the hood and places the noose around the neck of Captain Paul Lewis, High Toby. He nods to the carter, who flicks a whip at the nag; the cart jerks forward and the body swings out and falls straight, no cry or movement, and hangs twisting about as the nether member makes its last salute to life.

Tears trickle down tender cheeks, hearts aflutter at such an end. But Jamie sits as if struck by lightning: it is himself he has seen there on the scaffold, his own unruly member straining the silk of his breeches, it is himself, James Boswell, that he has seen falling into hell and damnation. His curiosity has been rewarded with horror. He wants to go back to his rooms and touch everything he owns, he wants get up and leave this place but he can't, he's rooted to the spot and he realises: there were two coffins on the cart, two for 'Jack Ketch' today, and the second is not going quietly.

Noticing her when the cart arrived, he thought: a large, unconcerned being, but now she's anything but unconcerned. An anger as big and powerful as her frame seems to possess her. Her name is Hannah Dagoe, a flower seller, an Irishwoman and a Roman Catholic of no great piety, if the Popish priest falling from the cart after a buffet from Hanna is anything to go by. Sentenced to death for robbery, she has stood quiet through Captain Lewis's end but now her fury has come to the surface; it is not that she wants to escape, but that somehow she wishes to vent her spite against the whole wide world before she goes.

An idler seated next to Jamie mentions that Dagoe stabbed the fellow who peached on her and was the terror of her fellow prisoners. Jamie can believe it as she rips her hands from the cords that restrain them and, bloody-wristed, grabs the hangman and spits into his face, daring him to hang her, the damned little scrub! The crowd is no longer in sentimental mood, half of them are shouting her on, the others shouting her down.

She takes off her hat and cloak, rips off neckerchief and apron and sails them out over the mob, laughing in the hangman's face as she denies him his perquisites. The Popish priest is hiding under the cart, a couple of constables hop up beside Hannah to restrain her whilst Jack Ketch struggles to get the hood and noose over her neck. She fights like a fury, her mighty fists making mayhem, her toothless mouth open, bellowing a stream of curses against God and all His creation.

Whilst the constables hold her arms against her body – both are big fellows and they are having to struggle – the hangman slips the noose over Hannah's head. The touch of the hemp gives her extra strength: she shakes the constables off like fleas, sending them tumbling in the hay, then thrusting her hand inside her skirt, she pulls a handkerchief from a pocket and after glaring again at the hangman, presses it against her face and, with a last howl of fury, throws herself from the cart with such desperate energy that when she reaches the end of her leap and the noose tightens, her neck breaks with an audible crack and she hangs stone dead.

The Story

'I felt a completion of happiness. I just sat and hugged myself in my own mind.'

James Boswell, *Journals*

James Boswell

It is a fine day in the summer of 1763 and James Boswell is strolling down the Haymarket. He's passing the Theatre Royal on his left and pauses to give the playbill a quick glance since, in his time, he's been devoted, besotted with the theatre and considers himself something of a critic.

Just lately he and a couple of friends have published a cutting review of *Elvira*, a tragedy by one Malloch, a Scottish gentleman who has changed his name and accent and now tries to pass himself off as an Englishman! There is, in the eyes of Boswell and his friends, no worse crime than this, though the tragedy, with its touching orphaned children – 'We would suggest to Mr Malloch introducing into one of his future productions the whole of the Foundling Hospital ... which would certainly call forth the warmest tears of pity and the bitterest emotions of distress' – runs it close.

The review made a small splash but young Mr Boswell, he's twenty-three, has recently made greater waves with a series of letters he and his co-critic Andrew Erskine have published, letters that reflect their high spirits and wit and intelligence and sophistication – they think.

Others are not so sure. Lord Eglinton, a friend of his feared and puritanical father Lord Auchinleck, mutters angrily that he wishes young Jamie would 'give over with that damned publishing'. And as for Erskine: 'I wonder at him, for he seems to be a douce, sagacious fellow.'

Boswell says disarmingly: 'Poor fellow, my lord, I've led him into this scrape. I've persuaded him.'

'He cannot be very sensible,' Lord E replies, 'if you have persuaded him.'

Boswell isn't sure upon which of the friends this reflects worse but tries to defend them both, exampling the letters of Madame de Sévigné as being about very little but of very great literary value.

'Yes, a few at the beginning; but when you read on, you think her a damned tiresome bitch.'

So much for literature.

It's probably just as well that young Jamie is spending a year in London since his odour at home is not of the best. But that's a problem for the future and not beyond solution. He has a feeling there is not much in this world that he cannot achieve or cozen into acquiescence with a pleasant face, an accommodating manner and his own unique genius. And this is fortunate, since there are a great many things in this world James Boswell wants very much indeed.

When he's five years old he passionately wants the Jacobites and Bonnie Prince Charlie to come marching in triumph to Arthur's Seat in Edinburgh and despite, or in spite, of his mother and father, he wears a white cockade and prays for King James – until his uncle, General Cochrane, gives him a shilling to pray for King George instead.

When he's eight he wants, just as passionately, to be ill so he can leave Mundell's school where he's learning Latin, English, Writing and Arithmetic but what he learns best is to touch his mother's heart with aches and pains. Instead of running around like a boy should he stays in bed and slumps in chairs, pale, anxious, ill, always ill, until his dear mamma lets him off school and keeps him warm and tucks him in and feeds him sweets and hot drinks and provides all sorts of pretty things to amuse him.

She also slips in little doses of guilt with the sugared plums, since she's a follower of George Whitefield, a hell-and-damnation Protestant who gives it up with the best of them when he preaches, roaring and red in the face, sweating with guilt and bellowing redemption. Quite a lot of Scottish gentleman don't really like these theatrics, particularly since actors are seen and often charged as vagrants, but he goes down well with mamma and other ladies, who don't get out to the theatre much, if at all. Mamma did go once but never again; she decided to lace her theatrics with predestination.

As well as the guilt, there is another thing for Jamie, a thing about truth, because somewhere in his tender soul his loved and feared and terrifying and magnificent father has planted the seed of truth (a hearty beating ... talking of the dishonour of lying) and this presents a problem. He cannot lie and yet, if he is to stay off school, he must be ill. What is to be done? He hangs his head down towards the floor and, by and by, a headache arrives, it's that simple, too simple, and at last it's decided to educate little Jamie at home.

When he's twelve, contrary as ever, he wants to get well. A new tutor has been engaged, Joseph Fergusson, a dry stick of a man, disappointed in his career as cleric, angry with the world and with the spoiled, intelligent child he's expected to educate. His lessons become eternities of fear and loathing for the boy, a foretaste of Calvinist doom where the spider trapped on the shovel is held above the burning fire in perpetual anticipation of suffering, intolerable suffering which must be tolerated for ever and ever. And there's nothing like fearful anticipation for summoning the black melancholy that has long been an unacknowledged member of the family. Jamie's younger brother John is already behaving oddly, his grandfather on his mother's side was illfaur'd and rarely happy, and now the patient himself is diagnosed as suffering from an extraordinary nervous illness.

Does the madhouse beckon, will he be shut away in a windowless room? At twelve all things are possible but what happens, after the best doctors in Scotland are called in, is a dose of common sense: he is sent to the spa at Moffat to drink the waters and, far more efficacious as it turns out, meet the other visitors on walks and at games of bowls and cards and in conversation. It does the trick, he is insensibly cured.

At thirteen he wants to know everything about the amorous passion that has his temperament in its grip. For instance, as he later wrote in his *Sketches*: 'In climbing trees pleasure, Could not conceive what it was. Thoughts of heaven. Returned often, climbed, felt, allowed myself to fall from high branches in ecstasy – all natural. Spoke of it to the Gardener.' Who, rigid with embarrassment, was unable to elucidate but made damned sure he didn't work under the trees when the young master was about.

Then there's love with Miss Mackay, a wonderful, spiritual emotion that brings out his better feeling and evokes withering contempt from the dour Mr Fergusson, still around but no longer so feared.

And following on from trees and Miss Mackay, 'the fatal practice': a small sin compared with fornication but, so far, the only one he can set his ambitious hand to and there is the risk that even the smallest sin, if repeated ad infinitum might grow into something very big indeed. He wonders if he should follow the example of the Christian Martyrs and cut off the offending member – but only, fortunately, for a moment or two; then the madness passes. The pleasure remains. It's a lesson for life, he thinks.

At sixteen, studying now at Edinburgh University, he wants to break out from the prison of shyness and make friends with two other boys, an Englishman named Temple, of the most worthy and amiable character, and a Scot named Johnstone, whose character is masculine and hearty. John Johnstone happens to be a very snappy dresser and it's the flash yellow lining of his coat that first catches Jamie's eye. He's a bit of bravo – not too much but just right for the retiring Boswell boy – and amenable and thus tends to agree with most of what his new friend suggests. He also shares a grand regard for Scottish history.

William Temple is English but only just, coming from the border town of Berwick-upon-Tweed. He's scholarly and the two friends talk about literature and religion; he is charming where Johnstone is bluff, and charm, as Jamie learns, is a powerful weapon. Temple is inclined to periods of depression during which the two friends walk the 'black dog' together and call each other Jimmy and Willie and tell each other everything there is to tell in a way that Willie will never do again in his life and of which Jimmy will make a habit. Perhaps it is for the best, though neither would think it as they stroll chattering past Arthur's Seat, that Willie's ambition is to attend Cambridge University and become an Anglican priest in some quiet country living. The two swear lifelong friendship and vow to keep in touch by letter, no bad thing, Jimmy reckons, if his amorous plans turn out as he hopes; his confessions will be easier for Temple to accept off the page than eye to eye.

When he's eighteen he wants to be a High Toby like Mr Gay's creation Captain McHeath with his gang of flash coves nimming and forking and moon-cursing the respectable folks. A bit of houghmagandie wouldn't go amiss, either, though he's already cultivating actresses at the theatre near the Cannongate that his friend Lord Summerville is supporting and where he recently saw the Magnificent Digges in the very role of McHeath:

> *If the heart is depressed with cares,*
> *The mist is dispelled when a woman appears;*
> *Like the notes of a fiddle she sweetly, sweetly,*
> *Raises the spirits and charms our ears,*
> *Roses and lilies her cheeks disclose,*
> *But her ripe lips are more sweet than those.*
> *Press her,*
> *Caress her,*
> *With blisses,*
> *Her kisses*
> *Dissolve us in pleasure and soft repose.*

Perhaps the theatre-hating Syndics of Edinburgh have a point: there's no telling where this kind of thing might lead, except that it's far more likely to take a fellow down wide, whore-infested Drury Lane than through the straight gate and along the narrow way to salvation's shore. Young Boswell loves it: the flaring gas lamps, the spectators piled high in the pit, flinging orange peel and nosegays at the stage; Jamie himself entertaining the *canaille* with cow impressions (cries of 'encore the cow' from the gods) the strutting actors with their pistols at the cock and the actresses, painted and powdered, all plunging necklines and silk stockings, playing delicious Polly Peachum, Dolly Trull, Sukie Tawdry and Jenny Diver.

At twenty he wants to live in London and convert to Roman Catholicism. In fact he is living in London, at the top of the Haymarket where he'll be walking one sunny day in three years time but now, in 1760, he's staying at the Lemon Tree Inn, just up from the Haymarket Theatre, which is providing a tempting stop on the Road to Rome. How did it happen, this sudden rush of holiness to the head which has driven the father into a seething rage – and no one seethes like Lord Auchinleck – and the son over three hundred miles on horseback to London? It's woman, a Mrs Cowper, one of those actresses, a good ten years older than the young man who has fallen head over heels in love with her and, quite reasonably, he feels, her 'Catholacism' as well.

Perhaps because Mrs Cowper has not allowed her admirer to prove the strength of his passion in the manner most befitting a twenty-year-old, he's redirected his enthusiasm towards religion and flaunted pamphlets and prayers about the house with predictable results. As his father points out, there's very little a professing Catholic can actually do in Great Britain. No career in the army or the navy, in the law (for which Jamie is meant to be studying), in parliament, the church; he cannot even inherit the family estate.

The youth gives not a fig and sets off for London with the address of a priest who will instruct him and set him upon his journey to Rome (he's thinking of becoming a monk) but not before he's got something half-way decent to repent and renounce.

In town he bumps into an old friend from Edinburgh who shows him the temptations of the world: fame – he meets Garrick and Laurence Sterne who has just published *Tristram Shandy*; theatre – he attends every performance he can manage; high life – his father's good friend Lord Eglinton finds him decent lodgings and provides good company, fine food and great wines as well as getting him into the Jockey Club; sex – in the beguiling person of Miss Sally Forrester who, in a room just off the Strand, lets him, for the first time, go all the way! Rome doesn't stand a chance.

James Boswell is beginning to feel, for all his Scottish pride, that a little bit of his heart will be forever English amongst the great, the gallant and the ingenious. And then there's the army. The Guards, to be exact. Social standing, a neat uniform and not a lot of actual fighting to be done. He lets his father know his change of plans. Lord Auchinleck tears his hair and moans: 'What have I done to deserve this?' He knows this new enthusiasm will cause endless trouble but reflects that at least it will be better for the family name than an apostate on his way to Rome. Boswell is hurried back to Scotland to complete his studies in law but he has learnt a lesson more important than torts: people actually like him in London. He is an agreeable young fellow, someone to invite back. And that is no mean thing in this world.

A year later, still in Edinburgh, he's thinking of:

~ *A glorious career as a Guards officer.*
~ *Social success.*
~ *The favour of politicians.*
~ *The adoration of beautiful, rich ladies.*
~ *Visiting stately homes.*
~ *Reading men and their weaknesses.*
~ *Mastery of science.*
~ *And the arts.*
~ *Touring Europe.*
~ *Being received at foreign courts.*
~ *Returning to brief the Prime Minister.*
~ *Becoming a secretary of state.*
~ *Raising a regiment.*
~ *Repelling an invasion.*
~ *Marrying beauty and one hundred thousand pounds.*
~ *Having many children of whom he can be proud.*
~ *Being universally loved and respected.*

~ *Honoured by all.*
~ *Painted and sculpted.*

It's one thing after another but, realistically, he'll be content with getting back to London, with its infinite variety keeping the mind lively, and meeting its most famous citizen, Dr Samuel Johnson.

He's read all the essays published in Johnson's monthly magazine, the *Rambler*, and absorbed their lessons, and the good doctor is by no means reluctant to offer lessons and exhortations to his readers: 'He writes like a teacher, he dictates to his readers, they attend with awe and admiration.' It's one of the aspects of the man that most attracts Boswell; that and his almost universal knowledge, attested by Boswell's friend Thomas Sheridan who celebrates the great man's commanding authority in conversation (and no one, least of all Johnson himself, is in any doubt that Ursa Major, the Great Bear, the Cham of literature is indeed a Great Man).

And then there's Lord Auchinleck's opinion that Dr Johnson is an overrated, pompous windbag, which adds the marmalade to the rowie for his son. The fact that Johnson returns the sentiment – 'Oats: a grain which in England is generally given to horses, but in Scotland supports the people' – is not going to prove too great a hurdle for the enthusiasm of James Boswell: he hopes.

May, 1763, and Boswell is visiting a new acquaintance, Tom Davies, an actor and bookseller who has a shop just off Covent Garden. He's back in London; his father has given his reluctant blessing and set up a legal disbar that will not, ever, allow his wayward son to fully inherit and thus waste his patrimony. There's a bastard child, of one Peggy Doig, a servant girl, who Boswell has tupped, paid off and more or less forgotten; there's a great philosopher, David Hume, miffed at Boswell's reportage of private conversations in the letters he has published with Erskine, though Boswell maintains it wasn't David Hume to whom he referred but quite another Scottish philosopher who, by an odd coincidence, also happens to be called David Hume;

there's hopes of finally getting that commission in the Guards; and, above all, there's the chance of meeting the Great Man.

So far, though, to be honest – and Jamie is trying very hard to be honest, writing himself notes on deportment, putting down his impressions in a journal – that quest has not gone well. He had counted on his friend Sheridan to be the means to his satisfaction but Sheridan is out of favour at present; one of those sudden, violent squalls that is always liable to brew up in the great man's vicinity. Tom Davies, however, is a good friend of Johnson's and has promised to introduce Mr Boswell, though a number of planned meetings have already fallen through and, on this May evening, the bookseller and the would-be Guardsman have no other aim in view than a companionable cup of tea and a chat in the back parlour of the bookshop.

Leaning in his chair, keeping an eye out for customers through the glass door, Davies suddenly leaps to his feet and announces, being something of a wag: 'Lo! He comes!' A shadow falls across the parlour, a vast shape cuts off the light from the shop and, as Boswell springs to his feet and the glass door crashes, very nearly smashes, open – Johnson is in the room. Nothing in his reading, in the tales he's heard, not even in his wildest imagination, has prepared Boswell for what he is about to receive.

First there is the sheer bulk of the man: not so much the arms, which are long, the legs, shorter; but a great head and a face, looming like a pitted and scarred moon and the body itself, a mighty block of planetary size, whirling into the space of the parlour, threatening to draw in and crush everything in its vicinity by gravity alone. Then there is the linen, the broadcloth coat, the breeches and shoes, the wig, the absolute – to a young man of more than fastidious personal taste – Africa of stains and smuts and smears and crusts and the dust of months and the gatherings of the streets and the remains of meals large and small and claret and port and brandy and snuff, a complete history of the gustatory world through which Johnson has passed over the last few days.

All this is as nothing, merely stage dressing for the character: lumbering, hunched, twitching, jerking, juddering, mumbling, shouting out nonsense words, shambling but to some strange pattern known only to himself; approaching the door counting the number of footsteps, the floorboards, his arms flailing, the hands going through series of repetitious movements ... and then Tom Davies announces 'Sir, here is Mr Boswell.'

The great shape turns.

Jamie, through his shock and awe, remembers Johnson's fabled dislike of Scotsmen and mumbles to his friend 'Don't tell him where I come from.'

Davies is a joker. He adds: 'From Scotland.'

Silence falls like the dust of ages. Boswell realises he has to come up with something fast or this meeting is going to be over before it has begun and, for all the shock produced by the physical presence of the man, by the fact that he could easily be taken for a Bedlamite out on a visit, Boswell still believes there is much to be gained from an acquaintance.

He searches for something clever, witty, disarming or disingenuous to say. He manages: 'I do indeed come from Scotland but I cannot help it.' Limp he thinks, very limp indeed. So does Johnson.

'That, sir, is what I find a very great many of your countrymen cannot help.' And he turns his back, and a very big back it is, and starts talking to Davies about a complimentary theatre ticket Garrick has declined to offer.

Boswell realises this man can be seriously rude. He's an artist of rude, a Shakespeare of rude, the Great Cham of rude bourn aloft on a spluttering, drenching sea of spittle: but Boswell also reckons that he himself is the champion jockey of persistence. Having been thrown off the conversation, he jumps right back on: 'Oh, sir, I cannot think Mr Garrick would grudge such a trifle to you.'

'I have known David Garrick [approaching squall] longer than you have done, sir, [rain storm] and I know no right you have to talk to me on the subject [hurricano!]'

A lesser fellow would have been washed away but Boswell is no ordinary cove; not only does he have his own particular genius waiting to bloom but he is now a five-times-a-night man. It happened a few months ago with a twenty-four-year-old actress called Louisa. She too had spurned his attentions at first but by dint of charm, a timely loan and persistence he persuaded the young lady to accompany him to an inn not a hundred yards from the very bookshop he waits in today. A cold January evening it was and whilst Louisa's maid got her out of corset and petticoats, Jamie took a turn in the inn yard: the night was very dark and very cold. He experienced for some minutes the rigours of the season, that he might make a transition from such dreary thoughts to the most delicious feelings. And so he did, slipping back inside the inn and softly into the room and thence into Louisa and 'five times was I fairly lost in supreme rapture!'

Johnson booms on but Boswell is certain that this Great Bear is no more proof against charm and flattery than pretty Louisa, in fact, when it's a question of slipping the flattery softly in, writers of fifty are no more sophisticated than girls of twenty.

It works. Johnson starts to feel guilty, as he often does, for his cruelty. He is not a cruel man by nature, quite the opposite: his rudeness is a defence. Like many who are afflicted with physical symptoms that might well appear to be those of a maniac or simpleton (as painterly Hogarth thought, though only on first acquaintance) Johnson sets warning traps for the unkind, his sallies are spring guns and only the hardy and true will risk venturing onto his estate. This young man, it seems, is one such and Johnson begins to include him in the conversation. Boswell makes little steps, being pleasant, offering no crass opinions, allowing the bear to lead the dance. And after Johnson leaves, Tom Davies says 'He likes you.'

Two weeks later Boswell beards the giant in his den in Temple Lane where he is received pleasantly and, when he leaves, Johnson shakes his hand.

On his next visit, two weeks later – he's playing it carefully – he brings up that first terrible put-down. 'Poh, poh, never mention these things. Come to me as often as you can. I shall be glad to see you.' A few days after this the two bump into each other – by accident or design – at a chophouse and arrange to have supper together at the Mitre Inn, just round the corner from Johnson's house. It's a real advance and as he walks down Fleet Street that evening, past Lintot's Bookshop and Hoare's Bank, James Boswell reflects that now he has the friendship he's desired, he really ought to mend his ways and try and live up to Samuel Johnson, particularly in matters of sexual morality. After all, has not the Divine Creator Himself ordained marriage for the mutual comfort of the sexes and the procreation and right education of children?

Which is perhaps why, on this summer day as he strolls down the Haymarket, his hopes and desires either achieved or a good way towards being so, the thing he really wants most in the world, of everything that this great city contains, this very moment, is to fuck the strong, jolly young damsel he sees loitering under the awning of the theatre. She wears a large floppy-brimmed hat which shades her twinkling eyes and curls which frame her pretty round face – she could be a milkmaid, with that simple but artful dress, though no maid that Jamie knows would have such flounces framing a plump and powdered bosom that would blind a man with delight if she hadn't draped a modest neckerchief across the shelf. Her dress, he notices, with its padding and hoops and the hint of the vertical festoons, owes something to Mrs Pritchard, recently seen again in London reprising her famous role as Clorinda in *The Suspicious Husband*.

Catching the maid's eye and receiving a sparkling smile in return, he is certain that she is what she is and not some respectable miss out in the fashion which such girls are affecting nowadays, to the confusion of many a sporting gent. She holds a hand behind her back and touches forefinger to thumb, making a circle, an O, confirming that she indeed looking for a 'friend'.

He thinks it would be a fine thing to do it standing on Westminster Bridge with the Thames flowing past underneath. And if there's one thing certain about London, it's that money can buy you, if not anything, then certainly a game pullet; in a trice the price is paid and Boswell takes his queen of the afternoon down the busy street, towards New Palace Yard from which point the new bridge starts its passage across the river.

Jenny or Suki or Molly, he isn't sure what her name is and doesn't really care, is concerned about the piers. People say they aren't safe. Boswell is mightily pleased at the thought that his rogering might bring down a bridge but reassures Betty or Sophie that the thing will assuredly stand, the stories come from the watermen who are losing trade and she need have no fears. And here they are, looking out over the ferries and wherries, Diana or Dolly or is it Polly leaning over as he lifts her skirts, petticoat and shift, unlaces his breeches – he wore the drop-fronts today, can it be by accident? – slips on the armour and plunges home. It feels good, no fumble-fingers he, Captain McHeath could not discharge his pistoleros with such brio!

A few days later Signor Gonorrhoea comes to call. Jamie decides to mend his ways. Again.

Mary Broad

How many miles to Babylon?
Three score miles and ten.
And can I get there by candlelight?
Yes, and back again.
If your feet are nimble and light,
You can get there by candlelight.

nd there's the sea which is always there and her mamma tells her to be careful of the water because it takes things away, it takes people away and she says it takes her dadda away and mamma says yes, but it brings him back, thank the Lord but sometimes those it takes never come home again.

A smell, what's the smell? It's good and warm and it tickles her nose and she looks up at the table so far above and sees mamma cutting yellow bread and dadda's strong hands reach down and lift her up and set her on his knee and there's the smell of salt and fish and tar and cake, not bread but yellow cake and she asks what that smell is that's so strong and mamma says it's saffron and dadda tells her a story about traders a long time ago who brought flowers from somewhere a long way away and the flowers were yellow and called crocus but when she eats the cake she forgets all about the story and when she tries to remember it later, she can't.

There's a horse in the streets and lots of noise and it frightens her but she wants to see what it is anyway so while mamma is putting on her new bonnet, she slips out of the cottage and hurries along the wall by the churchyard which is shady and smells damp but at the end she comes out into a square and there it is, leaping and snorting and waggling its head as boys and girls run shrieking around it, rushing in to touch and run away and even the grown up people are laughing and reaching out to touch the horse and all at once it stops and its big, wiggly-waggly head turns and looks down at her and she tries to shrink back into the shadows so it can't see her but she knows it can with its big eyes and its huge massive teeth and it starts to stamp and snort and buck, steel hooves striking sparks from the cobblestones, coming closer and closer and she keeps quiet as a mouse hoping it may go by but all the time she knows that she is in the terrible eye and ... Mamma lifts her up and suddenly it's only a little horse and mamma tells her it's a hobby horse, cloth and sticks with some wild boys inside it making it work and off it goes, clip-clop, with the crowd following, laughing and shouting 'Horsie, horsie ...'

And this and this ... her father's hands pull and twist the tarry thread, knotting faster than her eyes can follow, making good the tear in the net. He laughs and says they're filling the net with holes. She laughs too, even though her knots are slow and clumsy compared to his and her hands are beginning to hurt where the twine bites into them. He tells her not to fret, soon enough her hands will get used to the work and her back won't ache as she bends over the net. She won't even notice what she's doing, it'll come that natural to her. He has a stubby clay pipe between his chapped lips, no tobacco in it this afternoon, just a habit, he says, to keep a man happy.

She looks up from the nets. The tide is running in between the rocks and the stones, the seaweed and scraps of wood too small to salvage. The harbour is in shadow, the sun going down behind St Catherine's Fort on the headland but out between the two curving arms of the bay the sea is still bright and blue, as if it goes on forever and once the land was behind you, there would no reason ever to stop sailing.

She wonders what's out there at the end of everything and thinks about asking her father but stays silent, because he doesn't like those kinds of questions. No more does her mother. 'What's the point,' she says, 'of asking what can't be answered?' But if Mary holds up her right hand and brings the thumb and first finger almost together, they cover the land and seem to hold the sea, glittering, beckoning, in the O – then the calm water changes, churning as if a whole school of pilchard is passing between the heads, but it isn't fish, just the huge old chain that is hauled up from the sea bottom every night and hangs between the heads so no harm can come in or go out of the harbour.

Her father slaps her hand, not hard but enough to remind her where her fingers should be, twisting and knotting, and where her eyes should be – looking down at her work.

Winter evenings she sits with her mother and her big sister Dolly close to the candle, cutting down and sewing dresses and petticoats and darning stockings, telling old stories and rhymes and listening to the wind outside, whipping up and down the narrow, winding lanes of the town until it gets lost and begins to howl.

The girls think of their father somewhere at sea and hope he's safe. Needles catch the candlelight as they swoop and rise, like silvery mackerel sounding, making new seams in old cloth and Dolly says that tomorrow they'll go down to Readymoney Bay, where gold coins from the Spanish Armada still wash up after storms. Angrily their mother asks when anyone last found a dubloon or a piece of eight with the King of Spain's head on it. They'd do better to go out collecting furze for the fire, but mother has never been happy since their little brother died and neither of the girls looks up from their sewing.

Later, when they go to bed in their corner of the room, they play at being treasure hunters and wonder what they would do if they found the Pope's gold. Maybe they'd just be rich like the Rashlieghs and the Treffrys who have coaches to ride in and fine big houses and silver on their shoes and go to London to sit in parliament and see the King. That would be something, they think, but Dolly thinks being married would be better. Mary asks who but Dolly doesn't know, someone nice, she hopes, who will buy her a new bonnet and a new dress and on their wedding night all the boys in the town will gather under their windows to make rough music, banging cans and kettles and pans.

To make a Saffron Cake: Take a quarter of a peck of fine flour, a pound and a half of butter, three ounces of caraway seeds, and six eggs; beat well a quarter of an ounce of cloves and mace together very fine, a pennyworth of cinnamon bark, a pound of sugar, a pennyworth of rosewater, a pennyworth of saffron, a pint and a half of yeast, and a quart of milk; mix all together lightly with your hands thus; first boil the milk and butter, scum off the butter and mix it with the flour and a little of the milk, stir the yeast into the rest and strain it; mix it with your flour, put in your seed and spice, rose water, tincture of saffron, sugar and eggs; beat all up with your hands very lightly, and bake it in a hoop or pan, minding to butter the pan well; it will take an hour and a half in a quick oven; you may leave out the seed if you chuse it, and I think it the best.[2]

But they have no caraway, no clove and mace nor any cinnamon, nor sugar or rosewater, no fine flour, only a little coarse put by, no butter and only a farthing's worth of saffron because who has more in these times. Even the oven, Mary says, is slow. Her mother clips her round the head and tells her not to be so smart: 'smart will make you smart but it won't make you full!'

At the Ship Inn, the Mayor is giving a dinner and there's a hog's cheek at two shillings and a roast duck at one; lobsters here come cheap at ninepence and a piece of beef, well cooked at three shillings and six. Neat's tongues for two shillings, stewed pears at one and six, cream and tarts and mince pies at five shillings and butter at four. Tea and coffee, two shillings; ale, cider, punch and spirits – seven shillings and sixpence.

And she listens at the window, late that night, when the gentlemen go by, heavy heels cracking thin winter ice as they step carefully across the cobbles and the steam of their hot breath hangs in the frozen air and, after they have gone to their carriages, drifts away like tatters in the moonlight.

The wind catches them as they pass between the heads, the small boat heels alarmingly and she slides across the coiled rope, grazing her knee and almost slipping over the side. The deep blue water racing by makes her dizzy and she can feel herself falling forward. Her father grabs a handful of bodice and pulls her back aboard, sitting her down by the tiller. 'Take it,' he tells her, 'hold it steady, don't let the wind have its way.' Even as he talks, he's slacking off a line to the big sail which shivers as they fetch. He shows her how to run close-hauled without tacking for a pace or two before he lets go and the sail is caught aback, and they gybe before the boat finds her way and comes upright. The tiller bar, which had pressed against her ribs giving her, she's sure, a nasty bruise, now seems to move easily. 'Try it,' her father says, 'we're going to tack across the wind ...' The first time she tries, they miss stays but her father is patient and they try again and again until: 'See, that's how you do it,' and the sail draws, filling with wind. The boom steadies as he belays the line and the boat gathers way, the bow rising as it begins to race through the water, turning a long white furrow in its wake. 'Hold her steady, steady now, don't push against the wind or it'll break your arm.'

He's a good teacher and she's a good learner. This is something she likes, sitting in the stern of the little boat making it go this way and that with a touch of her hand; the sun now this side of the mast, now that as they yaw and tack, catching the westerly, heading down the channel and away from the little town and the hills that surround it on all sides, heading west, her father says, heading for the ocean.

And then it's time to turn back.

The church is cold even when it's full of people and a March Sunday sun is shining outside and it's so big from where they sit at the back on the hard seats that she can hardly see past all the heads to the front. That must be why they have the pulpit, made from the wood of a Spanish galleon and specially blessed in case any Popery hung around the timber, right up high so everyone can see the Vicar or maybe so that the Reverend Mr Corey can see all of them.

She doesn't want to be here smelling the old stone and the incense and the dust. So she looks up at the roof with its beams like the bones of a fish coming off the spine. It's an old roof, someone told her, and special, but where she's sitting, everything is old and nothing is special.

Bored, she starts to count the beams – she's not very fast at numbers, she's never been to school, but she can count because in all sorts of ways you have to. She can't read or write and she doesn't see any reason why she should. Soon she'll be old enough to go into good service at a local house or on a farm somewhere, maybe as a dairymaid and then she can think about getting married and ... one, two, three, four, five ...

Here they come, all the important people in the town. First of all the mace bearer, Mr Paine, strutting like a pug who's just won the All England championship, holding up the mace as if to say 'Do what I tell you or I'll give you such a whack your ears will ring for a month come Sunday!' Six, seven, eight ...

Then the mayor and the aldermen, following the mace like kings in a fairy tale, their heads held so high they must be counting the roof beams too and how their curled and powdered wigs and the little black velvet hats stay on, she can't imagine. And their long gowns with fur at collar and cuff and hem – how much stitching and how many candles would that need? – and peeking under the fur, the square points of their big buckled shoes ... nine, ten, eleven, twelve ...

And altogether they sit down in a row, their backs to everyone else in the church except the Rashlieghs and the Treffrys, who have their own private pews and only the vicar stands above them – on Sundays – and for the rest of the time only King George and God. That's the way of it. Thirteen, fourteen, fifteen, sixteen ...

And why not? It seems to Mary a very good way to be because ... just because that's the way it is. Was that sixteen or was it seventeen? Maybe she'll go back and start over again. One, two, three ...

Maybe she could be a maid in one of the big houses in town, that would be something, a maid at the Treffry's house! She might catch the eye of the young master and then and then ... There must be places and work for willing hands, as her mother says, and her hands are willing and she's not shy of hard work ... four, five, six ...

Glass on the pavements one fine morning early. Broken windows
as she hurries along the narrow street to the bakers. Cockades lying
crushed in the gutters, grey and blue, Whigs and Tories, but it makes
no difference to her which way such things go and she hardly notices
as she hurries on by.

Cousin Puckey says there's a war. Cousin Puckey says all the boys will
want to go for soldiers or for sailors but Mary doesn't think many of
them look ready to leave. What she does notice are the fishermen, the
boatmen, all the young fellows keeping a weather eye on the heads in
case a ship of the navy should come sailing through and steal them all
away.

   She remembers stories about fairies who would come in the night
and steal human babies and leave one of their own, something long
and strange in the crib in exchange but her father says these infernal
bumerees aren't fairies, they're the press gang and if ever Mary should
gaze out to sea and notice a ship standing in to shore that she doesn't
recognise, smart and Portsmouth-rigged, then let her run like the wind
and raise the warning and the men will hide inland and the fishwives
will be out in anger like they was down in Newlyn, to pelt the sailors
with rotten pilchards: 'Ho! Jack, your dancing days aren't over yet –
you had best lead a few outsides, cross-overs and foot it out of Fowey
before I can say black to your eye!'

Arthur Phillip

pril 1st 1765, the Portuguese frigate *Nossa Senhora de Pilar*, twenty-eight guns, a hundred and twenty-eight crew, flying north before the wind, all sails set including studding sails and skyscrapers; the captain stands by the helmsman, intensely aware of the gusts of the following wind, the drag of the sea, the risk of a line parting, canvas splitting or a spar carrying away, any one of a hundred accidents that would slow him down and lose him the prize they are dashing after.

The gutterings of the south-east trades are blowing strong, perhaps too strong. He rests a hand on the mainmast stay and feels the tension in the cable; it's thrumming like an iron bar which a legion of blacksmiths are beating with their hammers. He looks across at the frigate *Prezares*, heeling as she drives into the long Atlantic swell, and points upwards, indicating that he's going to take in his skyscrapers. Her captain, young Jose de Mello, waves agreement.

A word to the first lieutenant in fluent Portuguese and the command goes out: sailors swarm up to the highest crosstree, the inverted triangles of canvas are taken in, the bow settles slightly and the vibration in the preventer lessens. Is their progress just that little bit easier, are they beginning to gain on the chase? On the *Prezares* the skyscrapers shiver and fold under the ministration of her topmen and from here, Captain Phillip can see clearly that the other frigate is settling and gaining a little. He can hear De Mello urging his men on, as if he hears the roar of the broadside already.

Captain Arthur Phillip, at thirty-nine, knows that nothing is certain at sea except that nothing is certain. And that the chase hull down on the horizon is a seventy-gun Spanish second-rate newly off the slips at the yards in Cadiz, and could blow both frigates to matchwood with a single broadside. He also knows that the Portuguese squadron sailing in his wake is making no serious effort to overhaul the Spanish ship because every captain in the fleet, apart from De Mello and himself, has been infected with the defeatism of the commodore, Robert M'Douall, another English sailor, but one who, in Phillip's mind, and often enough on his lips, is a disgrace to the traditions of the Royal Navy.

Two weeks before a Spanish packet had been captured and the dispatches found before her commander could weight them and throw them overboard. They announced the imminent arrival at Montevideo of two seventy-gun ships. Once docked, they will renew stores and water and head south for the disputed island of Santa Caterina, to reinforce the Spanish Fleet. It is, Captain Philip maintains, imperative to stop them before they tip the balance of sea power in the South Atlantic firmly in favour of the Spanish.

How does he come to be here, inspiring a Portuguese crew to supreme efforts in pursuit of a vastly superior enemy? He is not what anyone would call an inspiring figure; no Hawke or Anson standing over six feet and square-shouldered on the aft deck scanning the horizon with keen blue eyes. He is, in looks, a very ordinary man; smallish, slim, round-shouldered, with a rather long and lugubrious face, a somewhat drooping lower lip and a long nose which you might call Jewish if Jews were not forbidden to be officers in the Royal Navy.

He is, in fact, half German. His father, Jakob Phillip, was a language teacher from Frankfurt; his mother, Elizabeth Breach, the widow of a navy officer. She became a widow a second time when Jakob died leaving Arthur and his sister poor and without prospects. His mother, calling on her old connections, applied for the boy to attend the Navy School at Greenwich Hospital on the Thames. He was accepted and his future was settled.

It had long been understood by those in power that whilst influence and preference were not, on the whole, any bar to rising in the army – after all, it takes no particular talent for a man to stand still and be shot at – when he is put in charge of an expensive item like a ship, lack of practical knowledge can easily send a hundred-thousand-guineas' worth of technology and firepower to the bottom of the sea. So the boys at Greenwich have the basics of navigation and working a ship drummed and often tanned into them; they also learn to get on with their fellows, not to make a fuss or blub because they're away from home, wash their face and hands every morning and their feet on Saturdays, to mumble on Sundays something approximating the thirty-nine articles of the Church of England and to recite, with absolute accuracy, the King's Regulations of the Royal Navy.

At the age of fifteen Arthur Phillip leaves school with his books and instruments of navigation, a couple of pea jackets, two waistcoats (serge and Kersey), a pair of best breeches and a pair for everyday, a drugget coat and matching breeches, five shirts – two white, three coloured – a hat, a cap and two pairs of shoes and an apprenticeship on a whaling vessel bound for northern waters.

The whaler's captain, William Readhead, is a hard driver, he has to be: the *Fortune* will be whaling in Arctic waters where a man overboard is a man frozen in seconds and hidden ice shelves project hundreds of yards beyond their bergs, ready to sink the inattentive. It is a world of white on white, where the endless, empty brightness of ice and sky make it impossible to judge distance and tire eyes which search every daylight second for the tell-tale sounding of their prey. And once harpooned and killed, the great whales must be dragged alongside and skinned – apprentices like Arthur slip and slide on the stinking carcase, struggling with yards of heavy blubber stripped off by the razor-sharp tools of the flensers, manhandling it into the boats and struggling to get it hooked and swung up on the whaler's decks where it can be fed into the huge rendering pots.

In the still, cold air the greasy black smoke from the operation hangs above the ship like something solid; the smell and the oil permeate every thread of cloth and piece of meat or bread until no

one aboard smells or tastes it any more. It becomes a background
to the backbreaking labour and the man or boy who isn't strong will
sooner or later break down under the strain.

Arthur isn't strong but he has a dogged will and the intelligence to
know that somehow he must get through this voyage without showing
his weakness; whalers have no compassion for those who don't pull
their weight or their blubber. He does so but in lasting out, he
reinforces a natural reticence: the less you tell your mates the less you
have to live down, or live up to. Do the job, day after day; stand your
watches, keep alert despite crippling tiredness. Haul on the block and
tackle as the great slabs of meat are winched aboard and never mind
what you feel about it, for feeling has nothing to do with the practical
business of being a sailor. It doesn't reef a sail or take a sounding; it
only gets in the way when you have to make it plain that this is where
you sling your hammock and devil take the next fellow; and when it
comes to pushing your arms into stinking blubber up to the chest, it is
of no practical value at all.

And perhaps you lose something of yourself in the process but
Arthur Phillip, as he steps ashore having survived his first voyage,
doesn't miss it. A second voyage comes around and he finds he's
beginning to settle to the life of a whaler but it isn't what he wants –
he wants to join the Royal Navy, where an ambitious man without too
much sensibility can make a real career for himself – and the French
are about to provide him with the opportunity.

Expanding in the Americas, France cannot but avoid rubbing up
against British interests and, by the by, give a young general called
Washington a little practice for the future. War is declared and Arthur
joins *Buckingham*, a first-rate commanded by a distant cousin of his
mother's, Captain Michael Everitt. He is rated captain's servant, little
more than a waister but one with pretensions of gentility who might, if
he strives and survives, rise to midshipman.

He sees bloody battle under the unfortunate Admiral Byng off the
coast of Minorca but, more to the point, he sees the consequences of
inaction when the politicians and civil servants have their own agendas.

He also begins to experience the consequences of his weak constitution and those months spent in the far north: he is discharged as sick and unserviceable and finds himself unemployed, without even the shaky crutch of half pay he would get as an officer, even a lowly midshipman.

His health improves slowly and by 1760 he is back at sea in Captain Everitt's new ship, *Stirling Castle*, sailing for the West Indies where the action is hottest in the war against France and her new ally, Spain. He is rated able seaman, not midshipman, that berth is full and rather than sit it out on shore and miss the chance of gaining experience and seniority, Phillip decides to sign on in whatever capacity he can. Besides, Everitt is a relative and in the wooden world, relatives, no matter how distant, count for a lot.

He's not wrong: within the year, he is promoted to fourth lieutenant and has his foot firmly on the rung that should, if chance, cannon shell and disease are kind, lead eventually to master and commander, and thence to captain.

The *Stirling Castle* is involved in the siege and taking of Martinique and Phillip goes ashore to look at the land: incredibly rich and yielding endless profit for its masters old and new, principally on the backs of the slaves stolen from Africa to labour and die after an average working life of seven years.

It is a strange experience for the young officer, one that is underlined when he inspects British possessions where the same system applies and the same profits flow back to the mother country. There are those back home, he hears, Methodies and bleeding hearts, who will not use sugar in any form to avoid supporting a system of which they and their religion disapprove.

He has little time for it; church is rigged on Sundays, the ship's Bible opened and read from and as long as the men believe that God is one hundred per cent behind the Admiralty and the chain of command, it suits him fine. And yet, for all that, there seems something inherently unreasonable about the practice of slavery. If we live in a free world, albeit with laws and rules accepted by the majority, doesn't the sheer, brute fact of thousands held in absolute bondage somehow stick in the throat? He doesn't have a theory about this, or anything else; there's not much time for theorising aboard ship, but the more he thinks about it, the more his sense of practicality, of what you can and cannot ask men and women to do, is offended by the very notion.

Captain Everitt transfers out of the *Stirling Castle* but Arthur stays, unlike many of the captain's followers who go with him, and serves under Commodore Augustus Hervey when the squadron is ordered to blockade the Spanish fleet in Havana. It is thankless work, holding station day after day under a broiling sun that sends tar dripping from the rigging onto the deck, in an ocean where vast curtains of weed attach themselves to the ship's bottom and impede its sailing whilst the Toredo worm slips under the copper and drills through the oak planks, leaving the hull like a sponge.

Havana is both well protected and well defended. British land forces are held up at El Moro, the heights overlooking the town, unable, even with the help of the navy, to get enough heavy artillery in place to reduce the Spanish. Hervey proposes to bombard the heights from the inshore waters and transferring to *Dragon,* leads a sortie along the cliffs. Unfortunately *Stirling Castle,* sailing ahead to draw enemy fire, falls too far back; the guns of the following ships will not elevate far enough to hit their targets and *Dragon* runs aground and has to sit it out whilst the Spanish use her for target practice. Hervey orders Campbell of the *Stirling Castle* to tow her off but he lacks the courage to press home and merely sails past; *Dragon* is blown to pieces by Spanish shot. It is a humiliation and Captain Campbell is dismissed the service.

The plan reverts to a land attack, this time with naval artillery transferred ashore to provide a barrage to clear the heights and support the troops, who have been reinforced by regiments stationed in North America. Getting the cannons ashore by rope and pulley and manhandling them up the cliffs to a position where they can take on the Spanish redoubt is a massive task; Phillip learns more, in a couple of days, about the logistics of moving cargo and directing masses of men to work together efficiently in a trying situation, than he would in a month of Sundays back at the naval school.

The operation is worth all the effort: Havana falls; it's a rich prize: as fourth lieutenant, Arthur collects in the region of £130, which he will need as the fleet is sent home and he is, once again, on half pay of only two shillings a day. It's another worthwhile lesson: succeeding triumphantly at sea one day, doesn't mean you won't be on the beach the next.

The year is 1763 – James Boswell is taking a course to get rid of the clap from the jolly, big girl; in Fowey, it will be two more years before Mary is born – and Arthur Phillip is twenty-four, he has a few guineas left in his purse, he has leisure and he decides to get married. Why not? It's what people do. Quite a lot of them do it for love; some do it for money, others because there's a blunderbuss with an irate father on the end of it pointed at their heads. Arthur gets married because she's there and the church is handy, just around the corner from where he grew up. Her name is Margaret Denison, though she calls herself by her middle name Charlotte; she's a widow of forty-one with considerable property in Dorset and more than £100,000 in the bank. Arthur signs a pre-nuptial agreement and relinquishes any legal claim over the property or the money.

They get married at St Augustine's on Watling Street and settle down near Hampton Court. Over the breakfast table he sees a slim, efficient rather than beautiful woman who has not suffered the rigours and risks of childbirth and is not about to. She has a good forehead, a steady gaze, a clear complexion, thinish lips, a chin that might denote character and shrewdness, a long neck and narrow shoulders that slope even more than his. Her build is on the modest side and so, unfashionably, if such a thing can be in or out of fashion, is her bosom; her carriage is upright and her nightgowns and dresses are quality but not flashy, English rather than French; her hair is brown like her eyes and her expression is, somehow, businesslike. She sees a plump young man in his mid-twenties who looks younger than his years. His complexion is neither here nor there but is still tanned by the Caribbean sun; the wig sits on his head somewhat awkwardly – style is not his metier; his nose is definitely there, you'd never overlook it. The lips are full and the chin, if he doesn't watch out, is going to double or even treble with the years. It's a round face whilst Charlotte's is definitely a long one. All in all, if it's not unpleasant, it's not memorable either. Reasonable is how one might describe it, undemanding but not really lively.

After a couple of years they move to Devon where he tries his hand at farming some of her properties with reasonable success. They buy more land, two extra farms, he does his duty as a local official and learns something of the way of things in the country: the sheltered cot, the cultivated farm, the never-failing brook, the busy mill, the decent church that tops the neighbouring hill. He also sees the advent of something else: enclosure, easing itself over the landscape, grabbing up common land to feed those that serve the manufactories of new Britain. In its wake, '... Desolation saddens all thy green: one only master grasps the whole domain ... Ill fares the land, to hast'ning ills a prey, Where wealth accumulates, and men decay ...'[3]

As do marriages if the soil is not regularly turned and ploughed. With no particular argument between them, Arthur and Charlotte start spending more time apart, then most of the time apart until there doesn't seem to be much point in this marriage going on since it is, so obviously, going nowhere. They separate and sign the indentures in the summer of 1769. Arthur undertakes to return any property of Charlotte's he might have and also agrees to repay certain monies should circumstances allow.

Then he goes away to Europe and travels and exercises his reason, studying fortifications and engineering; and there are those who hint that some of the fortifications he studies are in areas which happen to be of great interest to the Admiralty back in London, where they are concerned about the increasing pace of French shipbuilding. There is talk of fifteen first-rates on the slips and an equal number of heavy frigates. Augustus Hervey, Arthur's one-time captain during the blockade of Havana, is now a Lord Commissioner at the Admiralty, in charge of Intelligence in this matter, and what is more likely than that he might call on the thoughtful, dependable Lieutenant Phillip to take his good French, his artistic talent and knowledge of ships and sailing on a trip along the Mediterranean coast?

Nothing is said in public about the task but when Arthur returns and starts looking for a post in the peace-time navy, and finds very little is to be had, Hervey recommends him (one amongst thousands of half-pay officers) to the Portuguese ambassador in London, Mello e Castro, who is on the lookout for sailors-of-fortune to aid his country in the conflict simmering between it and Spain on the coasts of the New World.

The Portuguese and Spanish have been arguing for years over the control of the Rio de la Plata, the River Plate, on the western coast of South America. The Portuguese have been using it as a western port, a landing stage for trade goods which they go on to sell to the Spanish settlers inland. The Spanish object to this and have burnt Portuguese forts and retaken the territory, which the Portuguese have, in their turn, reclaimed and opened to British manufacturers. The markets are as potentially vast as the profits and Britain is by no means averse to helping out an old ally against the Spanish, who have recently been supporting France in the Seven Years' War.

Hervey writes of Arthur Phillip as being 'a discreet officer', and after consulting with his superiors, Castro offers him a position as captain, thereby jumping three ranks and thirteen years on half pay in one appointment. Castro is also keen to counterbalance the British officer who is currently commodore of the Portuguese fleet, Robert M'Douall, a disastrous appointment since M'Douall is one of those roast-beef-of-old-England sorts who has nothing but contempt for foreigners and their methods, whilst being himself an inefficient braggart and a bellicose coward. His political masters on the River Plate have come to loathe and mistrust him and have long given up any hope of him bringing the Spanish Fleet to action.

For them, Arthur Phillip, active and zealous, is the answer to a prayer. For Augustus Hervey, Arthur Phillip, with his cool eye and steady drawing hand, is an answer of another kind: the Portuguese have long operated a no-entry policy in the mountains of Minas Garais, where they mine the majority of their gold and diamonds. The government would very much like to know something of these forbidden lands and should Captain Phillip get the chance, he is to do his very best to bring back a 'compleat' report.

In the meantime there is a war to fight and a country to explore.

War is slow – orders and ships have to travel vast distances before even the chance of an encounter can occur. Phillip patrols the coast and disrupts local Spanish trade to such an extent that the Portuguese begin to worry that too much success might provoke a disproportionate response from their enemy and upset negotiations back in Europe. There the war seems to flicker on and off like a formal dance at a court function. Phillip finds this attitude understandable but frustrating; he points out to his superiors that one or two firm strikes against Spanish shipping will teach them to respect the Portuguese squadron and allow those on the spot, at the River Plate, to have a greater say in the disposal of their fortunes.

The Marquis de Lavradio, governor at Rio, fully supports this intelligent and active sailor who compels the Spanish to respect the Portuguese flag. He gives him command of a small squadron of his own and entrusts him with the sea defences of the coastal ports whilst leaving the inactive M'Douall to seek out the Spanish Fleet, which their intelligence warns them has set out from Europe. Escorted by twenty line-of-battle ships, ninety transports crammed with ten thousand troops are heading for the New World; this is intended by the Spanish to be the killing stroke and finish the conflict for good and all. M'Douall is given express instructions to seek out and engage the enemy. It is, as Lavradio and Arthur Phillip know by now, a forlorn hope.

Phillip is sent to reinforce the main squadron and shortly after he joins, on 17 February 1777, the Spanish ships begin to appear, first as individual dots, as the van comes into view, then as a string of beads as more and more ships follow, finally filling the horizon, port to starboard, with a wall of wood and canvas. Phillip advises attack – so does a young frigate captain, Jose de Mello – but M'Douall hesitates whilst the fleets close, then run alongside each other, carefully keeping out of cannon range.

Arthur is ready to eat his wig with frustration. The Spanish don't want to fight, their disposition is clumsy, their power to manoeuvre restricted by the transports that straggle and continually fall out of line; if ever there was a chance to play the fancy game and give 'Juan Dago' a good biffing, this is it! He suggests, he pleads, he begs, he writes a letter to M'Douall so it is set down in black and white: for the honour of England, for your own honour, do not hold back!

Over two days and nights the commodore considers. He orders a couple of frigates to see if they can cut out any stragglers, he waits, he watches ... as the Spanish sail into the roadstead at Santa Caterina, their fortified base. Then, having marshalled his forces, he moves into the attack: unfortunately the target is not the Spanish and the object is not victory at sea.

He calls all captains to the flag and over a tortuous afternoon in the sweltering heat of his cabin, goes over the events of the past days and reads, in excruciating detail, passages from his orders which, unsurprisingly, fully support his actions in not joining battle and in preserving the fleet. Arthur suspects that other, unread, portions of the orders make it quite clear that should an opportunity present itself, the commodore should take it and press home an attack but, without the document in front of him, he cannot disagree with M'Douall's version of events.

Young De Mello is unable to contain himself. Leaping up, he demands they attack at once, before the Spanish troops are fully disembarked. He turns to Captain Phillip for support: Phillip says an attack now would be possible but, given the orders as M'Douall reads them, they have little choice but to hold back. They are substantially outnumbered and though this would not have mattered had they joined battle as soon as the Spanish had come into sight, now the enemy is in harbour and protected by artillery as well as their own guns, any attack would risk the destruction of the majority of the Portuguese ships and would, therefore, go against the tenor of their orders. M'Douall has his victory: he presents a letter of agreement which all his captains are compelled to sign.

The governor has no choice but to support M'Douall, though his low opinion of the man is clear; he allows the squadron to refit and then sends them out again in April. Then the Spanish packet is taken and the imminent arrival of the two new first-rates discovered. They must be found and stopped or, with the newly arrived Spanish troops, the war will be lost.

M'Douall sights one of the Spaniards and gives listless chase with the squadron. Phillip and Jose de Mello, in fast-sailing and efficiently maintained frigates, draw ahead of the rest, using every speck of wind and every trick in the book to gain on the chase.

Throughout the long day of the 14th the pursuit goes on, with Phillip slightly ahead of De Mello. The Spanish are still well beyond the range of even the long chasers on the foredeck and both captains send their crews to dinner; there's no point in tiring the men, if they should come up with the Spaniard they are going to need everyone, sailor or waister, if they are to have the least chance of slowing the enemy.

Victory is not an option, both captains and their crews realise this: naval warfare, given the vagaries of wind and tide, is pretty much a science and the science is that of gunnery. The ship with the biggest guns wins because she can pound the enemy long before they get into range and reply with their smaller guns; it's that simple. And yet, as the sun goes down, Phillip and De Mello press on; they are so frustrated that even hopeless action is better than no action.

Night falls – not a particularly dark night and, far ahead, the white of the Spaniard's canvas glimmers in the O of telescopes. She is not attempting any moves to escape her pursuers; she is following a steady course for Santa Caterina, seeing no great danger in the present situation.

At dawn a following wind springs up which will favour the two frigates for a good while before it reaches the chase. The *Pilar* springs forward, her bow wave spreading like opening wings, as they skim across the waves. De Mello drives his frigate hard, determined to be the first within range but the disposition of Phillip's sails gives him the advantage and he draws ahead and closer to the Spaniard, who is identified as the *San Augustin*.

From his station by the wheel, Phillip can see across the whole curved sweep of the *Pilar*'s upper deck as the frigate drives before the wind. He orders the gun crews to their stations and soon the characteristic smell of slow and quick match wafts through the warm morning air. Below, the cook's fires are damped down and the bulkheads between officers' quarters removed. A silence falls; a sea silence in which the regular creak of rigging and crack of canvas, the rush of the sea alongside, the swinging of the lead or the ring of the bell are not counted as sounds. Moment by moment they are closing. Soon they will be within range of the *Augustin* and there's one question on everyone's mind: whether she will take the time to come about and present her broadside and send tons of iron sweeping back towards the frigates. One unlucky shot and a spar or mast might be lost; even a parted rope could slow them down enough to lose contact.

The air is split by the flat sound of cannon firing – but the firing is from behind: De Mello, young and enthusiastic, is unable to wait any longer. He has tried a couple of ranging shots. They fall short. The *Augustin* ploughs on. De Mello has lost way and falls behind. Phillip drives his topmen to ever greater vigilance: the wind increases, they are gaining, gaining and every man aboard her has a mental line stretching out between the *Pilar* and the Spaniard and marked on it, like the canvas markers on the lead line, two points: when *Pilar* will come into the *Augustin*'s range and when the Spaniard will come into theirs. And there's a big gap between the two, during which they'll have to suffer the weight of broadside after broadside.

Some might even wish the wind would fall away but it does not and the *Pilar*'s bow creeps along that line, closer to the deadly mark, then on it and every man flinches and holds his breath ... then past it by a yard, past it by a league and now, surely, the *Augustin* must turn and present. But she does not, and inch by inch they close on that second mark. Now they can smell the Spaniards' ovens, the tang of bread and garlic, soon they'll be able to hear the shouted orders. Can it be they are not even cleared for action? Surely she must come about any moment and wipe this irritation from the surface of the ocean?

Slow minutes creep past and still she does not come about and Phillip realises that the *San Augustin*'s captain cannot believe, cannot in his wildest speculations comprehend that a frigate would be insane enough to fight a ship of the line. He must think that the *Pilar* is a Spanish ship being chased by De Mello, an impression underlined by this morning's firing which, from so far ahead, might easily be mistaken for one frigate firing on the other.

Looking back, he sees De Mello has settled his crew and is once again coming on. If he can deliver a broadside and bring down enough rigging to delay the *Augustin*, De Mello will be able to join him, and together they might delay the Spaniard until M'Douall and the rest appear with enough force to finish her off. The sound of battle will surely stir even their torpid commodore – if nothing else he'll want a share in the prize money.

The point of attack is closing. Phillip commands the gun crews to lie flat, out of sight, and guard their matches. There'll be a chance for one broadside and then a desperate race to come round on the *Augustin*'s stern to escape the terrible weight of metal her broadside will unleash. Tar drips from the rigging but no one scurries to clean it off the deck. They are so close that they can see the white reflection of their sails in the lights of the Spaniard's stern cabin. An officer leans over the taffrail and waves in a companionable sort of way. Phillip waves back and calls out: 'Fire as you bear!'

The *Pilar* comes round, heeling radically so the guns are elevated and, in a rolling thunder, the broadside crashes out, sending case-shot, chain-shot and canister sweeping across the *Augustin*'s deck and into her rigging. For a moment everything is obscured by smoke as the *Pilar* comes about into the *Augustin*'s wake and the Spanish ship ploughs on, making no reply to the attack. Men race aloft whilst the helmsman struggles to bring the *Pilar* up to the wind but with every second the gap between the two ships widens; it is clear the *Augustin*'s captain has no intention of fighting, only of escaping and, as the powder smoke still hanging in the air makes clear, the breeze is falling and he has the advantage in spread of canvas. The distance between the ships increases, the imaginary line stretches out and by the time *Pilar* is once more in pursuit, the pursuit has become hopeless.

The cannons are secured, the men stood down. De Mello comes alongside and offers his condolences but points out that during the chase the *Augustin* has made considerable leeway and is sailing any number of points off her supposed course to the roadstead at Santa Caterina and will have to work inshore against current and wind. The Portuguese fleet, short of sinking or turning back, must bump into them and even M'Douall can't think that odds of fourteen to one are extravagant.

This turns out to be the case. The *San Augustin* is taken more or less undamaged and brought into the Portuguese navy. Arthur Phillip is appointed captain; in Europe negotiations proceed apace and, as often appears the case when the eternal stalemate in the New World seems about to be upset, peace breaks out and Captain Phillip finds himself without a position. He is still in good odour with the Portuguese authorities, however, and he requests permission to travel through the area of the Minas Gerais and the forbidden gold and diamond mines of Serra do Frio dos Diamantes.

Permission is gladly granted: Captain Phillip has given of his best for Portugal and now he sets off to give some more to Mr Hervey and the secretive officials who sit in their upstairs offices at the Admiralty.

Evan Nepean

Cornwall is a long way from the corridors of the Home Department and Under Secretary Evan Nepean, a slim, tidily dressed civil servant, is heartily glad of the fact. He's not a country man, he doesn't ride and he doesn't hunt and he hates the long, winding conversations with which his country cousins keep boredom at bay and recall headlines from their newspapers: An Astoundingly Large Hog shown recently at Bodmin Fair; a Nondescript Animal at Loose, savaging Farm Stock; a Curious Mushroom Collected, bearing the silhouette of His Majesty. None of this for him, but rather the pleasures of work. He loves the daily grind, the memos and letters, the meeting notes, the situation papers that pile up in mountains all around the building because they give him the long view and allow him to influence policy and solve problems without ever having to stand up and defend his solutions in the House, though he is called before their committees from time to time, where he takes care to appear no more intelligent than the average politician.

Evan's father is a shipwright on the River Tamar in Cornwall; a precise but practical man who passed on his pleasure in physical things to his elder son Nick who became an undistinguished soldier, and his prodigious work rate to Evan, the younger, who took it into the Royal Navy, not as an officer but as a purser, the one man after, or sometimes before, a captain who can set the tenor of a ship by the practice of his craft.

Traditionally as corrupt as the bosun, the purser controlled every cask of pork and water, every quid of tobacco and bottle of brandy or rum; he was the man to know on board and if you had the purser and the master-at-arms on your side, you were fit and fat enough for anything.

For Evan, it was a first taste of being the controlling presence hidden at the centre of a thing – this was the reward; he had no interest in corruption, if only because it would have been a slur on his efficiency. Not surprisingly, he rose and rose and by the time of the little local difficulty on the Potomac, he was Purser to the British Fleet and supplying rather more than just food and drink. Information had begun to flow his way through the contractors he employed; he discovered that even enemies who can see off your forces are not proof against the profits to be made in a trade-off of goods and information.

He moved from ship to shore, from country to country, always making friends, seldom upsetting anyone since emnity is the enemy of commerce. He realised that in a navy as far-flung as the British, acquaintances made on the Atlantic seaboard might be renewed or redeemed in the South China Sea and, as far as possible, he never met a man he didn't appear to like and who didn't like him in return. He returned to England in 1781 and became part-time secretary to Admiral Shuldon at Portsmouth; through him he made contact with Lord Rockingham, who took over the reins of government when Lord North let them fall after his miscalculation of these pesky colonists' ambitions. One of Nepean's first tasks was to deliver the news of his sacking to Lord North; he did it with tact and efficiency, as he did everything.

The times were uncertain: the Americans had won their freedom, the spectre of republicanism was stalking Europe and, when London exploded into the Gordon Riots in 1780, even the British Royal Family began to experience intimations of revolution. Evan Nepean was brought in to reassure the establishment. He knew ex-sailors and ship's corporals as well as lieutenants and captains, he knew merchants and farmers, idlers and sturdy beggars and he could ask a man to sniff around his local inn back in town or chat to his mates down a country lane; he knew what to offer by way of inducement and threat and what to pass on to reassure his patrons.

In 1782 he moved into the Home Department with a mission to reorganise its Byzantine structures and turn it into a modern, clear-thinking ministry capable of responding at speed to the crises of the contemporary world: and here he sits, his finger on more pulses than you'd meet in a month at Surgeon's Hall, with one big problem.

Convicts.

More and more of them, as a wave of criminality sweeps the nation. It might be the enclosures, which are taking – or stealing, depending on your point of view – common land all over the country. It might be seditious ideas from France, it might even be the sheer bloody-mindedness of the lower sort, but crime is up and so is the number of convicted criminals.

Ideally, as Bishop Berkeley might say, the majority would walk from court to scaffold and thence out of this world but juries have a nasty habit of not convicting on capital offences if they can avoid it. No one quite knows where this unusual sense of mercy comes from, though there are suspicions that Methodists and other low-church sorts may be part of the problem and the development of sensibility in the middling sort – put it down to that writer Richardson and his wretched heroine, Clarissa Harlowe – may also be part of the equation. Be that as it may, ordinary folk don't like the spectacle as much as they used to and are hanging fewer men, women and children. Who simply have to be sent somewhere.

The government thought it had the perfect answer a few years ago, in 1776, when the colonies erupted and it was no longer feasible to ship off convicts as indentured labour. Mr Duncan Campbell, a Jamaica merchant, the son of a divinity professor from Glasgow, came up with the idea of using decommissioned ships of the line as floating prisons. Nepean's naval friends might have chuckled 'Ho ho, what's the difference? They already are!' but Evan himself thought the idea workable and Campbell a decent enough man to put it into practice. The merchant had been in the America trade for years and done well, receiving a bounty for every convict delivered healthy to Columbia's shore. However, when Columbia held up her hand and refused entry, the prison service and the courts did not stop delivering convicted prisoners to the holding pens. Campbell had to come up with something fast and the idea of the hulks was born. It was either that or going out of business.

Campbell thought that male convicts could be set to work dredging the channels in which their prisons were moored, thus earning money and paying for their own upkeep. There was not a lot that women and children could do apart from housework and it was not considered likely that the class of person confined would be all that bothered with brush and duster; they would just have to sit out their sentences and keep the gaolers and marine guards amused.

Unfortunately, as Evan is well aware, there are a finite number of ships and moorings and very few coastal towns happy to have the festering, rotting wooden hulks moored off their shores. The smell, for one thing, is quite simply indescribable; then there is the risk of the prisoners rising, overcoming their guards (off Portsmouth: eight dead, thirty-six wounded) and swarming ashore like Blackbeard's crew avid for gold, chintz, daughters, domestic animals and anything else debauchable.

There is, in short, a crying need to find somewhere to send them and Evan's boss, Tommy Townshend, Lord Sydney, Secretary of State for the Home Department and Leader of the House of Commons, thinks his brilliant under secretary is the man for the job. And not just anywhere. Sydney is one of those who believes that man is improvable; he even has a sneaking admiration for the American colonists and his instructions to Evan contain a humanitarian subtext in which hard work and redemption play a not inconsiderable part.

Whilst Nepean is considering the question, Tommy dumps another task on his desk: South America. Britain is once again interested in gaining a toe-hold for trade in that area and it is suggested that a naval expedition be mounted, including at least one officer with experience of the place and the ability to keep his eyes open and make succinct notes about everything he sees. The job has been passed from the Admiralty to the Home Department. With it has come a recommendation from Sea Lord Sandwich, supported by a certain

Mr Shafto, a man of many names in secret circles, that Captain Phillip may be suitable for the mission. Evan interviews the man and finds that this is so; he has experience of working undercover for the Admiralty, he is discreet, not given to sentiment in an age which is excessively given to sentiment, not lacking in courage and ingenuity. He gets the job, sails away and the under secretary goes back to pondering the convict problem.

Africa, it appears, could be an answer. Evan is summoned before a Parliamentary Committee in 1785 and asked about the state of things. He tells the honourable members:

That the *Censor*, hulk, and the *Dunkirk*, hulk, a King's ship being in ordinary at Plymouth, has been appointed to receive prisoners from the West Country to ease the crowding amongst the rest of the convict fleet but that Mr Duncan Campbell can see no long term solution except that the inhabitants of said hulks should be moved on and moved through by means of transportation.
To where, sir?
A plan has been suggested for the transportation of convicts to the isle of Lemaine, up the River Gambia. I know of no other plan regarding Africa at present under proposal.
Why is Africa proposed?
These, in particular, are notorious felons, daily expected to break out from their confinement. They are a class of people too dangerous to remain in this country. There is no place in America to which they may be sent.

The Committee calls Mr Smeathan.

Sir, you have resided on the coast of Africa for a number of years?
Four years.
What is your opinion of the proposal?
If two hundred convicts were left on an island in the River Gambia without any medical assistance than that which they might offer each other, not one in a hundred would survive the

first six months. People confined for long periods in prison are particularly unsuited to struggle in an African climate.

The Committee calls Sir George Young.

You have visited Gambia, Sir George?
I have been four times and have always regarded it as the most unhealthy part of the coast. As for sustaining a colony of the sort suggested, no trader would approach it for fear of being plundered.
Could such a colony sustain itself by agricultural labour?
I believe it is not practicable for Europeans to sustain themselves by prolonged labour in such a climate.

Thank you, gentlemen.[4]

So, not Africa then. But where? And in the meantime it would be better to keep the hulks as much out of the news as is possible. Evan has a quiet chat with his friend Duncan Campbell at a Lodge meeting and asks him to do what he can to keep the convicts under wraps for the time being. Campbell rightly takes this as the nearest thing to a threat that Evan is going to utter in public and hurries off to clean up his act, if not the scuppers of his sedentary fleet.

However, unlike stories in the press, the basic problem will not go away and Evan begins to trawl through the proposals which have landed on government's desk these last few years. One such comes from a Corsican–American loyalist called James Mario Matra. He had sailed as a midshipman on Captain James Cook's first voyage to the South Seas and written an unauthorised account of the trip. He noted that it might be possible to atone for the loss of Britain's American colonies by establishing a settlement for trade on the coast of New South Wales. 'If a colony were established in the large tract of country and if we were at war with Holland or Spain, we might very powerfully annoy either state from our new settlement. We might, with a safe, and expeditious voyage, make naval incursions on Java and other

Dutch settlements and we might, with equal facility, invade the coasts of South America.'

It is not a practical scheme; New South Wales is thousands of miles away from anywhere – almost four thousand either way to Java or the coast of South America – and the voyages would be anything but safe and expeditious in those waters. However, looked at backwards, as it were, the isolation, the thousands of miles away from anywhere, might be an advantage if your aim was to be out of the way, rather than in it.

Evan mentions this to Tommy Townshend, who mentions it to someone who mentions it to James Mario Matra who comes back with an addendum that if convicts were sent they could not fly the country, they would have no temptation to theft and they would have to work to feed themselves or starve.

Sydney passes the idea onto Lord Howe at the Admiralty. He doesn't like it. His fellow sea lord Sir George Young feels it might be improved upon and, having done that, passes it on to Prime Minister Pitt, who doesn't like it either and sends it to the desk of the Attorney General, Pepper Arden, who does like it but comes up against Alexander Dalrymple of the East India Company, who doesn't under any circumstances want John Company's bailiwick in the South Seas or the east interfered with so the whole mess is dumped into the lap of a Public Enquiry under Lord Beauchamp, which arrives at this solution: send the convicts to Africa.

A frigate is sent to Upper Volta and comes back with the predictable news that the place is quite unsuitable. The Home Department turns its gaze back to New South Wales and to Botany Bay in particular. Messengers hurry round to Soho Square and collect piles of material from Sir Joseph Banks, who has, in the years since he visited the shores of *terra australis* as a young botanist aboard Captain Cook's *Endeavour*, grown in reputation and influence until it seems that nothing in the far southern latitudes can be decided without his advice. He is, on the whole, sanguine. Evan Nepean gets down to work putting together the outline, the heads, of a plan to transport a fleet full of dreadful banditti to the other side of the world.

Other considerations, annoying the Dutch and Spanish, controlling trade routes, cutting down tall timber for masts and weaving sails from the native flax plants, are added to the plan but, in truth, are not seen as being of any great importance. Evan reckons it will cost £29,669 to get them there; £18,699 to keep them over the first year, £15,000 for the second, £7,000 for the third and that after then they should be self-sustaining.

This is the kind of mathematics government loves and when Lord Sydney presents the heads of the plan to the Treasury he takes care to lard it well with dreadful warnings – all penned, of course, by his under secretary. There is no doubt, though, that Tommy can deliver a speech with the best of them. He fixes the financiers with a solemn eye and tells them that the prisons and hulks of Britain are so crowded with desperate villains and in such a state that the greatest danger is to be apprehended not only from mass escapes but also from infectious distempers which hourly may be excepted to break out amongst them and – though he leaves this unsaid, the Lords of the Treasury can read the tea leaves as well as anyone – amongst the general population. He then goes on to mention the trading advantages, the tactical reasons for annoying the Dutch and Spanish, the tall trees and the sails.

The plan is bought, though there are dissenters. East India Company nabob Alexander Dalrymple protests that so pleasant is the prospect of sunning themselves on a faraway island continent with every luxury provided, that surely thousands will actively set out to become convicts just to join the pleasure party. What's more, the wretches will be their own masters! Where, he cries, is the punishment to be inflicted?

But it's too late. The plan is in motion now and in September 1786 Evan Nepean writes to Duncan Campbell, asking him to start making lists of convicts in the hulks suitable for transportation. Campbell is not offered, and does not want, the contract to provision the fleet; he's been in the convict business too long and there's no great profit to be had out of this scheme. There is, however, no shortage of tenders and the contract is awarded to William Richards Jr, a merchant from Walworth in London who offers both a good rate and the prospect of delivering an acceptable standard of service.

For a few days Evan Nepean can sit back and congratulate himself on a job well done – but it is not, of course, quite finished yet. They need a man to command the fleet and run this convict colony that is to be established on an unknown shore on the far side of the world.

Mary Broad

The village lies on the edge of the forest, at the end of a long, winding track, past farmland and hills and a deserted tin mine. She walks slowly along the main, the only, street, running her fingers over the rough stones that form the cottage walls. Behind walk the others in the gang, vague presences here beside the ghosts of just a few months gone. There's no shouting, no 'hey, you, what do you want?'. There's no washing hanging on walls or lines, no smoke coming from chimneys, no quiet talk or loud gossip, no laughing, no crying, no children; there are no good smells of cooking or compost heaps, of sweat even, or burning wood or horse shit and cow dung. There are only the bad smells: the stink of cottages left empty, barns unused, the curdled milk of nettles creeping back along the roadside, choking everything in their way. It won't be long before the nettles stretch out across the flinty track and begin to climb up stone walls and in through the front doors and the back.

She stops, and the others stop behind her, looking uneasily around at this emptiness like the carapace of a dead stag beetle, eaten out by smaller predators. It is as if they are waiting for someone to come out from one of the dark doorways and explain what happened, why the people went away but there's no one left and they all know what happened here. Someone eases a cosh from their belt but there are no enemies to hit, unless your ambition is so great that you want to bring down the whole nation, and that's not going to happen this side of the Atlantic.

They walk on, none of them happy about staying here overnight. They'll find somewhere else to sleep; back under the cover of the forest maybe, not here where each corner and doorstep, each roof point and chimney, every wall and fireplace is heavy with the memory of lives lived richly over generations.

Perhaps the travellers are also abashed in the face of success, after all, their business is the business of relieving the unwary and the weak of what is theirs; stealing it from them under threat of injury or death, if it come to that. Here, bigger and better operators have taken the common land and made it theirs, sensibly dividing the country among opulent men, and done so legally, by act of parliament, to general approval and their own perpetual profit. 'For the Common Good, they steal the common, for whilst it is a sin in man or woman, to steal a goose from off the common, what then is his excuse, who steals the common from the goose?', as the rhyme has it.

The little group moves on, and after a while even the sound of their leather heels on the flint track, the swish of cloth and the sharper noise of buckles and metal on metal, the odd words they mutter, all of these are gone and the empty village settles back and waits for the nettles.

Nobody cares why the three women are in court. They are here as one more piece of business for the Lenten Assize at Exeter Castle. Judges Sir Beaumont Hotham and Sir James Eyre have already dealt with two days' worth of human misery, chicanery, evil and stupidity and these are not men to dabble with the reason why. What happened, who did what to whom, when did they do it and did anyone else see it. That's what they care about.

These are serious men who want to get through today's business and get on to today's dinner. And they don't much like these West Country juries either; close-faced men of the middling rank with a loyalty towards their own and a suspicion of the outside. Just try and get them to convict a free-trader, as they call the damned smugglers who deprive the nation of its import taxes! You might as well try and hold fairy gold.

Certainly, times are hard down here but they generally are and the economy has cycles like anything else. One might as well disagree with the orbit of Saturn as with the fall in the price of tin or, for that matter, the rise in the tax on salt. There is an invisible hand at work in human affairs and it is called enlightened self-interest; through constant and uninterrupted effort every man may better his condition and, as a result, enrich all and if those damned free-traders down in Cornwall should take it upon themselves to smuggle French salt as well as French brandy, then let them look to their lives because the law will have no compassion. What if they need it to salt the pilchards they fish? Let them pay the English salt tax, let them put up the price of pilchards and if customers don't buy those, then let them salt something else that they do want.

The court is two different worlds. One is quotidian, where habit and repetition have made each session like any other, where barristers and judges and tipstaffs are familiar with every circumlocution, since they've heard every plea, excuse and apology a thousand times, where even shock and horror are part of the daily business. The other, for the juries, the majority of defendants and witnesses, is something else, a step across the line between their world and a place where everything is heightened and the consequences are so real that you can almost feel them, like the rough touch of hemp round your neck.

The solid drone, it might be a hurdy-gurdy, of the clerk of session's voice drifts up into the roof beams along with spirals of bluish sulphur smoke and the herbs burned against the stink of prisoners who have been held months in gaol without water to wash. He clears his throat, spits accurately into a spittoon and begins: '... in the case of Mary Broad, Mary Haydon, also Shepherd and Catharine Fryer, at Exeter Assize this 23rd March 1786 ... of Highway Robbery ... how will you be tried?'

'By God and my country,' they answer.

Another voice chimes in, the lawyer, a bitter enemy to those in the flash way of life: '... the road into Plymouth Dock ... the evening of January ... three young women lie in wait ... a moon behind clouds ...'

A slim, dark-haired girl of nineteen, nondescript dress, breathing fast as she waits in the shadow of a doorway. Her hands are damp despite the cold evening and the mist that wreathes up from the harbour. Shouts and screams come from the alehouses and leaping shops down along the dockside. She can see a patch of lightness from Kate's dress across the road, where she waits in the mungy outlet of an alley, sewer juice flowing sluggishly under her shoes out into the slick moonlight where it pools like mirror glass.

Mary H stands as if lost, looking this way and that as the woman comes up. Respectable, of the middling to lower sort, wearing a silk bonnet and probably carrying her money in the indispensable stitched somewhere under her clothes. Mary's eye is good by now at totting up the profit on anyone's back. It's been a light time of late and this one will do.

Mary H moves into the centre of the road and catches the woman's attention: 'Ma'am, I'm looking for somewhere to sleep tonight, you would not ...' By now Mary and Kate are beside the woman, three skirts barring her way, a soft prison and the three women hard, merciless, voices shrill with the strain of it, a maelstrom of words to her and to each other – 'Your bonnet, nim the bonnet, Kate, under the mantle, it'll be there, find the yellow boys, give us the bung, shout and you'll not breathe again, you bitch!' – but something is wrong, she *is* shouting, screaming and flailing, fingers like claws. This tiger isn't giving up anything whilst she's got life in her to struggle with. A look passes between the three women: the play isn't going to plan, no words, just the need to run, get as far away from here as possible, and do it now.

They run across the slimy cobbles, out of town but it's luck, just plain bad luck or maybe Mary's bad choice that leads them in the wrong direction and there are lamps and people and the shouting of male voices, blows with fists and sticks and a flurry of falling and then being taken up and here comes that damned shrill baggage wailing about her bonnet and her valuables. It isn't long before Mary and Kate and Mary H find out what pleasure a crowd may have with three thieving sluts and, in the end, all are glad to be locked up, locked in and locked down and taken in front of the magistrate next morning.

Where they learn that the spinster Agnes Lakeman was relieved of her bonnet and other goods to the value of eleven guineas. This makes it pretty much a certain thing that the three young women will, in turn, lose their lives; that commodity is set in this case, in law, at forty shillings in value and to step across the forty-shilling line is to step into eternity.

The lawyer finishes his account. The case stands baldly, ready to be answered. The other questions – how did the child who grew up in Fowey and sat by the sea mending nets, the child of Grace and William the fisherman and the sister of Dolly, the little girl who sat in the church counting the roof beams and wondered how you made a saffron cake, how did she come to be here standing beside Catherine Fryer and Mary Haydon alias Shepherd – aren't questions that have any relevance today.

> Was Agnes Lakeman attacked, did her assailants intend to rob her, did they do so and in doing so, did they cause her physical harm? *Yes. To all.*
> Can you offer any reason why judgement should not be passed upon you?
> *No.*
> Then for feloniously assaulting Agnes Lakeman, spinster, on the King's Highway, putting her in corporeal fear and danger of her life in the said highway and violently taking from her person and against her will in the said highway one silk bonnet, value twelve pence and other goods to the value of eleven pounds and eleven shillings, her property, you will be taken from this place, back to the prison where you are being held and from thence to a place of execution and there hanged by the neck until you are dead and may God have mercy on your soul.[5]

Being merciful men, the judges, according to custom and having dispensed justice and protected the landed, turn their minds over the next couple of days and a prodigious amount of claret, port and brandy, to those who will be pardoned.

Sir Beaumont and Sir James no more question the system of condemning men and women to death and then, pretty much on a whim, pardoning some of them, than do those who have been sentenced and are sitting in the cells contemplating their crimes and easing the irons that rub flesh raw and bone into ulcers. Not one of them so much as wonders if this is fair. Certainly not Thomas Ruffel, steward, charged with murdering his master and mistress, whose trial was hard and tenaciously fought and lasted the unprecedented length of almost three hours; not Susannah Hanford, charged with procuring an abortion from a local apothecary, who managed to kill both herself and the offending baby in her belly and so was tried in absentia; not James Martin, alias Martyn, a likely lad sentenced to the long drop for stripping pounds of lead from a roof belonging to Lord Courney. You might as well ask the rats and mice that patter through the straw on the floor of the cells, vying with the occupants for crumbs, or the fleas that leap and sip blood or the crab lice that infest the hot, damp, filthy human crevices of the prisoners whether they think it fair.

It is just *so*. The judges decide that Mary and Catherine and Mary H and James Martin and a dozen others who were convicted of felony will be the grateful recipients of the Royal mercy on condition that they are transported beyond the seas for and during the terms of seven years, and that said warrant has been (pre) signed by His Majesty's Principal Secretary of State, the Right Hon. Thomas, Lord Sydney.

'So where shall they send us?' asks someone.

Someone else thinks America but then a third remembers when the war with the colonists started and thinks that the King lost that war and the Yankees aren't British any more.

'So where shall they send us?' asks someone.

'Probably to the hulks, until they can think of what else to do with us,' comes the answer and all three young women shudder because the hulks are every bit as bad as the worst prison on land with the sea and the isolation added and not so many ways to earn half a ned. And money is the stuff that makes the world go round and nowhere more so than in prison. What can't be paid for can't be had. Want your irons removed? Pay up. Want a place to sleep, something to eat or drink, a corner to call your own, a bit of protection? Pay up. Need medicine, a cloth for the time of the month, brandy to make things tolerable or a pinch of tobacco? Pay up. And if you ain't got the rattler, you better have something you can sell, Sukie, or you won't be long for even this floating hell.

The yawl pulls away from the Devonport hard. It's a grey, unforgiving day with cold rain spitting in the breeze and their faces are raw as they huddle amidships, but in some ways even this weather is preferable to the months inside Exeter gaol deprived of light and the touch of the wind, where the damp stone reached out fingers that picked at flesh and left it leper pale and hanging in tatters like thick lace. The crew stay clear of them, even though they are female; these jacks can buy all the jills they need ashore and coming within a yard of this lot would guarantee infestation.

The bow goes up and crashes down, setting a jarring along the deck planks and into brittle jaws where teeth are already loose in their sockets through scurvy. Mary and the others hug their tatters to themselves not out of modesty but because they have learnt a hard lesson these past months: until you're lying in your long home, everyone has something that can be stolen. Mary is determined that she will keep what she's got because she's already seen enough poor souls who have given up, little by little, everything they have until there is nothing and no reason left to take the next breath. Like steam from piss in December, they have drifted away into nothing. She won't. She'll survive because that's what she does: she wakes up every morning.

The crew of the yawl stuff little twists of tobacco up their noses. The prisoners look at each other and wonder: what on God's ocean stinks worse than us?

The motion of the yawl becomes less and looking over the side they see a stain covering the water like grease on the top of a thin stew. The stain surrounds them and stretches out ahead, the gleaming slick of a slug track across the water to the slug itself, a great slab-sided hulk wallowing and oozing from every scupper and plank. There's not an opening to be seen, not a port or a window; the landward face of this thing is utterly closed off.

As they approach, the vast side climbs higher and higher above them, blocking out the weak light. The planking is stained black, the copper corroded and now they begin to smell the thing itself. A sailor spits a thick quid of tobacco over the side and shouts 'Nine to come aboard!' The mate growls out an order, the marines come to what passes for attention and the yawl slips under the stern and along the seaward side of the prison ship *Dunkirk*.

Now they know what stinks worse than any gaol on land. On this side the ports and scuttles are all open and bars can be glimpsed and from them thin shouts and jeers and cheers sound out – 'New chums, new chums!' – as the yawl bumps against the entry port and lines are thrown and secured. One of the prisoners vomits what little she has in her stomach; the others squint against the burning stench of piss and shit, mould and rot, old blood and new, bilge water, sweat and dirt and despair blowing like the hot breath of Satan in their faces.

Dunkirk: they've heard of it whispered of as the worst of the hulks, a place where the torment and official thievery got so bad that government was forced to step in to stop the horrors; and in their dark world, where horrors are everyday, that brings a chill to the soul of the gamest chicken amongst them, because who knows if *Dunkirk* has really changed or if the terrors are still waiting.

The boatmen want to get them off, the marines want to get them aboard and, men and women, they are pulled and pushed out of the light into the shadow of the ship where they are dragged along narrow, low passages, down, down to the orlop which, someone shouts at them – because no one ever talks in this place – is the receiving area. They state their names and their sentences; they are searched without much enthusiasm, even the prettiest amongst the women, and then herded up on deck and stood under a pump whilst sea water is sluiced over their shivering, bitterly chilled bodies. There is nothing to dry themselves with as they are herded off below again, given small beer and tuppence worth of bread and cheese, though most can't keep it

down, and issued with a coarse blanket and told off to their new homes
'tween decks.

The prison runs the length of the ship, fore to aft, men and women
separated by thick oak bulkheads studded with spikes. The inward-
sloping sides are lined with sleeping shelves inches above wooden
decks which are sticky to the touch. There's no light to speak of;
Mary and the others exist in a permanent twilight that veers between
arctic and tropic in temperature and is filled with noises. Argument
and complaint are just the ground from which the variations spring:
screams and bellows of anger as disputes flare into fights; howls of
anguish from the waking and the sleeping; the wails of the mad, but
who can tell who's mad down here; the crash of marines' boots and
musket butt against flesh and bone; the occasional screech of childbirth
and the thin cries of infants whose stay in this floating world is
inevitably short; the sharp iron clatter of the chains and manacles
(sixteen pounds to drag and lift every step of every day) that those
who can't afford to bribe the gaolers still wear; bellowed orders from
above; gasping sobs of agony from those who suffer convict justice,
like the peacher who got twelve dozen on the arse and would have
screamed the hold down only they shoved two needles through his
tongue so he couldn't get it back in his mouth to use it; the ship itself,
creaking as the timbers move sluggishly against each other, shrieking
as the stumps of the masts shift against the blocks and keelson; the
constant squeak and thump of the pumps clearing the top few inches
of the bilge water that swills sluggishly back and forth in the well
and the curses of the male convicts told off for this task; the threats
hissed viciously into ears too close for comfort and the endearments,
whispered into ears close for comfort ... In this purgatory there is no
silence.

Mary knows one thing. Seven years is a long time and if she's going to
get through it without ending up like some of the old twats down here,
she needs to shift for herself. She needs a handle and there's only
one way a girl of twenty without cash but with looks is going to get it:
it's smock alley for her, lovers' lane, she needs a willing prick to pay

the toll on this turnpike. She's lively, she has good eyes and a good complexion, she knows a trick or two to please any 'Captain Standish' and his master. She has only a few weeks before this place pulls her down and wastes not a moment of it upon the subject of what's right or fair; those impostors have drowned long since, somewhere down in the scuppers. She's done her time on the pad, didn't they write her in the book at Exeter assizes as a Toby, one of those wild women who ply their trade on the highway, a scamp, a nasty girl not afraid to put up the maulies to get what she wants? Most in here are not the desperate sort but more the sad and lonely, gooseberry fools and farm girls who hid their babies in the hedges and tried to forget all about them. She can take what she wants from them and as long as she sleeps with one eye open and gets out of here soon, she'll survive and she'll make the climb, deck by deck, from gaoler to marine to officer's cabin.

James Boswell

The year 1784 and it's been a long time since 1763 and the day he made Westminster Bridge tremble with that big, jolly girl – a lot of water and a sight more claret, port and brandy has flowed; quaffing and quiffing and the corporal and four and he's not the man he was but he does know, at last, what he wants to be: the great biographer. He's going to write a biography like no other in the world about the most important thing in his life: the figure who has bookended the last twenty-odd years of his life, in a way held him upright for that length of time, Dr Samuel Johnson.

Of course, being Boswell, that's not all he wants. Fame and respect are still there, he feels, for the claiming and the best place to get these must be London. Which means leaving Auchinleck, where he is now the laird, married to Margaret, rewarded with four children, another on the way, who worry him to distraction: should they be brought up in London where they might acquire a metropolitan gloss and risk the unsuitable habits that James knows all too well or should they stay in the north and learn the Scottish way of decency, probity, honesty, coarse accent, coarse manners and lack of polish?

He feels he'll have to bring them all down to London sooner or later but his wife Margaret has always been of tender health, consumption stalks her days and nights and he loves the woman (though it makes not a jot of difference to his philandering), and does not want to put her through the rigours of travel. And, of course, there is always the material question.

The estate at Auchinleck brings in an income which just about covers the family outgoings, if you overlook the huge mortgage on the place. His practice before the Scottish Bar has brought him a certain respect – he is by no means a bad lawyer when he puts his mind to it – but this has not resulted in fortune, promotion to the bench like his father or the realisation of his dreams of political fame. An acquaintance in the legal way of business has mentioned to Margaret that Boswell's jocularity has rather stood in the way of him getting a judgeship. He's never yet got hold of a really big case, the kind of national event which can make a man's name and career. And the House of Commons, which can only be reached by being elected, rottenly, corruptly or, very occasionally, because the voters actually want you in there, depends totally on those local landowners who control the vote and James has never quite managed to get in with these gentlemen. He's either been too convivial or too learned or too snobbish or too early or too late or, sometimes, too naïve.

The idea that writing pamphlets, even very witty ones, against a political tendency is not likely to endear you, especially in the land of grudges, to its adherents has never quite settled in his head. Even his adored Sam Johnson had suffered from this lack of social nous.

Edward Thrale, the wealthy London brewer of Thrale's Entire ('Porter, happy produce of our isle, Can cheer each Manly Heart!' as his advertisement has it) who, with his wife Hester had more or less adopted Johnson, giving him the run of their houses and lives, had died in 1781. Johnson missed his old friend who for fifteen years had offered untainted respect and affection – and a damned good table too, since though he cared little for the intellectuals, eating, along with Hester, was Thrale's pride and joy. In the end it killed him.

Boswell has never really liked Hester, who has the double temerity to be a woman who both resisted his charms and exerted her own upon Johnson. So he penned a facetious poem upon the subject of mighty Sam's supposed wooing of the tiny widow and their resultant conjugal happiness.

My dearest darling, view your slave,
Behold him as your very scrub,

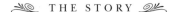

Ready to write as author grave,
Or govern well the brewing tub.

To rich felicity thus raised
My bosom glows with amorous fire:
Porter no longer shall be praised;
Tis I myself am Thrale's entire.

Not only are our limbs entwined,
And lip in rapture glued to lip;
Locked in embraces of the mind
Imagination's sweets we sip.

It was funny, yes. It wasn't true, Johnson would never have ventured on an amorous relationship with Mrs Thrale any more than she with him; he would never have set aside his strict moral code or opened himself to ridicule. But it was funny, and Bozzie just couldn't resist declaiming it here, there and everywhere and simply didn't see that anyone, even Johnson himself, might find it objectionable. After all, you only have to know Jamie to love him because he is a such a sweet, pleasant creature.

Unfortunately, not everybody has a sweet tooth and those who control political influence and consider themselves wise in the ways of the world tend to like their beer bitter and their music with a bit of bite, which is why Joseph Haydn's slow movements go down rather more easily than Mr Boyce's. And why both went down better than Boswell's chance of getting a parliamentary seat in Scotland.

He thinks his only route of preferment now lies in England, and where else in England but London. That is his natural stamping ground, not some damp North British moor with sheep. Only there is the material question: to live means to live in a certain style, he is a Scottish gentleman, the descendant of a fine line and owes his ancestors that much. And to live well means joining the English Bar and picking up clients on the various circuits. He has, in preparation, performed the arcane ritual of eating the correct number of dinners in the Inner Temple and, though English law (based on common law) is a long way from Scottish law (based on Roman law), he has no doubt that he can pick up the knowledge with a stint of sustained study. He might ask himself when it last was that he sustained anything more than an erection but he does not. He is, after all, a sweet, pleasant fellow and bound to succeed. Only a year or so ago, just before Johnson's death, he had taken himself off to see his old acquaintance Henry Dundas to seek his opinion on a move to London.

A friend of Margaret Boswell's, Dundas is a man whose powers of concentration and application are the polar opposite of Boswell's. The two had known each other slightly at university, though Dundas was two years below the Boswell–Johnstone–Temple set and had never become close; he was derided by the older boys for his obvious ambition of which he made no secret. What wasn't so obvious, was an unmatched sense of political timing, the ability to read and cultivate men more powerful than himself and a deep understanding of political and legal structures. It was as if he carried a map drawer in his mind and could pull out a plan of the Scottish legal system, the Admiralty finances, the Home Department in London at a moment's notice and find his way around with perfect facility.

At the time James found himself knocking on Henry's door, Dundas was known as the uncrowned king of Scotland. He had been appointed solicitor general at the age of thirty-three, he had spotted William Pitt's potential and been the man who advised him to go for power after the fall of Lord North, he was a deputy governor of the Bank of Scotland, he controlled upwards of thirty parliamentary seats. Everything he touched turned to gold and Boswell had, on many an occasion, wondered why the wight should be so lucky. On another occasion he had considered challenging the fellow to duel over a remark passed about Boswell's father. The affair came to nothing – had Dundas been the challenger there's little doubt his man would have been dead and buried in a trice.

Boswell can never quite make up his mind how much he despises Henry Dundas; it generally depends on how much he wants something from him and what chance he has of getting it but somewhere, deep within himself, he suspects that Dundas thinks James Boswell is a shallow man.

Dundas thought the move to London a good idea, as long as Boswell could afford something in the region of £1000 a year to support his family; Boswell admitted he'd nothing like that amount; he could reckon on £500 if he was lucky. Dundas hummed, ha'd and more or less came to the conclusion that it might not be such a good idea; on the other hand, when Boswell raised the question of getting a seat on the Scottish bench, a seat which Dundas had already bought and sold, the whole venture began to look just a little more possible and Boswell, at least, left thinking he was set fair for fame and London.

He left behind him seething resentment in just about every political breast in Scotland as the result of a pamphlet – *A Letter to the People of Scotland* – which he'd written against a parliamentary move, generally supported north of the border, to reduce the number of Lords of Sessions which Boswell took as an abuse of the Articles of Union between England and Scotland. It was a position which any man of spirit might take if he had set out to become a thorn in the side of the establishment; a Wilkes would have tossed it off and walked away laughing. Boswell, despite his sanguine nature, has an uneasy suspicion that such an attack upon men he knows, including Henry Dundas, will neither be forgotten nor forgiven so easily.

To begin with, everything does indeed look rosy in London. True, Johnson is no longer there but Boswell has decided to begin his presumptuous task of biography with a trial run, putting his diaries of their jaunt though the Hebrides in 1773 into book form which he now intends to issue to test the waters.

He's met up with a lot of old friends and acquaintances and, on some occasions, actually got home reasonably sober after spending time (three times!!!) with various new friends. He's spent dreary hours observing the law courts and has given a splendid dinner to celebrate his calling to the English Bar; he sets off on the Northern Circuit, hoping to pick up a few clients and begin his new, English, legal career with a flourish.

Unfortunately, he is, though a good deal older than most of his fellow councils in terms of custom and experience, the actual Junior on the circuit, who has any number of onerous duties to perform, including arranging lodgings and settling bills. It is galling to a man of spirit and pride but he is able to congratulate himself on cutting a fine figure with the Lancashire ladies and is more than capable of keeping up with his young companions when it came to the bottle. Their jokes, handing him a fake brief that he falls for hook, line and sinker, are harder to cope with; he doesn't enjoy looking like a flat but he puts up with it all in good-ish humour and enjoys the picture he makes as an advocate.

Back in London, a different picture awaits him. The *Tour to the Hebrides* has been published to general enthusiasm. Reviews and sales are good, except where the reviewer has an old score to pay off and after the *Letter to the People of Scotland*, there are quite a few of those and they don't hold back. Boswell has never been reluctant to sound his own trumpet and in the *Tour* he has blown an orchestra-full but what most reviewers catch on to is the very thing that gives the book its lively, lifelike qualities and make it a delight to read: the author's use of conversation and asides, letters and confidences, his successful attempt to present Johnson as a man in full, moving through a world reported exactly as it was in every particular.

Boswell's friend and collaborator on the book, the Shakespeare scholar Edmund Malone, has cautioned about the inclusion of conversation; Boswell replies that he does not intend to withhold any part of the story, no matter how ludicrous. It is exactly the spirit that allowed him to write an insolent poem about the Doctor and Mrs Thrale and hector the people of Scotland without thinking of any comeback. Malone points out that whilst in a biographer Boswell's style is not only unique but very near an invention of genius, in a man who still wants to make a public career it is not only stupid but very nearly suicidal.

Jack Lee, the English Attorney General, tells him straight: it won't help his career at the bar if his clients think he is a blabbermouth.

Malone manages not to say 'I told you so', but can't resist reminding Boswell how much mischief the *Letter* had done.

Boswell says he expects a certain amount of criticism on the style of his book and has inserted a sort of apology, mentioning Shakespeare and Dryden, speculating on what pleasure it would have given us now to know their petty habits, their characteristic manners, their modes of composition. All these are irrevocably lost.

Close friends like Burke and Garrick feel no easier after reading this. Garrick even proposes that Boswell should be searched for pens and paper before being allowed to drink with his friends. Boswell snorts that he doesn't need notes to remember conversations, he carries them all in his head. One Alexander Tyler, a Scots advocate mentioned in the *Tour*, decides to settle that by blowing off Mr Boswell's head. The travellers had met the advocate in Edinburgh, where they had engaged in a learned dispute about Gaelic poetry in the course of which Johnson had forced Tyler to admit that he knew not a word of the language. Boswell thought he'd got permission to publish an account of the meeting; he hadn't. It now looks as if Tyler is going to demand satisfaction. He doesn't get it; mutual friends intervene and the matter is settled amicably.

Then a letter arrives from Sir Alexander MacDonald also demanding satisfaction. It begins to look as though there's a queue of duellists ready to plant lead in James Boswell's forehead. It's all very upsetting; he isn't sleeping, he's quite naturally distracted by the thought of killing or being killed. It's bad enough realising (memento mori) that death is certain, but knowing it's waiting at precisely eleven in the morning on Tuesday week is particularly depressing. Letters are sent back and forth and, at last, after MacDonald is assured that the disputed passage will be removed from all future editions, the matter is settled.

At the end of the *Tour* an advertisement appears for the forthcoming life of Samuel Johnson by James Boswell; whatever the fuss occasioned by the test run, the overwhelming response has been highly favourable and even with half a dozen other Johnson lives promised to the public, Boswell is still the favoured runner. And then it all rather goes flat.

Melancholy, as he'd once written, is like the fever or gout and is incident to all sorts of men, from the wisest to the most foolish. Then again, it is not every man who can be exquisitely miserable, any more than exquisitely happy, and Boswell often thinks himself the most miserable of mortals, his prostrate soul heaving beneath a load of huge imagination, his heart fluttering with guilt in a guiltless breast.

Well, more or less guiltless, since he feels very real guilt over deserting Margaret so much of the time when she's struggling against the consumption; and then there is guilt over the fate of his children, stuck in the far, uncultured north. Sometimes he wanders the streets of London weeping with sheer depression and lies abed all morning, unable to get out up and face a hopeless future in which he never finds another client, and the piles and piles of notes and journal pages for the *Life*, or the *LIFE* as it is rapidly becoming, are a constant reminder of his dilatory and changeable nature. His father had been right: he'll never amount to anything and now there is no Sam Johnson to shake him by the shoulder and tell him to buck up.

One morning he has breakfast with an old friend, James Mario Matra, who is going off to be ambassador to Morocco and has some wild scheme about settling a colony on the shores of *terra australis* and Boswell, exiled in his own mental *terra australis*, makes up his mind to bear his mental pain with quiet fortitude. He goes out and calls on Malone and chats over the *LIFE* and has coffee and tea and stays to a dinner of pickled salmon and sits till one o'clock over port and madeira and good conversation and feels as full an enjoyment of life as at any time.

Two days later he is feeling wretched again but Matra recommends an emetic, which seems to do the job, and Boswell sits down to write a letter to Henry Dundas asking for a position as Lord of Sessions that will keep him and the family afloat until he begins making money at the bar. The last time he wrote to Dundas had been in the *Letter*, specifically attacking him for abolishing said Lords, so the uncrowned king of Scotland may be a trifle surprised at receiving what amounts to a begging letter. He puts off answering for the time being.

Two days after this Boswell confines himself to his rooms – a new London house is being built for the family in Great Queen Street – and spends the next three days eating toast and tea for breakfast and boiled milk and toast at night whilst he pulls the first part of the *LIFE* into shape.

It is his intention to carry on working for a fourth day but Malone drops by at about four o'clock and invites him to take a trip into the country and dine at Dulwich. Boswell can hardly decline so handsome an offer and they set off, first on foot, then by coach. At Dulwich they visit the College and find a good inn where they eat bacon and eggs – Boswell notes the intensity of the taste after three days of milk and dry toast – followed by mutton chops. They drink madeira and small ale and walk back to town where they eat cold beef and drink wine and water. Small pleasures, perhaps, but none the less the future begins to look a little brighter, particularly after Boswell takes his courage in both hands and moves his family down to the new house on Great Queen Street. Schools are found for the boys, Sandy and Jamie, and the girls, Veronica and Euphemia, where they can pick up English manners, accents and education.

However, Boswell's career prospects in the law aren't improving, he's only managed one client since arriving at the English Bar and even dinner invitations seem to be drying up: he is reduced to playing draughts with a young friend who, somehow, always manages to get the better of him. And then, out of the blue, things begin to look dazzling when the sun of Lord Lonsdale rises above the horizon and Boswell launches himself happily and innocently into hell.

Like so many things in his life, it starts well. A week after the tea-and-toast writing marathon Boswell receives an invitation to dine with John Lowther, Lord Lonsdale, an acquaintance he has long been courting. A man of immense wealth and powers of patronage, Lonsdale is a legendary figure in London and in the border country, where he rules like a medieval baron, controlling his tenants and supporters through a mixture of charm and threat. His control over any number of rotten boroughs offers a first-class seat inside the coach all the way to parliament and on a number of occasions, including in the *Letter to the People of Scotland* and the *Tour*, Boswell has managed to include flattering references to a man he actually wants to flatter. He's tried to get close to the Great Lowther through a number of mutual acquaintances, particularly Lord Eglinton, who has – for whatever reason – blocked off his access.

On the Sunday after receiving his invitation Boswell, walking with Malone in the Strand, bumps into Eglinton and casually mentions that he is to dine with Lonsdale later in the week, where a turtle is to be served. He enquires: 'Pray, my lord, do you dine there too? I have got a card to a turtle!'

Eglinton, obviously miffed, replies that he does not and that, anyway Lonsdale is a great bore: 'He'll tell you a long story of ...'

But Boswell breaks in and, assuming an insider's look, expresses his surprise and is about to confide – as it were – the deeply private and fascinating matter that will be discussed at the dinner when he catches Malone's eye and says: 'But I must follow my friend,' and hurries off, leaving Eglinton to chew over what he might be missing. Boswell gleefully confides to Malone that this is not 'tantalizing' Eglinton so much as 'turtleizing' him!

In fact Boswell doesn't dine with Lonsdale; he is otherwise engaged and can't be absolutely certain the invitation isn't a joke against him so decides against turning up at a house from which he might be turned away. The invitation is genuine but Lonsdale doesn't take the refusal amiss; six months later he sends Boswell a note asking if he would be so kind as to serve as the mayor's counsel in the forthcoming elections at Carlisle, a town in which his lordship has some interest and influence.

This is good news. His legal career is not prospering; the *LIFE* is progressing but slowly; Boswell is adamant that nothing of relevance should be left out and that every fact, every phrase must be as authentic as he can make it. There is a vast net of correspondence opening up across the nation as he writes to old and distant friends and acquaintances of the doctor for any scrap of information they might be able to provide. Then there is the black dog, which often drops by for a week or even a month at a time and causes all work to cease. Carlisle is a godsend: the position will pay, though not a lot, but could lead on to an appointment as Recorder of the town bringing in £20 a year without too much effort. He tells his Lordship's representative that he is at his disposal and can head north at a moment's notice.

Once installed as counsel, Boswell has to check the credentials of the voters and exclude those who will vote against the Lonsdale ticket whilst authenticating those who will vote for it. The work is simple enough: election agents, bribes and bully boys have sorted the pros from the contras; however, getting on with Lonsdale is anything but easy and Boswell begins to suspect that he has attached himself to a tyrant of Neronian dimensions.

The rules are simple: do whatever Lonsdale wants, whenever he wants it and keep your mouth shut; never, ever, complain; don't go to sleep at table whilst he tells his interminable pointless stories; don't ask for good wine or even bad wine because he won't give you any, even though he's drinking the stuff himself; don't expect him to offer anyone else at table an oyster, even though there's a good few dozen; don't argue or he'll challenge you to a duel and do his very best to kill you. Lonsdale is an over-indulged three-year-old with a fortune as vast as his selfishness and the invaluable bully's talent of recognising who not to annoy, though there must have a been a few warm moments at the Hell Fire Club when he was a member unless, perhaps, he kept his mouth shut when in company with that band of devil-may-care rakes and roisterers.

Boswell, unable to call on Auld Nick to spirit him away, sits through a series of endless, wineless dinners listening to Lonsdale's harangues and his blatant rudeness whenever anyone dares to interrupt, even to agree with him. He bellows down the table 'you will hear!!' and drones on, occasionally putting in an aside about the look of a man's wig – the victim whistles tunelessly under the insult – and goes on and on and on until half the table takes refuge (as did Nero's hapless audiences) in feigning sleep and even, Boswell is tempted, death. In the end, Lonsdale begins to snore and the bruised, battered, hungry and thirsty diners slope away for a drink and a cutlet in more convivial surroundings. This servitude comes to an end at last and Boswell leaves Carlisle with £150 in his pocket book; it is good money hard earned, though he might have reflected that Lonsdale now considers Mr Boswell to be bought and sold and one of his people.

Boswell returns to more normal, if less profitable, pursuits for the next few months, plodding away at the *LIFE* and carrying on various affairs, principally with Mrs Rudd, a fascinating woman who has been deeply involved in a sensational case and has only just escaped with her life.

Coming from a poor background, Caroline Rudd used both her looks and her brains to forge a career as an upmarket whore, sleeping with and later blackmailing wealthy men. She fell in with a couple of high-class crooks, the twins Perreau, and married the elder, Daniel, a financier with an extremely dubious background. The marriage took hold, the couple had three children but Daniel's skills were not equal to the stock exchange and there was never enough money to go round. It was Caroline, many said, who introduced the idea of forging promissory notes as an easier way of making a profit and make a profit they did: the three lived in high style until the forgeries were discovered in 1776.

The Perreaus said it was all Caroline's fault, she was a conniving bitch who had fooled them totally; Caroline simpered and said she'd go King's evidence. The prosecution, accepting that two gaolbirds on the scaffold were better than one – even a pretty woman – accepted her offer to the extent of securing a conviction against the Perreaus. Then, in a rather underhand manner, Caroline found herself on trial but was more than equal to the task of convincing the audience of her innocence. There could be definite advantages in being considered the weaker, gentler, more tractable sex and in her widows' weeds she sold her innocence to the jury who came out with a verdict in her favour in under thirty minutes.

The case has been the talk of the town and Boswell, along with every other rake in London, felt himself drawn to this fascinating woman who had, unlike her accomplices, escaped the gallows by a simper. He thinks she is an enchantress and wants to be enchanted; he knows she very nearly ended up a corpse – and as a man who is fascinated by death and spends days at Newgate chatting to the condemned, watching them swing and then studying, with the most minute attention, their dead faces – he finds Caroline Rudd irresistible and thinks that like water corrupted and grown fresh again, her art is become purest simplicity:

SHE: I'll show you a miniature of myself if you'll return it upon your honour. This was taken when I was in confinement, in case of an accident.

HE: What, Madame, do you talk with so much ease? Do you mean losing your life?

SHE: Yes.

HE: What, being hanged?

SHE: I assure you, I should never have been hanged, I had taken care of that.

HE: What! You had resolution to destroy yourself?

SHE: I promise you, I'm not afraid of death. I am above it. I have too much virtue to be a prude and too much sense to be a coquette.

HE: You could make me commit murder! But you would be sorry afterwards to have made so ungenerous a use of your powers. You have no occasion to be convinced of your powers over the human heart. You know it. I dare say you could make me do anything. (DELIRIUM SEIZES HIM) Is a pretty ankle one of your perfections?

SHE: Yes.

HE: Your eyes ...

SHE: Poets and painters have told me enough of them.

HE KISSES HER

SHE: I have heard I have a fine mouth.

HE KISSES HER AGAIN – WITH PASSION.

HE: Adieu!

AND AGAIN

Adieu!!!
AND AGAIN
God bless you.[6]

After that, the pair don't get together again until Boswell's return to
London in 1785, a meeting he thinks so wonderful it brings on an
attack of the thees and thous: 'how much do I owe to thee who hast
made the greatest pleasure of human life new to me!' Which is some
feat, given Boswell's expertise in the field, the bed, the couch and
coach and bridge and just about every other location in which a man
might screw, snabble, split, shag, hump, drill, prod, punch or put four
quarters on the spit. 'Thou hast shown me it,' he rhapsodises, 'pure
and free from evil.'

Mrs Rudd is very, very good at her job and Boswell becomes a
constant friend and customer, not that the money is flowing that
freely.

The *LIFE* is going well enough with Malone's help and encouragement. There are other biographers – Mrs Thrale amongst them – but
Boswell is happy to let them appear first; he has confidence, most of
the time, that his will supersede theirs with no trouble at all.

The big problem is keeping his wife and family fed and housed in a
suitable style and when, at the end of 1787, he gets a note from Lord
Lonsdale stating that the post of Recorder of Carlisle is once more
available and that his lordship is minded to offer it to Mr Boswell, he
jumps at the chance, presenting himself, as requested, at Lonsdale's
house at nine in the morning, to the very second, on 21st December
ready to leap aboard the coach for the journey north.

Two hours later he is still waiting, as he is four hours later and
six hours later until finally, as it begins to get dark, the coach moves
off, empty. Lonsdale never boards his coach outside his own door but
always sends it a street or two away and walks the first few yards of his
journey. One of his companions tells Boswell that this is a school that
all who hope for the lord's favour must pass through. Boswell mutters
that it is harder than the school of Pythagoras but since he needs the
£20 per annum which the position will bring him – and there has also

been a clear offer of one of Lonsdale's parliamentary seats if Mr B pleases – he sets aside his concerns and walks along with the little group, learning his lessons.

Once aboard the coach, Lonsdale is anxious to get on and upbraids postilions, drivers and link boys as they head north: 'Boys, I'm in a great hurry and if I have to call you again, you shall have nothing. If I must waste my lungs I must save my cash.' Boswell sings songs from *The Beggar's Opera* to pass the time and tries to keep warm. They arrive at Lonsdale's estate, Lowther Castle, on the 23rd to find the house icy and no fires likely to be lit; dinner is meagre, late, accompanied by Lonsdale's complaints and followed by the reading of an entire tragedy to which he has taken a fancy. In the morning, Lonsdale's general factotum, Satterthwaite, ensures that Boswell and the other guests for the festive season have a roll and butter in their rooms before breakfast, but only on condition that they 'beware of telling'!

Satterthwaite also confides to Boswell that Lord Lonsdale expects 'his' MPs to do as they are told and vote as he bids them. This casts a damper upon Boswell, who is missing his wife and family and Mrs Rudd and London in equal parts; that night he has a dream in which his father appears to him and chides him for being so subservient.

Christmas is a dreary business with interminable dinners, not enough food and drink and far too much hectoring. Boswell groans within as the snow falls and the days pass: is it really worth all this just to be Recorder of Carlisle and get into the House of Commons? Well, yes, it is; James Boswell MP would be a man to respect; in one leap he'd gain that *gravitas* which has, hitherto, always escaped him. No more Bozzie the drunk, the joker, the listener, the good fellow to be sure but ... but ... Yes, being a member of parliament will surely get rid of the 'but' in his life. So he sits it out with gritted teeth despite moments of homesickness that, on one occasion, lead to a hurried bag-packing and an expedition, through the snow, to the staging post for the London coach.

On 31st December, Boswell asks his patron when exactly he will be elected Recorder. Lonsdale replies he doesn't know, he hasn't thought about it yet. This isn't promising. The next two weeks seem set to last a lifetime. Letters came from London: his wife Margaret is in indifferent health and his daughter Veronica has been ill but there are no more details and he frets and once more asks Lonsdale when he will be appointed. He receives the same throwaway answer: 'I am thinking of it.'

On 6th January, he receives a letter from his brother David in London telling him that Margaret's health is far worse than she admitted and that Boswell should be home and by her side. It puts him in a panic: he is far from the perfect husband but he loves and respects his wife as the keel, the mainmast of his life; to be without her is a truly ghastly prospect. He becomes desperate to get away.

Finally, on 10th January, Lonsdale allows him to leave the gloomy halls of Lowther Castle and travel to Carlisle where he meets the mayor and corporation and, on the following day, is duly elected Recorder of the town. It should be a great occasion; he's suffered enough to be there but his mind is full of anxiety about Margaret and as soon as the ceremony is over, he grabs his cases and boards the coach for London.

Three days later, he races along Great Queen Street, certain that he is too late, that Margaret is dead. Then he sees the front door knocker tied up so as not to disturb the invalid. She is alive, thank God, but when he reaches her bedside, he sees clearly that she has been at the gates of death. He is, for all his relief, plunged into a great melancholy. Perhaps it is the result of all his efforts over the last weeks or of Margaret's illness or of his inability, despite Malone's urgings, to get back to work on the *LIFE*, but all the vitality has drained away and with Margaret in bed, there is no influence to keep him away from the drink in a search to find himself again.

Never a man to do misery by halves, he begins visiting Dilly's Gambling House where, after drinking more than is good for him, he plays whist, loses, tries to recoup his losses and ends up all of nineteen pounds, seven shillings and sixpence down. He takes to his bed, too miserable to answer the door to anyone, which leaves Francesco Sastres, an Italian friend of Johnson's, unable to deliver a collection of letters he has promised Boswell. He gives them instead to Mrs Thrale for her collected *Letters to and from the Late Samuel Johnson LL.D.*

Then his agent writes from Auchinleck telling him that a local merchant had defaulted on bills due for the sale of woodland and there is only £34 in the kitty, with about £50 overdraft left with the Ayr Bank. After feverish calculations it becomes clear that he has, in all, about £129 to support his family for the next nine months. It simply isn't enough.

He talks it over with Margaret; her anxiety brings on a fever – more guilt – but she comes up with the only possible answer: they must leave London and go back to Scotland. But, that confounded 'but' again, the only answer is utterly impossible: it will mean putting the *LIFE* aside and be the end of all his ambitions for cutting a fine and respected figure in town. Margaret tells him that he cannot give the application necessary for the practice of the English law and that he leads a life of dissipation and intemperance, so that he does not go on with his *Life of Doctor Johnson*, from which he expects fame and profit. She says that he is even being neglected by those who used to invite him when he first came to London, 'for people shun a man who is known to be dependant and in labouring circumstance,' as he writes in his journal.

Boswell is stunned and Margaret takes the opportunity of adding that if they do not go north, their children must suffer in their health for want of good air and exercise.

Her arguments, he thinks, have very great weight.

Arthur Phillip

When Arthur Phillip returns from South America he finds that some things never change: the situation in England is the same as when he'd last been on active service. France and Spain are in alliance and threatening British prospects with a combined fleet insolently sailing up and down the English Channel. One thing, however, has changed: he left as a lowly fourth lieutenant and is, on his return, bumped up to first, jumping two whole steps, and is posted to a first-rate, the *Alexander*, during her fitting out at Greenwich. As first lieutenant he is responsible for overseeing all repairs, and the loading and making and mending necessary to get the ship ready for sea. He is clearly climbing the ladder of promotion and, given his lack of family influence, is at the age of forty in a good position to make the next step to master and commander once a suitable ship – a frigate – becomes available.

Alexander joins the Channel Fleet in July 1779 and patrols the western approaches; the combined French and Spanish Fleets come within telescope distance on a number of occasions but wind, weather and naval policy mean that action is not joined. Phillip does, however, receive his promotion when on return to port he is given command of the *Basilisk*, an ancient frigate no longer able to keep up with the main fleet, which has been recommissioned as a fire ship.

A less sanguine man than Arthur Phillip might see such a command as no very long-lasting thing; the *Basilisk* is designed to sail as close as possible to a potential enemy – presumably a very slow enemy – grapple and secure and set light to herself and burn the enemy to the waterline. However, once the dockyard mateys begin to look her over it becomes plain that the ship is so old and decrepit that even the efforts necessary to creep and combust are beyond her. Nevertheless Phillip has occupied the position of master and commander, and though this, unlike the godlike rank of captain, is not substantive, it is an important rung on the ladder and reflects the Admiralty's satisfaction with their intelligence agent's reports, if nothing else.

At a bit of a loss, Arthur applies to join the *Victory*, patrolling in the Channel, as a volunteer; there is no action in prospect but the fleet purser is an ambitious young civil servant named Evan Nepean, who is putting out feelers and making contacts in every direction he can with an eye to his future influence.

Cruising on the *Victory* is not likely to advance Phillip's prospects, however, and he begins to badger his acquaintances and former spymasters at the Admiralty. Augustus Hervey has retired but Lord Sandwich, an Admiralty Lord with a finger in many pies, personal and professional, does see him on at least a couple of occasions, though without any immediate results. There are, however, letters of recommendation which Sandwich reads, from his Portuguese employers and from a certain Mr Shafto, a shadowy gentleman who swims in the clouded waters of international intelligence; it is clear that Arthur Phillip has delivered and is waiting for some sort of reward for his undercover work. And wait he does, going onto half pay, relieving captains when they have to be absent from their ships, killing time travelling around Britain and finally, on 10th October 1781, receiving promotion to post captain. Now all he has to do is remain alive long enough without blotting his copybook and he will, in the fullness of time, become an admiral and fly his flag.

His new command is a frigate, *Ariadne*, which is directed to sail to the Elbe to collect a detachment of German troops en route for India. On arrival, he finds himself iced in and has to spend a tedious winter waiting for the thaw and settling the endless quarrels which arise amongst the bored and fractious soldiers.

When the ice melts, he frees his ship from the protective mud into which he'd driven her, delivers his cargo and takes the *Ariadne* out on patrol. It's an uneventful time but at least he's in work whilst many others are not and when, in the autumn of 1782 he is promoted to the command of a sixty-four-gun ship, he can count himself a success, despite spending, as his fellow captains must have noticed, a lot of years away from the Navy and off the promotion ladder.

The situation in the New World is becoming explosive, with a revolt in Peru and considerable tension between Spanish and Portuguese settlers. Tommy Townshend, Lord Sydney, the minister at the Home Department, needs information – maybe the time is right for a British expedition to the River Plate to establish a presence in what has become known as the Spanish lake. After all, Britain is still at war with Spain, though it is a fairly desultory affair; peace negotiations are in the air but the Spanish demand for the return of Gibraltar is holding everything up. A swift reminder of British naval power on the shores of their own Empire, might concentrate Juan Dago's mind on the matter in hand. Sydney, as usual, passes the problem down to his new secretary, Evan Nepean, who calls on the South American experts to supply him with relevant information and come up with a few alternatives; and who is better informed about the Latin American theatre than Arthur Phillip?

In November 1783 a squadron of four ships of the line leaves Britain for the coast of Spanish South America. Captain Phillip commands the *Europe*, a sixty-four-gun fourth-rate. The weather is typical: winter storms plague the little fleet from the moment they leave port and the weather in the Bay of Biscay is so bad that they became separated; three of the vessels are so badly damaged they have to sail back to port to effect repairs. The fourth, *Europe*, ploughs on and, despite more bad weather and scurvy amongst the crew, arrives off Rio de Janeiro in the spring of 1784.

Proceeding into the estuary of the River Plate, the *Europe* passes the Spanish defences without mishap but when approaching the Portuguese shore, she is fired upon by the Portuguese fort at Santa Cruz. They are not the best shots and all the balls miss; Phillip is also aware that the Portuguese will fire at any ship unknown to them or about which they nurse suspicions. He does not, however, consider himself to be a suspicious character, nor the Union Jack to be unknown; on landing he tells the Governor that, though he has not so far returned fire, if there isn't a full and prompt apology for this grievous insult to his Majesty's flag, he will take his ship back into the roads and blow the fort to rubble. The apology is instant and full: everyone knows and respects the English captain who was an old friend to Portugal; it is all an unfortunate mistake.

Entertained ashore, Phillip takes every opportunity to look around and make notes on Spanish and Portuguese dispositions. It won't take much, he notes, to overcome Spanish resistance in the area; the Spanish have no line-of-battle ships and only a couple of frigates; their troops are disorganised and, for the most part, dispirited.

After making necessary repairs, the *Europe* sails and falls in with a small convoy of merchantmen who inform Phillip that the Spanish have withdrawn their demand for Gibraltar and that peace with Britain has been concluded; his mission is also concluded. He makes for Madras, where his orders direct him to join the India Fleet under the command of Sir Edward Hughes, who is more than grateful for the supplies the *Europe* brings with her; however, he is less than happy about the general state of repair of the ship, particularly with the monsoon season coming on. *Europe* is attached to a squadron under the command of Sir Richard King which is sailing back to England to refit.

The journey home begins well with following winds speeding them across the Indian Ocean, but as they approach the Cape of Good Hope their luck runs out and they find themselves tossed hither and yon in a series of violent storms. They make port at Cape Town but the Dutch governor is at first reluctant to allow them to land their sick and make temporary repairs: his government has been allied with the Spanish and he is not yet aware of any truce or peace talks. Fortunately, Commodore King has orders from Admiral Hughes that make the cessation of hostilities plain and the weary, battered and bruised mariners are finally allowed ashore.

The Dutch are grudging hosts; they knew perfectly well that Britain has a hungry eye on their possessions in the east and they must also be aware, at some level or another, that their own subject populations would be more than happy to exchange their brutal, blood-soaked exploitation for the comparatively humane exploitation of John Bull. Phillip notes, in a report to the Admiralty, that the majority of Dutch sailors he has spoken with would infinitely prefer to enjoy the plum-duff of British naval discipline than their own, and that Albion might well crew half her navy with Hollanders.

The land around Table Mountain is a delight to all: fine and airy prospects, beautiful gardens, fruit to be had for the picking, exotic animals from the hinterlands to be observed and drawn in notebooks. There are prostitutes by the hundred – all of them slaves, for whilst methodistical Britain had discovered its aversion to the cruel practice, the Dutch, like the Brazilians and the Americans, still find it a perfectly workable economic tool.

Once temporary repairs are made, the fleet leaves harbour and makes for roast beef and Old England, though the *Europe*, being the fastest of the group, is sent on ahead with Admiral Hughes's dispatches noting the difficulty of dealing with the Dutch and the advisability of having an alternative British base somewhere in the southern seas. The dispatches are delivered and the ship's crew paid off in May 1784.

Arthur Phillip takes a holiday in newly friendly France at the invitation of Evan Nepean, who has heard a whisper that the French are building up their supplies of timber. The Home Department is concerned about French ambitions and to be forewarned is to be forearmed. Phillip is by no means the only tourist with a notebook in the south of France that summer but his eye for detail and knowledge of ships and shipfitting allows him to deliver the firm judgement that something other than sea spray is in the air.

Back home he has, for once, time to himself. It's not a state he enjoys; Arthur Phillip is a man who needs to be kept busy because on the other side of 'busy' is sentiment and feeling and emotion, the great enemies of reason. He occupies himself with farming, a job that requires hours almost as early as that of sailing a ship but it is always second best; he is not one for lonely walks o'er the lea or chatting across a gate and he waits impatiently for a letter from the Admiralty offering him something, anything else.

A few days after his forty-eighth birthday one does come; Arthur Phillip receives a letter from Lord Sydney at the Home Department, though he must suspect that it is the work of his old spymaster and friend Evan Nepean. After the conventional flowery greetings, Tommy Townshend – in the name of King George – gets down to business:

> 'We have ordered that about 600 male and 180 female convicts now under sentence or order of transportation whose names are contained in the list annexed, should be removed out of the gaols and other places of confinement in this our Kingdom and put on board the several transport ships which have been taken up for their reception. It is our Royal will and pleasure that you do take them under your protection and proceed in the Sirius, with the said transports to the port of the coast of New South Wales situated in the longitude of 33' 41" called by the name of Botany Bay.
>
> 'According to the best information which we have obtained, Botany Bay appears to be the most eligible situation upon the said coast for the first establishment, possessing a commodious harbour and other advantages which no other part of the coast hitherto discovered affords. It is our will that you do, immediately upon landing, after as much as possible taking measures for securing yourself from any attacks by the natives of the country, proceed to the cultivation of land, distributing the convicts for that purpose under such regulations as may appear to you to be necessary for procuring supplies of grain and ground provisions.
>
> 'You are, by every means possible, to open an intercourse with the natives and conciliate their affections, enjoining all our subjects to live in amity and kindness with them. You will endeavour to procure an account of the numbers inhabiting the neighbourhood of the settlement and report your opinion to one of our secretaries of state in what manner our relations with these people may be turned to the advantage of this country.'

There is an extra paragraph tacked on the end about the rites of the Church of England and the vigilance to be pursued in ensuring that no unworthy or scandalous persons are allowed to assume the position of minister in the new land – and warning that the Bishop of London will be waiting to hear his report about that on his return. The thirty-nine articles are still a mighty band of iron protecting the people of Britain from Popery, no matter where in the world it might raise its head. Two Roman Catholic priests, on hearing of the plan, have offered to go, paying their own way: 'We rely,' they write, 'on the known humanity of government.' The offer is rejected.

However, the expedition chaplain, when appointed, will be well armed against apostasy with fifty copies of Syng's *Religion Made Easy*, twenty-five *Plain Exhortations to Prisoners*, two hundred *Exercises against Lying*, fifty Woodward's *Cautions to Swearers*, a hundred *Disuasions from Stealing* and another hundred copies of *Exhortations to Chastity* included amongst the essential supplies.

By the time Phillip receives his commission, the scheme has been some time in the preparation and is virtually up and staggering. William Richards Jr, the naval contractor chosen by the Home Department – effectively Evan Nepean – has been organising transport ships for the fleet. He hires three store ships: *Borrowdale*, 272 tons; *Fishburn*, 378 and *Golden Grove* at 331 tons, and six transports for the convicts: *Alexander*, 453 tons; *Charlotte*, 346 tons; *Scarborough*, 418 tons; *Lady Penrhyn*, 338 tons; *Friendship*, 278 tons and *Prince of Wales*, 333 tons. There are also going to be two Royal Navy ships, an armed brig, the *Supply* (eight guns) and the flagship, the converted merchantman *Berwick*, now renamed *Sirius* and fitted with twenty guns – guns which can be turned against enemies, but equally well back on the transports and their reluctant passengers. Phillip, whose commission will be as the governor of the colony or settlement – or in fact, prison – is to be commodore of the fleet with Captain John Hunter, another Nepean friend, in actual command of the *Sirius*.

Being Evan Nepean's friend is no mean lever in this business. The First Lord of the Admiralty, the celebrated Lord Howe, victor of the

Battle of the Glorious First of June, has no very great opinion of the proposed governor, noting: 'that the little knowledge I have of Captain Phillip would not have led me to select him for a service of this complicated nature.' He puts forward a candidate of his own, but it is just that 'little knowledge' that leads Howe to underestimate the man who is about to begin a struggle with the forces of bureaucracy that will become a small epic in its own right. Nepean has a better grasp of Phillip's talents and stiffens Lord Sydney's sinews enough to carry the day and get his man confirmed. Lord Howe is not pleased.

The transports have been fitted out under the aegis of the Navy Board well before Phillip receives his commission; the dockyard workers have fallen back on the old design for the America trade, taking no chances and making no concessions to a voyage that is going to last eight months rather than six weeks.

Adapting from the pattern used in the transporting of troops, the 'tween decks, with a maximum height of five and a half feet, are cleared end to end with basic shelves lining the sides for sleeping purposes. A space of roughly seven by six feet is allotted for every four convicts, regardless of size. The bulkheads forming dividing walls along the course of the deck are studded with nails and have small access holes for musket barrels so the felons might be fired upon – should the need arise.

When he inspects the ships, Phillip reflects that should the need indeed arise then the scuppers will run with blood and his command will end in ignominious failure before he has even arrived on the far side of the world. This commission may be offered as a reward, but it's a double-edged one at best and it will take luck and judgement to get out of it with his reputation intact.

The hatches which allow the convicts to climb up out of their enclosed and fetid quarters are secured with crossbars, bolts and locks whilst the upper deck has a three-foot barricade topped with iron spikes to confine the convicts within their designated exercise area. Armed guards will be placed at all hatches and in commanding positions whenever the convicts are allowed the privilege of going on deck for an airing or a soaking.

The conditions are not good, though they are not that much worse than those endured by the sailors on the average British ship. However, the sailors are fit and well fed; they are used to slinging their hammocks in the tiny space allowed and to eating where they sleep and they also have the habit of cleanliness: a stinking man would not last long in the crowded messes between decks. The convicts, when they came on board, will have undergone months or years of deprivation, many will be suffering from scurvy before starting on the voyage and just about the only parasites and pests they won't be bringing with them from their gaols will be the rats – and the ships have enough of those already.

As the lists of provisions and stores begins to cross his desk, Phillip makes notes on everything. He's spent his whole career being fitted and supplied by the Navy Board and he well knows that what goes down on paper doesn't always arrive in the hold. There are supposed to be forty crosscut saws at ten shillings each and forty frame saws at sixteen shillings. One hammer for every four men which, if numbers hold steady, would be somewhere in the region of a hundred and fifty, at a shilling each, any number of which might go missing; thirty wheelbarrows – vital to any building; two thousand spike nails and two hundred hinges; hooks, lines, needles and nets to the value of £100; scythes, but only six of them and sixty razors; clothes for each convict for one year, including jackets, drawers, hats, shirts, frocks, trousers and shoes at £2.19s.6d per man – though considerably less per woman since, no matter how hard Phillip looks, he can't find any record of their clothing being delivered to the ships and there are no provisions at all for buying cloth to make their clothes at a later date. And, like the cloth, if a thing isn't there, if the axes aren't in the crates or the cooking pots and door locks are missing there's no way in the world they can be replaced. What the fleet doesn't land with, they'll have to do without or improvise on their own behalf.

In a letter to Lord Sydney, Phillip writes about the general lack of everything: 'I am prepared to meet difficulties, and I have only one fear – I fear, my lord, that it may be said that the officer who took charge of the expedition should have known it was more than probable he lost half the garrison and convicts, crowded and victualled in such a manner for such a long voyage.'

He makes it clear that he does not want the general public and his peers in the navy to assume that any losses have come about because of his lack of professionalism. But Tommy Townshend has not got where he is by putting his hand up in answer to the question of who is responsible; he keeps his head well down and leaves Phillip to get on with it.

Phillip begins to put together a statement of his feelings about the scheme. He's experienced enough to know, considering his own clandestine past and the deniability of intelligence matters, that conversations and assurances vanish into the air, only documents survive and he wants his views down on paper.

He requests more seeds and plants and, noting the lack of livestock, suggests that the fleet buy in animals for husbandry at the Cape. He notes the shortages of supplies and asks that they be made up or found, though the women's clothes never are; he suggests that stores and equipment be spread through the fleet, each vessel taking a proportion of the saws, lead shot, etc., so that should any one or two sink or fall out due to damage – not unlikely on such a voyage – the colony won't find itself denied a vital article. He asks for more medical supplies and antiscorbutics since he knows how easily scurvy can spring up at sea, with a resultant loss of morale; on the other hand, he doesn't want his passengers to be too lively and will be sparing of the amount of time they are allowed on deck. The greatest villains amongst them will, he writes, be separated from the rest so as not to influence their behaviour.

Reasonably, he concludes, that if he can make the majority of convicts aware that their future, indeed, their very fate is in their own hands (he intends to visit each transport a number of times during the voyage) he is certain that some amongst them at least will reform themselves and become useful citizens. And it will be as citizens, and not as convicts, that they will help lay the foundations of an Empire. Not that he is naive about the prospects of reform, his years of experience in the navy and throughout the world have knocked any liberal notions firmly upon the head; he considers it right that the convicts and ex-convicts should be separated from the rest of the colonists and any genuine settlers who might come later.

Rewards and punishment will remain in the governor's hands. Death, he hopes, would never be necessary. 'In fact I doubt if the fear of death ever prevented a man of no principal from committing a bad action.' He notes that 'there can be no slavery in a free land and, consequently, no slaves'; convicts will be treated as convicts and the natives will not be coerced into becoming the servants of the newcomers. There will, however, be efforts to make contact and make friends and persuade some to settle near the colony where Phillip will furnish them with 'everything that can tend to civilise them and give them a high opinion of their new guests – for which reason it will be necessary to prevent the transports' crews from having any intercourse with the natives if possible. The convicts must have none, for if they have, the arms of the natives will be very formidable in their hands, the women abused and the natives disgusted. Any man who takes the life of a native will be put on trial the same as if he had kill'd one of the garrison. This appears to me not only just, but good policy. It will be a great point gained if I can proceed in this business without having any dispute with the natives.'

It might be advisable, despite those hundred copies of the *Exhortation to Chastity* that the chaplain will be handing out, to allow a certain amount of prostitution in the colony to tap off some of the tension produced by prolonged abstinence during the voyage. Though excessive activity in the male might result in loss of heat, sallowness and general poor health, a reasonable exercise of the sexual faculty will promote a more temperate character. And since it is generally known that many women's problems arise from the lack of sexual congress – the need of the colder, wetter female body for the balancing dry heat of semen – the practice will settle those females engaged in it as well. It will also put a stop to the Gomorrhans and their damnable habit of faggotry ...

At times Phillip feels that he is writing to the spirits: the many government departments he's dealing with (Navy Board, Home Department, Treasury, Admiralty) never seem to respond to his notes and letters. By January 1787 he is complaining that the conditions aboard the transport *Alexander* are already so crowded that more convicts can not possibly be put aboard; in addition sick and injured are being sent whilst the *Alexander* has neither surgeon nor surgeon's tools to help them. The other transports have to be emptied and thoroughly fumigated before their passengers can come on board, which necessitates hiring a lighter to receive them temporarily and guards to keep watch over them whilst the process is carried out.

He is particularly furious about the state of the female convicts loaded aboard the *Lady Penrhyn* in January. 'The situation in which the magistrates sent the women on board stamps them with infamy – tho' almost naked, and so very filthy, that nothing but clothing them could have prevented them from perishing, and which could not be done in time to prevent a fever, which is still on board that ship, and where there are many venereal complaints, that must spread in spite of every precaution I may take.'

These last-minute problems are eating away at the budget and producing a climate of frustration and anger. Finally, an official at the Navy Board suggests that Phillip start calling personally at the offices of the departments concerned so he can talk over his problems and needs and get a prompt response. It is, he thinks, a brilliant idea and civil servants all over Whitehall come to dread the firm tread and the brisk naval knock at their office doors.

There are complaints: 'Captain Phillip has so increased the orders for stores and implements for Botany Bay that they will occupy three hundred tons' worth of space! I was obliged to put a stop to his wishes still to add.'

But Phillip is unstoppable; he has the kind of persistence which allows him to go on and on at officials where another man would tear off his wig and dance on it. Having Evan Nepean on his side is no disadvantage either, and he is able to call on the extensive network of professional obligation the under secretary has built up over the years.

There are disappointments. He dearly wants to fly a commodore's flag on the *Sirius*, it would be a considerable step up in his career but Lord Howe at the Admiralty will not hear of it; the old hero of the Glorious First of June has never enjoyed being bested by anyone and now he has that damned civil servant Nepean caught on a lee shore with his gun ports shut, and he doesn't hesitate in delivering his broadside. 'Captain' Phillip, he thunders, simply doesn't have the seniority to warrant the appointment (and what's more, it's true: Phillip is, from a strictly technical point of view, trying a slightly impertinent move here) and as the governor of the new colony, he won't be a navy man at all but rather a civilian administrator. Yes, the admiral could have winked and let the appointment past – if Phillip has need of a navy ship it would make it easier for him to commandeer it if he is senior to a post captain – but heroes don't win battles by winking and Lord Howe gains satisfaction for his earlier reversal and Phillip, though commodore in name, will not be able to fly his flag as such.

There are compensations. The same official who earlier tried to block Phillip's re-ordering of the fleet and its provisions is, by the end of the year, forced to admit that the ships 'are better fitted than any set of transports I have ever had any direction in.'

Whilst the ships are provisioned, the officials who will run the colony under the new governor are being chosen; Phillip has a say in some of the naval appointments. Philip Gidley King had been second lieutenant of the *Ariadne* when Phillip had her. A Cornishman and the son of a draper who had worked his way up from captain's servant, very much like Phillip himself, King is a diligent and active officer and something in his quiet manner and lack of show brings him to Phillip's attention 'as one of the most promising young men I have met in the service.' He is to be second lieutenant on the *Sirius* and, on arrival, have the responsibility of setting up a daughter colony on tiny Norfolk Island where Captain Cook saw fine tall pines that will make splendid replacement masts and spars. King rather hopes the island will also provide splendid material for his diaries.

Captain John Hunter, a mutual friend of Evan Nepean, is to be second captain of the *Sirius* and, he hopes, the writer of an instructive volume on the expedition – he will, in effect, have the command whilst Phillip has overall direction of the fleet and the colony.

The Lieutenant Governor and commander of the marine detachment is Major Robert Ross, as yet unknown to Phillip; a career soldier noted for his active and fiery temperament and lack of literary ambition. Under him will be two captains, Campbell and O'Shea, and one captain acting as judge advocate, David Collins, already making notes for an exhaustive volume on the expedition. A step down are two captain-lieutenants, James Meredith and Watkin Tench, the latter of whom also thinks this story is going to be a palpable hit with the reading public and is sharpening a witty and incisive pen with the intention of instructing and amusing his audience.

There are nine first lieutenants and four second lieutenants including a young man called Ralph Clark who, even as he receives his commission is already busily scribbling letters to Captain Phillip in a blizzard of sensibility. Lieutenant Clark is 'devastated' and in 'agony' at the thought of leaving his wife, 'dearest Betsey', in England and 'begs' the governor to grant him permission to carry out Mrs Clark and their son, little Ralph, to New South Wales. It is not to be, Phillip replies, Lord Sydney himself decrees it: no officers' wives. In a spirit of heedless abandon Ralph renews his supplications, this time addressing them to Lord Howe. There is, in the young man's heart, the true spirit of a romantic hero and he needs all his fortitude when the old salt's withering reply burns its way back: 'The Lieutenant requested this posting – Which will require as much attention as if it were active service – Matters of a Domestic Nature are neither wanted nor needed on active service. Your humble servant, Howe.'

The refusal is all the more galling since the non-commissioned officers (twelve sergeants, twelve corporals, eight drummers) and the one hundred and sixty privates have a passel of twenty-eight wives – and seventeen children – trailing in their wake. Sometimes, Ralph reflects, it is better to be ordinary and unburdened by the sensibility of a fine soul.

The chief surgeon is John White (he also has a book in mind), at thirty a man young for such an important position, but he has the ear of Evan Nepean and the strength of character to impose his will on his three assistants, Considen, Arndell and Balmain and, if they don't listen, he's not afraid to stand up with a pistol and shoot it out. Never afraid of coming forward, White is more than happy to support Phillip in his requests – demands – for more and better supplies and improved conditions for the convicts who are being loaded aboard during February and March 1787.

The legal work is being hurried through by various committees who lay down a framework that both allows the crown to claim New South Wales and the new governor to administer it, appoint justices of the peace, declare martial law, establish land ownership and permit fairs, marts and markets and generate the hundreds, indeed the thousands, of other civil, military and commercial processes that empire builders need if they are going to build and hold their empires.

It is suspected that the French have a presence in latitude 33; the explorer and navigator Jean-François de la Perouse was known to be heading that way with three ships and though international tensions rarely effect scientific voyages – Captain Cook would not have been attacked by French or Spanish warships on his expeditions – La Perouse has the reputation of being another Cook but with a smoking pistol in each hand. When mapping the west coast of America he had taken the time to capture two English forts on Hudson Bay and the Admiralty Lords have no intention of seeing him repeat the trick in New South Wales. The legal annexation of Botany Bay (breathtaking sleight of colonial hand though it is) will be backed up by the guns of the *Sirius* and the *Supply*, and if necessary, Second Captain Hunter will be able to fight a campaign at sea whilst Governor Phillip establishes himself and his people on land.

Phillip arrives for a last meeting at the Admiralty on 6th May. He receives his instructions and his orders; he states his belief that the colony at Botany Bay will, once established and growing, prove to be a most valuable acquisition for Great Britain. The officials from the

Home Department breath a sigh of relief: acquisition be damned, at last they are getting rid of some of those wretched convicts! They even send a frigate, *Hyena*, to provide an armed escort for the fleet in case desperate convicts stage a rising and try to get back to land. The frigate is to stay in company until the transports are beyond any hope of return.

At Portsmouth, Phillip has his chronometers checked for accuracy and proceeds on board the *Sirius* which is lying at the Motherbank, protected from the Channel winds by the Isle of Wight. There are still supplies due: extra musket balls and clothing for the female convicts, but they don't arrive. However, the wind is favourable and musket balls and clothing can be bought at one of the ports of call on the journey (Phillip has checked that he may buy missing goods in this manner) and he gives the order for the fleet to set sail.

The transports don't move; not an anchor chain stirs. Phillip decides to investigate this personally and takes his cutter across to the nearest merchantman. It appears that there is a dispute over pay. The merchant crews are, to tell the truth, about as keen on this adventure as the convicts they carry; they complain that the ships' masters are holding back pay due for the time they've spent at anchor, in some cases up to six months. This is not unusual though it is unfair. The masters reckon to prevent their men buying supplies for the voyage ashore; by paying them late they have only the ship's shop, with its vastly inflated prices and no other choice at all – it's pay up or go without. Phillip has no time for this stuff: he needs to get away and shows that when necessary, he can be tough. The protesting sailors are sent into the *Hyena* under naval discipline and the frigate transfers out as many sailors as are needed to work the transports.

On 13th May 1787 Phillip gives the order to up anchor and proceed down channel. It becomes clear once they reach open water that the transports *Charlotte* and *Lady Penrhyn* are heavy sailers, wallowing and slipping in the comparatively calm local waters; once the fleet gets into the Atlantic they are going to cause considerable delay. Just keeping his fleet within sight of each other over thousand of leagues of sea room is going to be a major problem. On the third day, *Sirius* comes about and each ship passes in review; they discover that the provost marshal of the settlement has been left behind or, since no one has seen him for weeks, chosen to remain behind.

Contrary winds prevent the fleet getting clear of the Channel until the 16th and on that day, as they head out into the Atlantic, there are rumours of a plan being hatched by the most desperate amongst the convicts to take over the transport *Scarborough*.

Mary Broad

here is a torment worse than creeping around in the crowded filth between decks dragging your chains behind you, always alert for the hand that is going to snatch what little you have or strike out because there's no one else to strike at – and it is the monotony of day after day when nothing changes because nothing can. Even the light, from winter to summer, hardly manages to creep through the scuttles and down the companionway to the filthy deck, so you live in a perpetual twilight with never a lamp to vary it, for lamps have flames and flames can burn wooden walls and for those whose lives are passed within those walls, sometimes death by burning is preferable to life without hope.

They aren't philosophers down here; they don't think about the future or tomorrow and the day after or the day in seven or fourteen long years when they'll be free. Most of them live for now and now is bad: boredom or backbreaking work, hunger always there at the edge of everything and violence humming in the air you breathe because this is a world of violence, where the quietest word is shouted and official kindness is a shove in the back with a musket butt rather than a flogging or extra chains. And it's about to get worse.

The words circulate like a spark across black powder and flare into incomprehension and deep anxiety. Where is Botany Bay, what is it, why us, how far? Is it further than Exeter – London – Hull – Babylon? The other side of the world doesn't really mean a lot down here in the half light; an extra half ration, now that's worth fighting for; a scrap of cloth and a needle, illicit rum brewed over a still in the men's section, they're worth something but this news from the world outside, what does it mean, really what does it mean?

It means that a young woman sits huddled in a corner weeping without cease over the loss of her baby – they took it from her on the cart as they brought her and twenty others from the prison to the hulks, they tore it away as she was nursing it and sent it to the poor house where she knows it will die. She should stop crying, there's no use for it but she can't because when they laid hold of the baby and took it away, her life went with it.

It means that the space you have to live and sleep in is suddenly cut in half as dozens more wretches are delivered and decanted through the process, shivering from the winter cold, many shaking with fevers that have been stoked by damp nights on the road, crushed and chained in some barn before another day of being jolted so hard that scurvy teeth shake free of shrunken gums. They are all asking the same questions: what is it, why us, how far?

And what does it mean to Mary? She no longer lives in that dawn-and-dusk world. Light from a port falls across her face which is clean, powdered even, with hair that doesn't hang limp and filthy, but is dressed by one of the girls from down there whose skills allow her to come up here. Mary's clothes are clean, or as clean as anything ever is in the filthy breath of the hulk *Dunkirk;* an attempt has been made to cut a little fashion into the drop and sway of the mantua and the stays have something to take hold of, a little flesh to squeeze and more bosom to show.

She's an upper-deck moll now, with a real live protector of her own. There's something about her, a gleam of success but also, if her man knew where to look, a slight swelling of the belly because on her journey up, through gaoler and marine to lieutenant, the food and drink got better at every stop, she regained her flow and became a woman again and now she's a pregnant woman. She hasn't told him, why would she – to him she's a trip up Cock Lane with a pretty face; to her he's three decks and a cabin with a window and no manacles.

She's perfectly content with that: she's a seller in a buyer's market and as far as she's concerned, they both got a bargain. She's cheap, he's there.

It probably won't last though; if she's learnt anything, she's learnt that much. They take it away from you, whatever it is and whoever they are; everything changes and you better change with it or you'll be like the rest of them down there.

There's been something in the air besides the stench for a few weeks: whispers and questions, a general tightening of discipline amongst the turnkeys, better pipeclaying on the marines' belts and facings, orders snapped out with a will, all indications of the excitement that change in an unchanging world brings about. Words, whispers at first ... the bay ... other side of the world ... a long way to come home again. Wales? New Wales?

Botany Bay, New South Wales – she remembers the arms of the bay back in Fowey, the way the sea opened there and went on forever. Will it be the same? Perhaps that's where she's going: for ever? She doesn't like the idea one bit; there's something in her that says no. Not that it'll make any difference, not now; her officer isn't going to fall on his knees and offer marriage and a house in the country. He's going to slip her a coin or two, allow her to keep some of the clothes, say goodbye and go back to his duty and buy another mort.

Then it's all over. Tenders bump the sides of the ship and marines come swarming up like rats, rousting out anyone who has found a warm hole to hide in. Her Haymarket Jack is nowhere to be seen, an easy way to save saying goodbye. Mary grabs what she can hide under her skirts and puts on the face she hasn't worn for months: scowling, angry, stay clear of me. On deck a thin rain – the curtain to all her moves, it seems – soaks rapidly through her cotton and linen but she's better off by far than the leper-pale shapes who came staggering up from below, some of them seeing clear daylight for the first time in years, crying out with the sheer pain of the brightness, though to tell the truth it's a grey old day in Plymouth. It's hard to see as far as the dock through the spume and drizzle and now what light there is begins to fade as the January night comes on, calling up a clammy damp mist from the Channel.

Wasted white flesh seen clear through rips that couldn't take thread even if there was any, shoes compounded out of anything that will hold together, precious bundles it would break your heart to open; they carry with them the rags and tatters with which they've made their nests below because they're scared about what will happen now the very last thing they had is being taken away. They hiss and whisper and twitter like birds amongst themselves, clustering fearfully as if the devil might take the outermost.

Mary can't stop the shudder that passes through her whole body when the locksmith's hands go round her ankles with the irons and hammer them shut. She thought she'd lost this for good. Another lesson: nothing is forever.

A growl, deeper, angrier as the men come up from their quarters bringing that stink of maleness with them like a meaty blanket of sour broth in the cold evening. Those that can, still strut in their anxiety about the future; others drag themselves and their chains and find somewhere to lean. Most of them work ashore or on deck and the light is no stranger; the women, however, separated by bulkhead and iron bars below, now they are something that makes noses twitch because even in the state they are in, they are still women and most of them are young. Twenty, twenty-three, twenty-five: it's all the medicine the young prison bucks need and the calling and whistling starts and is answered with laughs and retorts. For a few moments, before the musket butts start hitting the deck and bellows, whistles and rattles drown out everything, they are just boys and girls again.

The names are told off and the convicts are sent in small groups down into the tenders which take them through the choppy waters of the harbour to the land. Many are sick due to the different motion; they're not used to going anywhere. At the harbour wall they're dragged up slimy steps, chains rattling behind them, and herded past small groups of onlookers into a warehouse where they'll spend the night. Some have relatives outside who have come to see sons and daughters for the last time. There are tearful farewells and the handing over of gifts, food and keepsakes which the turnkeys allow not because they are compassionate men – it's not really in the job description – but because they have been bribed.

Mary has no one except the child growing in her belly but as the evening draws on and the great space of the warehouse begins to fill with the noise of some two hundred men and women talking, the steam from soup cauldrons, lamp black, wood smoke and tobacco smoke too, she begins to look around, at the prospects of survival: at the men who stand out from their companions by virtue of their confidence, the tradesmen who will have something to sell in this place on the other side of the world.

There's a Cornishman with an easy way about him, probably not been inside that long. She asks who he is and someone tells her he's a fisherman and his name is William Bryant and he's a free-trader who was caught and charged with receiving contraband. She remembers the name and the man.

Early next morning, before daylight has even greyed the greasy cobbles, the sleepers are rousted out, fires lit under the kettles and thin gruel heated to give the felons something to puke up on the trip back out – but this time they'll be heading for the transports *Charlotte* and *Friendship* which are to take them beyond the sea. Nobody dresses since nobody undresses unless they want their duds stolen; they just wrap them around a little more and shuffle out into the cruel cold. Children are crying; wherever there are women in the hulks there are children crying but the thin wails have a particular poignancy on this morning, saying goodbye to a shore they'll likely never see again.

The two ships look very small in the harbour and some spirits rise; surely they can't be going that far in such tiny boats. Two gentlemen stand apart from the soldiers on the hard watching the embarkation; one of them, a doctor someone says, reminds the officer in charge that only the men are to be in irons once they are on board. The officer – Mary knows who he is, General Collins, a cold man it is said, whose son is going with them to New South Wales – nods; the women's irons will be removed.

Mary huddles down out of the wind into the deep well of the tender. Canvas cracks, orders are shouted and lines cast off as they race out into the harbour, the bow throwing up curtains of spray. Amongst the marines, watching the progress of the boat, stands a young officer; he seems to make notes – his name is Watkin Tench and Mary, sitting with her back to the wind, watches as his figure gets smaller and smaller and is finally lost altogether in the spray and greyness of the dawn.

Lieutenant Ralph Clark

He wants to be on board the *Charlotte* sailing to New South Wales but he doesn't want to be here at all because he's missing Alicia Betsey and their son, little Ralph, so much it's like a sword in his heart. During the day he thinks about her constantly and at night he often dreams of being at home with them. He tried to get them passage but it didn't work and perhaps, after all, it's for the best.

A convict transport is no place for a woman of sensibility and certainly the worst of all possible worlds for a child. The influences are so ... depraved is the only word he can find for it; a lack of standards, a lack of anything that might be called civilised behaviour. Even whilst the *Charlotte* was in port, the sailors broke through the bulkhead into the woman's quarters and did the women repel them or call for help? Not a word or a cry, apart from the beastly howling of rutting animals.

How can the governor hope to build anything of value in the antipodes if the women, the very foundation and meaning of society, the means by which man's brute passion is turned to sentiment and becomes civilised, have become debauched? He knows that they will cause nothing but trouble, these abandoned wretches. He recalls the fleet leaving harbour and the calls of 'wither bound?' shouted out from the dockside. He also recalls the answer – 'The arse-end of the world, matey' – and feels so depressed that he goes up onto the deck and looks at the porpoises playing in the sparkling waters beneath the bows.

One of the sailors tells him that they've made seventy-three miles in the last two days. That's good progress; they are racing down the Atlantic, he says, and the seaman, in the way of his kind, adds that these fortunate winds will never last, the porpoises are proof of it, they never play like that except when a storm is due.

The storm comes and Ralph finds himself flat in his bunk, dribbling vomit weakly into a bucket and worrying about little Ralph who was suffering from smallpox before they left; is he better, is he worse? Until he gets a letter from home he cannot know that the boy is even alive. It's a horrifying thought and for three days he lies there as the cabin around him swoops and falls and spins and rolls and rolls, dragging his guts as he worries and worries, sicking up whatever scraps remain in his stomach until only a thin bile comes. He's never been drunk but he knows a lot of officers who have – Lieutenant Maxwell of the marines, for instance, who is doing his best to drink himself to death – and this sounds like the very worst of their experiences; but whilst they can always say 'never again', the fleet still has twelve and half thousand miles to cover. It's a sobering thought.

On the fourth day the sea is slightly calmer. They are, the ship's mate says, at latitude 47′ 52″ north, longitude 12′ 14‴; Ralph only wants to be left alone, until the mate tells him that the commodore has come about: their escort frigate *Hyena* will parting company and ... Ralph needs no more: the last chance to send a letter back before Tenerife and after that, Rio. He pulls himself out of his bunk and writes like a demon, sending a thousand kisses to Betsey and Ralph and wishing he could fly back to them with the letter.

On deck everyone aboard who can write is handing down letters into the jolly-boat which is about to row across to *Hyena*. Word comes from the flag, reminding merchant masters of Captain Phillip's instructions that once the *Hyena* is out of company, the irons should be struck off the male convicts. Ralph is not so sure about it: they've a desperate lot of villains aboard and there's the example of the *Scarborough* convicts to encourage them; he discusses the matter with Captain Meredith and they agree to recommend that only a proportion of the men be freed at any one time.

The weather begins to improve and the seasickness abates somewhat; Ralph wishes it gone for good and starts making a diary note every day he remains free of the curse. Dr White, who is also aboard and has often dropped by to offer a slime draught or a black powder to the sufferer, tells him of an odd incident that has occurred whilst Ralph was *hors de combat*. One of the marine corporals had been taking muskets from the arms chest. For some unaccountable reason, one of them had been loaded and primed and, on being laid on the deck, it fired – sending the ball smashing into the corporal's ankle. This deflected it so that it went through a barrel of beef and shot dead two geese, standing on the other side; the officers' mess will be eating the geese shortly and the doctor hopes Ralph will be well enough to join them. It is a curious story and all on board find it oddly heartening, though nobody quite knows why. The doctor has great hopes of curing the corporal.

The days begin to settle into the order of the voyage; little routines, visits amongst the ships when conditions permit, broken nights and days still spent missing Alicia Betsey and little Ralph. They pass the Salvages and on 3rd June the command comes from *Sirius* for the fleet to tack and make anchor in the roadstead at Santa Cruz, Tenerife.

Frances Davis and Some Others ...

On board *Lady Penrhyn*:

Name	Age	Trade	Crime and sentence
Frances Davis	22	Service	Robbery, 14 years
Anne Yates	19	Milliner	Housebreaking, 7 years
Mary Love	60	Service	Lamb stealing, 14 years
Ann Colpits	28	Service	Privately stealing, 7 years
Elizth. Lock	23	Service	Housebreaking, 7 years
Mary Gamboll	37	Service	Defrauding, 7 years
Olivia Gascoin	24	Service	Theft, 7 years
Mary Tilley	30	Service	Housebreaking, 7 years
Sarah Davis	26	Glove maker	Shoplifting, 7 years
Ann Inett	30	Mantua maker	Housebreaking, 7 years
Mary Wilkes	21	Service	Privately stealing, 7 years
Elizth. Bird	45	Service	Lamb stealing, 7 years
Ann Dawly	23	Service	Highway robbery, 7 years
Sarah Bellamy	17	Service	Privately stealing, 7 years
Mary Davis	25	Service	Housebreaking, 7 years
Mary Mitchell	19	Service	Privately stealing, 7 years
Mary Bolton	29	Service	Housebreaking, 7 years
Mary Dickenson	26	Barrow woman	Stealing, 7 years
Amelia Levi	19	Furrier	Shoplifting, 7 years

Name	Age	Trade	Crime and sentence
Elizth. Hall	18	Service	House robbery, 7 years
Margt. Fowness	45	Service	Highway robbery, 7 years
Hannah Mullins	20	Service	Forgery, for life
Elizth. Beckford	70	Service	Shoplifting, 7 years
J:Jones/Osborne	28	Service	Robbery, 7 years
Elizth. Colley	22	Service	Housebreaking, 7 years
Elizth. Lee	24	Service	Housebreaking, 7 years
Mary Brenham	17	Service	Housebreaking, 7 years
Elizth. Hipsley	28	Needlework	Picking pockets, 7 years
Ann Read	22	Service	Street Robbery, for life
Susan Hufnall	24	Service	Receiving, 7 years
Eleona M'Cave	24	Hawker	Robbery, 7 years
Mary Finn	26	Service	Robbery, 7 years
Martha Eaton	25	Service	Receiving, 7 years
Mary Greenwood	24	Service	Street robbery, 7 years
Elizth. Cole	20	Milliner	Shoplifting, 7 years
Catharine Hart	19	Service	Privately stealing, 7 years
Mary Hill	20	Service	Picking pockets, 7 years
Margaret Dawson	17	Service	Privately stealing, 7 years
Sally Smith	25	Book stitcher	Receiving, 7 years
Elizth. Dalton	21	Service	Shoplifting, 7 years
Elizth. Marshall	29	Service	Shoplifting, 7 years
Mary Moulton	21	Service	Shoplifting, 7 years
Ann Morton	20	Service	Shoplifting, 7 years
Elizth. Evans	28	Service	Shoplifting, 7 years
Mary Humphreys	20	Service	Picking pockets, 7 years
Ann Ward	20	Lacemaker	Shoplifting, 7 years
Elizth. Needham	25	Maker of child's bed linen	Shoplifting, 7 years
Lucy Wood/Bran	33	Service	Picking pockets, 7 years
Ann Martin	17	Service	Shoplifting, 7 years
Mary Harrison	34	Silk winder	Misdemeanour, 7 years
A Sandlyn/Lyon	33	Needlework	Petty larceny, 7 years
Ann Green	30	Mantua maker	Privately stealing, 7 years

Name	Age	Trade	Crime and sentence
Rebecca Davison	28	Needlework	Picking pockets, 7 years
Mary Cooper	47	Chair woman	Stealing, 7 years
Ann Davis	29	Service	Shoplifting, 7 years
Ann Dutton	25	Service	Privately stealing, 7 years
Mary Carroll	36	Mantua maker	Privately stealing, 7 years
Ann Thornton	32	Service	Privately stealing, 7 years
Mary Smith	25	Shoe binder	Picking pockets, 7 years
Esther Howard	22	Service	Privately stealing, 7 years
Mary Cockran	32	Dealer	Receiving, 14 years
Ann Caulfield	19	Hawker	Perjury, 7 years
Sophia Lewis	29	Service	Shoplifting, 7 years
Ann Morton	20	Service	Shoplifting, 7 years
Mary Jackson	31	Hawker	Picking pockets, 7 years
Elizth. Fowles	22	Hawker	Housebreaking, 7 years
Mary Adams	29	Service	Privately stealing, 7 years
Mary Parker	28	Service	Privately stealing, 7 years
Mary Dicks	29	Stay maker	Picking pockets, 7 years
Mary Williams	39	Needlework	Privately stealing, 7 years
Margaret Bourne	25	Service	Picking pockets, 7 years
Ann Powell	35	Service	Privately stealing, 7 years
Dorothy Hamlyn	82	Dealer	Perjury, 7 years
Sarah Daniels	22	Hawker	Stamping, 14 years
Mary Lawrence	30	Service	Privately stealing, 7 years
Sarah Partridge	22	Mantua maker	Shoplifting, 7 years
Mary Slater	23	Watch-chain maker	Shoplifting, 7 years
Sarah Piles	20	Service	Picking pockets, 7 years
Jane Creek	48	Service	Privately stealing, 7 years
Phoebe Norton	26	Service	Privately stealing, 7 years
Elizth. Bruce	29	Service	Privately stealing, 7 years
Elizth. Anderson	32	Service	Privately stealing, 7 years
Susan Trippet	22	Artificial flower maker	Picking pockets, 7 years
Nancy Conner	28	Hawker	Shoplifting, 7 years

Name	Age	Trade	Crime and sentence
Catherine Henry	36	Hawker	Shoplifting, 7 years
Elizth. Fitzgerald	26	Service	Felony, 7 years
Mary Allen	22	Service	Picking pockets, 7 years
Mary Jackson	22	Service	Picking pockets, 7 years
Martha Baker	25	Service	Picking pockets, 7 years
Martha Burkett	33	Service	Picking pockets, 7 years
Charlotte Sprigmore	30	Silk winder	Misdemeanour, 7 years
Thamasin Allen	32	Service	Picking pockets, 7 years
Mary Marshall	19	Service	Picking pockets, for life
Mary Springham	21	Hawker	Picking pockets, 7 years
Ann Smith	30	Nurse	Stealing, 7 years
Sarah Purdue	23	Mantua maker	Robbery, 7 years
Maria Hamilton	33	Lace weaver	Privately stealing, 7 years
Charlotte Cook	20	Tambour worker	Privately stealing, 7 years
Sarah Hall	46	Hawker	Privately stealing, 7 years
Elizth. Haward	13	Clogmaker	Stealing, 7 years
Sarah Parry	28	Milliner	Felony, for life
Isabella Lawson	33	Mantua maker	Privately stealing, 7 years
Jane Parkinson	30	Milliner	Died on passage
Esther Abram	20	Milliner	Shoplifting, 7 years
Mary Harrison	25	Service	Stealing, 7 years
Maria Martin	20	Service	Stealing, 7 years
Sarah Smith	35	Hawker	Stealing, 7 years
Frances Anderson	30	Dealer	Robbery, 7 years
Susan Blanchard	25	Service	Robbery, 7 years
Margaret Blades	25	Pedlar and chapwoman	Defrauding, 7 years

Surgeon John White

enerife, to John White's detached, scientific eye, is a hotbed of Rome; the annual budget of the Bishopric is five times that of the civil administration. The streets are crowded and colourful, the women provocative and highly disgusting, or does he mean enticing? The ices are delicious, especially at midday under the broiling sun and the Spanish almost as taciturn as the English visitors, neither side quite ready, after years of war, to trust one another.

On board the fleet as it rides at anchor, it is clear to White, going from ship to ship, that there is already an improvement in the general health of the convicts; a better diet and regular airings have started to make a real difference and so far, the only death on the voyage is of one Ismeal Coleman, worn out by lowness of spirits brought on by prolonged and close confinement.

Convict John Power, aboard *Alexander*, finds a different manner of escape; during the afternoon exercise, he takes advantage of the general relaxation brought on by the landfall and conceals himself; that night he slips overboard and swims across the roadstead to a Dutch East Indiaman where he offers himself as crew. The Dutchmen can see the *Sirius* with its gun ports, clear even in the moonlight, and Power is sent on his way. He steals a rowing boat and makes for shore, hiding in a cave overnight. In the morning a search party apprehends him and takes him back to his confinement where he is put into irons and kept there until he prevails upon a literate mate to produce a petition to Captain Phillip, who does not want to keep anyone in irons for longer than necessary and frees the fellow.

On 10th June the fleet weighs anchor and heads out into the Atlantic, making for Rio. The further south-west they sail, the hotter and damper it gets; thunderstorms flicker continually on the horizon and moisture seems to ooze out of the air and cling to everything animate and inanimate. There are frequent rainstorms and White has insisted that the marine guards on every transport keep a good lookout and ensure that convicts airing on deck are got below before the squalls reach them. They have no means of drying themselves and White knows well the effect of continual damp in these latitudes. Overall, there is a smell of tar oil, which the doctor supports fanatically as a universal benison: 'it resists putrefaction, destroys vermin and insects and overcomes all disagreeable smells whilst being itself both agreeable and wholesome.'

The women below are beginning to suffer seriously from the damp heat; wind sails are rigged, they are aired as often as possible and the hatch covers are left open at night but even so there are continual outbreaks of fainting followed by fits. White is concerned for their health and puzzled about their morals: despite the conditions, which turn any effort at all into a perfect bath of sweat, the night-time opening of the hatch covers unleashes a frenzy of promiscuous intercourse between them, the sailors and the marines. It is the same all over the fleet, wherever men and women are confined on the one vessel: endless assignations, meetings, congresses as if there is a need not just to satisfy their brute appetites but for something more between one and another.

Through the rest of June and the first two weeks of July the fleet creeps across glassy seas. Often the sails hardly move for hours on end and the bows cut through the ocean with no more disturbance than a water rat in an English pond; at night the ships leave luminous trails behind them and fire seems to flicker round the masts and spars.

They cross the Equator on 14th July, accompanied now by a nightly carpet of sparkling will-o'-the-wisps. White is delighted and makes notes on the phenomenon, convinced that fish whirling just beneath the surface somehow create the brightness. He relentlessly checks the convicts and marines on board *Charlotte* for any signs of illness or scurvy: teeth are tested for looseness, gums prodded for the spongy signs of fungus; he scans for blotches or ulcers and dullness of eye and dispenses essence of malt by the bucketful but despite all his efforts the master of the *Alexander* – something of a bad luck ship – sends across the message that several marines and convicts have suddenly and inexplicably been taken ill. It is a message that sends a cold shiver down spines even in these latitudes; fever raging on a boat at sea is almost as terrifying as fire. Helmsmen sail close-hauled to get the best of the wind and ease their ships unobtrusively away from *Alexander* whilst Dr White gets his medicines and descends into the *Charlotte*'s cutter.

The crew is none too keen as they pull through the sluggish water towards what has already become the plague ship; Billingsgate fishwives gossip less than sailors and the fleet already has the yellow jack at the *Alexander*'s mast head and fever raging aboard her. White is made of sterner stuff though he is concerned; every precaution has been taken; the water ration is at the maximum allowable by stores, there's fresh food from Tenerife, fresh meat and fish, though seamen will go a long way to avoid eating it – so the cause must lie elsewhere.

The cox'n calls out '*Charlotte*' and willing hands reach down to help Dr White aboard. The deck is bleached white under the sun and the heat is immense; the mate advances, his face screwed up against the glare and White notices at once: the brass buttons on his coat are turned almost black. He sniffs but hardly has need to, the stench hangs around the deck like thick mist. How is it that no one aboard noticed, it cannot have crept up unbeknownst? He asks to be taken below, to the lower deck cabins, and here he confirms his judgement: the wooden walls are as black as the buttons and if you listen you can actually hear the bilge water slopping back and forth with the motion of the ship. For some reason no pumping of the bilges has been done aboard *Alexander*, no washing through with sea water. It is almost unbelievable. White calls for the hatches to be undogged. When it is done and they are cracked open, the eye-watering, corrosive stench is so great that those gathered round fall back and some fall over. Old seamen, salts who have spent their whole lives afloat, can remember nothing like it; no wonder convicts and seamen alike are falling sick. Dr White is furious. At his request, before sailing, Captain Phillip had issued a general order to the masters of the transports to pump the ships every day and if the vessel wasn't making water enough for the purpose, to throw bucket loads down the hatches and into the bilges.

Calling for his longboat, White goes on to the *Sirius* where Phillip hears him and sends Philip Gidley King across to the *Alexander* to sort the business out.

Almost as if the weather has been waiting, once the cleansing salt water starts rushing through the *Alexander*'s scuppers, the airs begin to lighten and a wind springs up; the fleet is on the move once again and everybody's spirits begin to improve. Some of the marines are so sanguine that they think they'll cut a hole through to the women's quarters aboard *Lady Penrhyn*; Major Ross, the deputy governor and marine commander, discovers the plot and the unfortunates are caught, tried and flogged, to the vast amusement of the convicts, who are never flogged: their worst punishment is the re-application of their irons.

On 3rd August the fleet enters the port of Rio de Janeiro where Captain Phillip is well remembered as an old friend of Portugal and, as a tribute to the service he has done, the officers of the fleet are welcomed ashore and allowed to wander as they will, with no controls at all; the first time such a thing has been allowed to any foreigners visiting the city.

With food easily available the convict ration for the period of the visit is increased to a pound of rice, a pound and a half of beef, fresh vegetables and as many oranges as they can eat. White is convinced that most of his charges are getting a better, healthier diet then ever before. Both he and Phillip realise that if the convicts are to prove any kind of resource once they arrive at Botany Bay, they must be fit enough to work. For if they are not, if they are sick and lethargic and will not or cannot work, the colony and all who are part of it, will perish.

Despite Phillip's best efforts, the transports are soon surrounded by clusters of bumboats offering goods and services and within a few days it becomes apparent that some of the convicts aboard *Charlotte* are passing counterfeit coins. The Portuguese are not pleased; the

British are embarrassed, a thorough search is made of the male convict quarters and one Thomas Barret is discovered with a hoard of silver dollars. He admits that he made them out of marines' buttons, shoe buckles and pewter spoons. Dr White examines them closely: the milling, impression and character is perfect; he reckons that were it not for the unsatisfactory nature of the metal itself, the coins would pass for mint. A further search is made for the dies, which must have been manufactured and used to create the counterfeits, but nothing is found and Tom Barret keeps his mouth firmly shut. White can only apologize to the authorities, who take it in good part, and wonder at the ingenuity and cunning, not to mention the sheer skill of the convicts involved in the plot. He wishes they might have used these qualities to a better purpose but reflects that if Governor Phillip can harness such energy and sense of purpose then perhaps the colony does have a future.

White spends some of his time comparing notes with his Portuguese colleagues (assisting in the amputation of a limb) and wondering at the length to which their wives grow their hair (one lady reveals that her undone hair hangs to the floor); he goes sightseeing and superintends the loading of fresh meat, livestock, rum and wine. Phillip is out making good the oversights of the contractors back in England, stocking up with musket balls, bolts of cloth and seeds and plants that will, he hopes, take to the climate of New South Wales, including vines, various fruits, cocoa and coffee.

On 6th August, in a light breeze at six in the morning, the fleet weighs anchor. Passing the fort at Santa Cruz, the *Sirius* is accorded a twenty-one-gun salute, which is returned in like manner. Everyone is relaxed after the visit and one of the convicts Thomas Brown, takes advantage of the easy atmosphere and offers an insolent answer to a ship's officer. He is given a dozen lashes – to the amusement of the marines.

On the evening of 8th August Dr White is summoned to the women's quarters where a convict is about to give birth.

Mary Broad

Worst are the bugs, the fleas, the lice that come crawling out of the wood as it gets hotter and damper and her belly gets bigger day by day and even the least movement brings you out in a sweat that is, like as not, going to turn into a rash. Sometimes she just lies for hours on her ledge, taking up more room that she ought but the others give her a little extra space because of her reputation and her condition – she's a bit of a mascot for them all, a baby being a new hope. Bets are cast on boy or girl, other bets that she isn't supposed to hear about, on whether it lives or dies – yet others on whether she lives or dies.

There's very little that a convict can't bet against: the size of the water ration, how long they'll be allowed on deck, the number of bugs you can kill in a limited time – it's a bit like terriers and rats – the number of rats you can kill in a limited time, the weather tomorrow or the day after, when landfall will come, what it's going to be like when they finally get there; will there be cannibals, giants, bears and tigers? There's a strong rumour going round that this Botany Bay is close to China and a determined lad or lass might easily get over the hills and escape to the lands of the east and one thing everyone knows, China is a big place and they'll never find you there. Of course, the officers all deny such a thing but then they would, and some of the sailors have told the women that yes, for sure, they've been to China and it's just over the hills. They've even offered to provide compasses drawn carefully on pieces of papers to help find the east but no one aboard *Charlotte* wants to be taken for a flat so they're not opening their legs for that one!

In the Brazils the motion of the ship stops at last and Mary is able to get a little sleep; because the shore is close the guard is doubled but they are allowed up on deck in small parties – Mary is hardly in any condition to escape – and the wonderful mountains and dark green of the trees and all the colours of the port are something to see; but even more wonderful are the bells, big and small, tinkling and clacking, that go on ringing all day and half the night. Someone says it's to summon the 'Portugees' to church but surely no one, not even a Haymarket whore, could spend that much time on their knees. There are smells too, drifting across the still green water to the boat: some they recognise – meat cooking, animals – but most they don't. Rich smells that tickle your nostrils and make your eyes water.

During the day the crew are busy loading more supplies. It seems like the ships will go down under the weight of all those oranges and limes and lemons, the animals and big lumps of dark wood that the officers are buying to make themselves cupboards and chairs in Botany Bay.

All this means nothing as the pains begin to come and Mary is helped back down the hatchway – no easy matter – into the twilight below. It's hotter than ever down here, the cotton that was cool and dry in the wind on deck is soaked in seconds as she staggers across to her shelf and falls back, the pains coming faster and faster.

An old dame mutters that it's no great thing having a brat, its what women do. Mary grits her teeth against an answer: the woman is the nearest they have to a midwife amongst themselves and giving birth is what women do, so is dying and Mary knows one thing above all at this moment: she wants to live and go back to Fowey, where the fingers of land almost touch at the head of the bay and the water outside goes on forever and inside there's the smell of warm saffron bread and ... the pain rips through her and she pushes and sees a male face leaning over her: a face she remembers from Plymouth.

He tells her she's doing well but she doesn't really hear him. All around are the women she's come to know over the thousands of miles they've travelled together; some reach out and pat her, others look on in curiosity – haven't they never seen a brat born before –

still others shrug, as if to say: she won't last long in this place. But cows do it, sheep do it and sows do it and she can do it too and she won't die, neither. She settles down to the business of getting the child out; in time it is done and the thin first cry changes something for all of them; reminding even the hardest hearts of other, kinder times.

The doctor says it's a Stepney girl because every child born at sea is registered in the parish of Stepney. Mary smiles, at her daughter and at him. Someone takes the baby and washes her down and then gives her back. There's a sip of grog and she slips away into sleep. When she wakes everything will be as it was before, except that now she'll have a daughter to look after as well.

James Boswell

hree days after the birth of Mary Broad's daughter, James Boswell wakes up to a London morning feeling somewhat dreary as a consequence, he rather fears, of not having drunk enough the night before at dinner with Sir Joshua Reynolds. Sad slavery, he reflects, if it is so!

Captain Watkin Tench

e notes a high degree of satisfaction in the demeanour of the majority of convicts though for some, the pang of being separated, perhaps for ever, from their native land, cannot wholly be suppressed. 'Some natural tears she dropp'd, but wiped them soon,' as his beloved Milton put it in *Paradise Lost.* And there was that business aboard the *Scarborough* before the fleet had even started when desperate men plotted to rise up and take the ship. Fortunately Captain Tench has the consolations of philosophy and art to wrap about himself and the spur of an almost insatiable curiosity, its attack eased by charm and good nature. Even Ralph Clark, still wrapped in visions of his paradise left behind ('dreamed of seeing my Betsey in her new gown'), is glad to see Captain Tench when he visits aboard *Friendship* and even if Clark does stick to lemonade, he's still happy enough to sit in with the rest of the mess as the bumpers are drunk and the port and brandy sink down inside of the bottles.

The voyage from the Brazils to the Cape is uneventful, except for William Brown, a well-behaved and trustworthy convict, who, whilst collecting some clothes he's hung out to dry on the bowsprit end, slips and falls overboard. *Charlotte* is clipping along at six knots and though Tench and others race to launch a boat, by the time they get it into the water and row back to the spot where Brown went down, there is nothing to be found, though Tench thinks this isn't surprising given that the ship must have passed directly over him, buffeting and bearing him down into the blue-green Atlantic depths.

Day by day the longitude goes down and the latitude creeps up as the little fleet makes its crabwise progress east across the map and the daily business of this floating community is recorded by the scrupulous diarist: eleven marines sick on *Alexander*, five or six convicts on board *Charlotte*, Dr White and Captain Meredith have a furious argument about a piece of wood and Captain Meredith raises his hand against the doctor. Lieutenant Clark, the only one who isn't drinking, threatens to clap both of them in irons if they don't behave: 'A piece of wood, forsooth!!!!' he writes in his journals.

Four seamen on *Alexander* are suborned by John Power who reckons to make another escape attempt and they hatch a plan for a mass rising at the Cape, but are betrayed by an informer: fortunately for them since the Dutch run a tight and brutal regime with no mercy given to criminals. The weather becomes colder and winds increase; Elizabeth Barbur gets drunk on home brew and swears blue murder and bloody mayhem and swears she'll see every bugger in the fleet overboard before they reach Botany Bay; the *Borrowdale* loses her topmast; the Commodore gives a dinner for Major Ross, Captain Hunter, Captain Collins, Captain Meredith, Lieutenant King, Lieutenant Maxwell and a jolly time is had by all; a convict woman using the seat of ease manages somehow to fall through the head and into the sea but is rescued; Captain Tench stands looking out over the bow at the endless, seamless ocean wondering when the wished-for day will arrive and the Cape will appear over the horizon.

Captain David Collins

'Relieving the tedium of many a heavy hour,' David Collins writes in his journal; he intends to publish an official history of the English Colony in New South Wales and has decided, in the interest of authenticity, to preserve as much as possible in the printed version the virtues of an on-the-spot journal – whilst preserving his own privacy. He's not a man to show his feelings, more like Arthur Phillip than Ralph Clark or Watkin Tench, whom he regards as perhaps a little too clever for his own good. Collins' approach will lay out the nuts and bolts, the screws and hinges, the seeds and hoes and the laws of the settlement, since he is to be judge advocate and, as such, the primary law officer. He's not afraid of the task; he served with the marines in America – fighting at Bunker Hill – and acted as adjutant, learning a good deal about the day-to-day administration of justice. He comes from a military family; his father Major-General Collins is in overall command of the marines at Plymouth and has set an exacting standard for his son David to follow.

In the spirit of completeness he notes that at Rio the fleet acquired one bull, one bull calf, seven cows, one stallion, three mares and three colts as well as a great number of rams, ewes, goats, boars and breeding sows. On arrival at the Cape, he notes that amongst the seeds acquired were fig, bamboo, Spanish reed, sugar cane, vines, quince, apple, pear, strawberry, oak, myrtle, rice, wheat, barley, Indian corn, etc ... The Cape is run by the Dutch East India Company and, on the whole, Collins approves of the perfection of the fruit, both tropical and familiar; the wine from Cape vineyards has a fine, rich and pleasant flavour, whilst meat animals are excellent, particularly the fat-tailed sheep. The commodore has bought widely amongst the fruit, vegetable and meat markets and every day large quantities of fresh food arrive on board the ships of the fleet: everyone – except the convicts – is aware that the long final leg down towards the big seas of the Southern Ocean is going to be the most rigorous part of the voyage. Phillip is determined, and Collins agrees, that their charges should be as well fed as possible before starting, since conditions will mean many days when hatches must be battened down, and all on board will be thrown around like rice in a rattle by the winter storms.

Taking advantage of his hosts' invitation to wander round freely – a privilege not enjoyed by the numerous slaves held in bondage by their Dutch masters – Collins visits, as fellow law-officer, the court house and prison. He notes the good order and generally well-behaved population and the good regulation of the police, who seem to be everywhere; he is, however, taken aback by the execution and torture grounds. Inside their looming walls he is shocked to see six crosses used for breaking prisoners, in the sense of breaking a vase or a carriage: the taking apart of, the disjointing, pulling, scraping, carving pieces out of the prisoner to be broken. There are other tools for the same purpose, some with the novelty of being wheels, with the added piquancy of having the broken bits still attached and the severed hands nailed to the axles, yet others are spiked, for the impalement of parts, whilst some – blocks, pulleys, gutters and wedges – are for the infliction of partial rather than total damage. And, of course, there's a gibbet or two for that final, merciful, release. The parts thus separated are displayed around the town, as it were a hand here, a head there, to encourage obedience to the law. Over the entrance to this horrible place, Collins reads the sentiment *Felix quem faciunt aliena pericula cautum*: happy is he who is made wary by the misfortune of others.

There are two fine churches at the Cape: the Lutheran and the Calvinist and not a smell of incense to be sniffed in either. The Lutheran pastor has a fine pulpit and preaches by the hour-glass; the Calvinist does not even offer that much to luxury as he instructs his congregation in the awful punishment awaiting the unjustified sinner. David Collins notes the facts but recalls his pleasure in attending the feast of Corpus Christi at Tenerife, when he knelt as the colourful Catholic procession passed by with all its tinsel and trapping and censors, and he joined with sincerity in offering 'the purest incense, that of a grateful heart.'

The commodore has made it known that he'll be transferring to the tender *Supply* and sailing with as many carpenters and other useful tradesmen as he can gather from amongst the convicts. Three of the fastest transports, *Scarborough*, *Alexander* and *Friendship*, will accompany him. He intends to set up a reception camp at Botany Bay where the rest of the fleet can land and find some kind of shelter ready and waiting for them. Captain Hunter is left in charge of the main fleet. Major Robert Ross, the deputy governor, is not best pleased that he has not been taken into the commodore's confidence – Collins decides not to note the fact.

Mary Broad

She is twenty-two and stands in the little church of St Phillip's at the Cape, holding the baby in her arms. It is wrapped not in a christening gown but in the best that the women below can find and make. Light floods in from the windows high up in the plain walls. The Reverend Johnson looks up from the prayer book and holds out his hands for the child. Carefully she passes her over and saying the words easily, he tips the water and receives Charlotte Spence Broad into the body of the church.

It has been a long time since Mary stood on solid ground without carrying the weight of manacles and chains and for a moment she wonders if there could be a future in front of her in this new land but all her hopes and ambitions are still waiting there in England: for the moment she returns and she knows that, no matter what, she will never settle in Botany Bay.

The vicar hands back her child, his secretary signs as witness. There are some smiles and why not? Charlotte has done nothing wrong, she's free; all she wants is milk and her mother's closeness. Not a lot to ask.

Lieutenant Ralph Clark

At last something is being done about the more unruly of the women convicts aboard the *Friendship*. The worst of them – Margaret Hall who shat between decks; Elizabeth Barber, a hell cat who told the doctor he might want to fuck her but he could kiss her arse for all the chance he had of climbing up her shift; Sarah McCormack and Elizabeth Pulley who broke through the bulkhead to meet with sailors – are transferred out of the ship. They are, all of them, damned whores he reckons, who will end up no better than they deserve, which probably means the gallows. He can't understand why they will not allow their finer feeling as women to blossom; can it be because they have none? What does that say about the fair sex, the sex that his beloved Betsey Alicia so dignifies, and they so revile?

Is that why he keeps dreaming that Betsey is dead? Captain Meredith, who bunks with him, is getting fed up with being woken in the night by heartfelt cries of loss.

On 8th November, the weather gets up and even in harbour the motion of the ships is such that no one wants to eat a thing. It's a foretaste of what's to come, the old hands warn, but then the old hands are forever practising upon the tyros so no one quite knows what to expect. Over the next few days the weather improves and Clark and his friends visit around the ships in harbour: a Dutchman, a

Portuguese, a Londoner; they exchange old news of Europe, entrust them with letters and copies of letters for home.

On Tuesday 13th November, the *Friendship* receives a signal from Captain Phillip to follow in the wake of *Supply*, weigh anchor and stand out to sea. The wind is high, the water choppy and grey and Clark, Captain Meredith and the assistant surgeon, Thomas Arndell, get a thorough soaking as they stand looking back at the last settled and civilised land they'll see for a long, long time. A couple of nights out, the officers' sleep is disturbed when the alarm is raised: young Thomas Bennet has sneaked into the longboat, where the convicts who are allowed on deck store their bread ration to keep it dry under the canvas cover. It is a good system just so long as nobody abuses it; Bennet has spent the day eating everything in the boat and was so stuffed he simply couldn't climb out at lock-down. Meredith and Clark decide a spell back in irons will cure his greed, if not his criminal tendencies, which are, no doubt, incurable. Clark is of the opinion that once they reach land young Master Bennet will not long avoid the hangman.

A night later Clark dreams that Betsey is dead – again! – and wakes howling in his bunk, 'Oh my God, what a dream!' The next night he dreams that Betsey is pregnant: 'Gracious God, I hope nothing is the matter with her!'

It is a Sunday and when he wakes up, he washes, dresses and puts on a flannel waistcoat because he has a pain in his breast. Perhaps it is his heart aching; he takes her miniature from its black velvet bag and kisses it. He only allows himself this relief on a Sunday in case, by excessive devotion, he might wear the dear image away.

It blows hard and a great sea follows the fleet, day after day of squally weather that allows little time on deck without being soaked, and drives them ever onwards towards a destination that seems less welcome the closer they get. By 4th December the wind has fallen and a mist surrounds the ships, isolating each within clammy grey walls; when it clears they see they are hardly a cable's length from two other transports and all three hurriedly pull away from each other.

Clark is reading the tragedy of *Lady Jane Gray* and is much affected by the poor woman's dilemmas; he misses seeing a good play almost as much as he misses Betsey Alicia and that night he dreams of slipping his hand under Betsey's clothes – 'dear sweet dream it was honey to my soul' – but in the morning he has sticky sheets and pains in his own breast and thinks of getting bled. A few nights later he dreams of shitting his breeches. He needs something to keep himself busy and starts to investigate a convict's complaint. It seems that a small gang have cornered the beef and bread ration and are doling it out according to their whim; Henry Lovell and Henry Cable, two rogues who have convinced everyone they are to be trusted and are allowed the run of the ship, have been stealing beef, and wood to make a raft, whilst they are supposed to be pumping the bilges. Clark puts them in irons and resolves to keep a sharp eye on the pair once they reach Botany Bay because they'll have the teeth out of your head if you don't …

Christmas is a dreary day with supplies running short; the commodore does not want to breach anything earmarked for the colony, and the officers make do with a leg of mutton sent along by the ship's master. Clark toasts Betsey Alicia with a glass of water; everyone else gets drunk. A whale accompanies the ship for a few leagues and then swims off to find better company.

Surgeon Arthur Bowes

owes is not a young man, in his forties now, the best job he can get is surgeon aboard the transport *Lady Penrhyn*; he's not that much of a doctor, either, just good enough for convicts and merchant sailors and one thing's for sure, he won't be putting up his plate in a fashionable or unfashionable town and buying a carriage for visiting his patients anytime soon.

After dropping its load in New South Wales, *Penrhyn* is bound for China where Bowes may hope to gain an interest in certain trade goods that will bring the voyage to a profitable end. He is well aware of the conviction amongst many of his charges that China nestles somewhere to the back of Botany Bay and finds it impossible to disabuse them – the mind, when set upon a thing, is as headstrong as a wild horse and as immovable as an oak. His more immediate concern upon setting out was the state of his cabin, recently occupied by Jenkinson, the *Penrhyn*'s mate who died of a putrid fever; the cabin has been fumigated and repainted but it was a few weeks before Bowes was able to breath easily in the confined space.

Now, approaching the coast of *terra australis*, he feels a great sense of relief tinged with impatience: he has come to feel nothing very much for his charges, he cares more about the trousers which he was washing the other day, trailing them behind the ship on a line when a shark surfaced, swam along behind them for a passage, gave an insolent look (he's certain it was insolent) at Bowes and the others standing on the stern, and took the trousers with one mighty bite and swam off with them!

The convict women are no better – blink and they'll have the trousers off you too – they are dead to any finer feelings and will take and steal without conscience and, what's more, encourage others to do so on their behalf. One Thomas Kelly, a convict who had been an ostler, was sent on board to look after the horses; he broached a puncheon of rum and shared it with the women between decks. The Lord knows what would have occurred had not the noise given their game away; Bowes has no doubt that the horrid hussies put Kelly up to the theft to satisfy their relentless thirst for ardent spirits and lewd behaviour.

They have been treated too well: beef and pork have been theirs for the eating; the fleet, so Bowes has calculated – and he is a man who loves to make lists and add things up – carries two thousand different sorts of medicine for their benefit. He himself was issued by government, for the use of sick convicts: forty pounds of moist sugar, six pounds of currants, six pounds of sage, one pound of almonds, mace, cinnamon, rice, barley; ten gallons of port wine, portable soup, tea, lump sugar, essence of malt ... He's seen soldiers of the King sent overseas with less than this abandoned bunch of harlots and harridans.

Nothing will induce them to behave like rational beings. They steal from each other; their common conversation, even as they go about their ordinary concerns, far exceeds anything you'd hear in the worst pits of London; they return the little kindnesses done for them by the sailors with ingratitude, tempting, using and abusing the fellows for their own ends. Confinement below, gagging or returning them to their irons makes little difference, even flogging – not enough of it, by far, on *Penrhyn*, and impossible at certain phases of the moon – seems to produce only a temporary reform and once strength returns, depravity comes along with it. Shaving the head seems to be the one punishment they truly dislike, striking as it does at the roots of their beastly vanity and even that they circumvent: Mary Davis, being unsteady, fell down a hatchway straight onto her head and would have been killed except she was wearing so much false hair that she escaped without injury at all.

The seas this far south are huge: vast swells that roll on for thousands of miles under grey skies, hiding the ships of the fleet from one another as they rise and fall from trough to peak. The peaks themselves are often a mile apart and come racing and foaming past the ships, burying the decks in white water.

One night a great sea breaks through the weather scuttle of the stern cabin where the officers and surgeon are dining, and crashes in a mighty stream along the deck, through the door, flooding the officers' cabins, and down the companionways into the convict quarters, whence come screams and howls of fear and anger. On deck it foams through the roundhouse, carrying the mate, who is eating his dinner on duty, through the door and over the deck. Only a frantic struggle to cling to the mizzen mast saves him from being cast overboard into a sea that would claim him in seconds. No one sleeps that night. The next morning, the mate's plate and knife and fork are found far forward, caught in the mizzen chains.

William Bryant

He's a fisherman born and bred. In the howling, swaying darkness that is the male convict quarters, he hangs onto a stauncheon as the sea breaks through and sits steady, watching as the rest are washed across the deck, clinging to each other in a scrambling, wailing ball of humanity. He knows the sea and knows that if the ship breaks up, there's no hope for any of them down here; he also knows that the *Charlotte*, though no great sailer, is a hardy little craft and will likely dig her way out of trouble and forge on through the weather.

He's known a good few tricky moments himself, not just at sea hauling the nets in but close inshore, under a smuggler's moon and the dark shadow of the Cornish cliffs, when kegs and barrels are unloaded and passed from man to man through the surf as it unwinds like white lace along the beach. It's an old business, almost as old as fishing and, the story goes, had Christ waited until night alongside the Sea of Galilee, at least two of his disciples would have been free-traders.

William is not a clever man – even his best friends wouldn't say so – but he is dependable, though given to moods when despair comes down and all seems lost; now, though, when they are almost within reach of this Botany Bay, his mood is anything but low. Major Ross, a tartar of a man all the convicts reckon, has been about the transports picking those who have the skills that will be needed once they land. William, by some chance, is the only fisherman amongst the lot of them. In fact, the chance is more ill-luck than anything else.

He was caught red-handed with contraband in his possession, there was a chase, a fight with the revenue men, a few bruises but nothing that would lead to the scaffold; in the end William Bryant found himself up before Launceston assizes in the spring of 1784. The case was clear: caught dead to rights and the judge, Sir Beaumont Hotham, was reaching for the black cap as the jury filed in and gave its verdict: not guilty. Well, they must have been simple to expect a Cornwall jury to convict a free-trader; half the goods on their tables, in their decanters and pipes and on their backs would have come into the country under a smuggler's moon: what kind of message would it send to the boys in the boats if they thought they'd be doing hard time whenever they were nabbed?

The judge is not so happy; wigged heads confer and William Bryant is stood up again for using an alias, one Timothy Cary, which can, if you try very hard, amount to a charge of forgery. The jury has no problems with that: guilty. The judge cheerfully hands down seven years' transportation which means Launceston gaol, one of the worst in the country; it's straw on the floors, a hundred years of filth uncleaned, one tiny window and they don't even have a jakes. In that place any man would feel despair.

Out here, on the southern seas, approaching a new land where there will be a crying need for a man who can catch fish and feed a hungry multitude, the future is beginning to look a little brighter for William Bryant, convict, with three years left to serve.

Captain David Collins

he main fleet makes slow progress and as the new year creeps onwards, every man who can is taking observations to see how far distant the South Cape of New Holland lies. On the evening of 5th January, the sky is lit by the shifting bands of the aurora australis, the southern lights, and strange luminous shapes flicker in the waters around the transports. It is as if they are entering in at the seaward gates of a new world and two days later, at ten o'clock of the forenoon, it is estimated that land lies seventeen leagues away; and by five minutes past two – Collins makes meticulous notes – land is sighted.

A thick mist hangs over the contours of the shoreline as ship's and marine officers line the rail with telescopes hoping to make out the nature of the place – which is rocky, climbing towards bare hills pitted with small caves and, Collins thinks, snow. As they proceed along the coast, they spot thick forests and though they see no smoke during the day, at night the light of fires twinkles across the leagues and some, the more thoughtful amongst the newcomers, wonder what the natives will be thinking of them.

On the 8th the wind shifts to the north-east and the fleet is obliged to head out to sea to avoid being driven onto the shore by the numerous squalls and foul winds that seem to spring up from nowhere. The weather stays against them, progress along the coast is slow, and it is not until 19th January that they make Captain Cook Point which marks the approach to Botany Bay. It is too late to enter this night, so the fleet lays up. The next morning they enter the bay and join the ships of the advance guard. Musters are taken, lists consulted, convicts counted and manifests checked.

Collins notes in his journal: 'Thus, under the blessings of God, is happily completed in eight months and one week, a voyage which, before it was undertaken, the mind hardly dared venture to contemplate, and on which it was impossible to reflect without some apprehension as to its termination. In the above space of time we have sailed five thousand and twenty-one leagues and have touched at the American and African continents without meeting any accident in a fleet of eleven sail, nine of which were merchantmen that have never before sailed in this imperfectly explored ocean. And when it is considered that there was on board a large body of convicts, many of whom were embarked in a very sickly state, we might be deemed particularly fortunate that, of the whole number in the fleet, only thirty-two died since leaving England and one or two of those could be deemed accidents.'

David Collins is in no doubt at all that this is an astounding, a terrific achievement: Dr White agrees; to see so many safe and in good health is a sight truly pleasing.

Second Lieutenant Philip Gidley King

As the sails shiver and collapse and the way comes off the *Supply*, Lieutenant King, who has transferred out of the *Sirius* with the commodore, stands looking over the rail at the vegetation that encloses the bay with a keen sense of ... disappointment. It doesn't look that good, even after thirteen thousand miles at sea it doesn't look good. The ship moves gently through the calm water under its own momentum, ripples gently fanning away from the bow. Lieutenant Ball, the commander, nods and down in the cable tier a sailor lets go the anchor. Almost unnoticeably, as the curve comes out of the cable, the tender stops with the slightest of jerks. They have arrived.

Over the last few leagues they have drawn ahead of the advance party and anchor in the centre of the bay, so as to be easily visible once *Scarborough*, *Alexander* and *Friendship* are in the offing. As always after time at sea, the smell of the land is strong, resinous, with a certain sharpness about it. The light too, now that the uninterrupted horizon is filled with objects, is clearer and brighter as if reflected in a crystal glass and everything it shows gives rise to a feeling that this place is not a place where Europeans are going to be comfortable. That may be fine for the convicts, they aren't supposed to be feeling on top of the world – which they aren't, they're firmly on the geographical bottom – but King wonders how the officers and officials, those who don't owe either allegiance or friendship to Arthur Phillip, are going to react. New South Wales is not going to give anyone an easy passage; the newcomers are going to have to earn the right of residence here.

Whilst running through the heads they saw some of the native population waving their spears in no very friendly manner and running off towards the bay, as if to await and repel the invaders. Most of the officers have prepared themselves for their close encounters by reading of the journals of Captain Cook and Sir Joseph Banks and uneasily recall the great navigator's reports on his first contacts with the local people.

As Cook's *Endeavour* entered the bay it passed through a group of men fishing from dugout canoes, none of whom appeared to pay the ship any attention at all – for those aboard it was a dreamlike experience, drifting silently past these people who can never have seen any machine as large and complex as a ship in their lives and yet, for all the difference it made, it could have been a floating island.

However, later in the day, after *Endeavour* had anchored and Cook and Banks attempted a landing, matters were to be arranged somewhat differently. This time, approaching the shore in a long boat, they were met with the brandishing of spears – about eight feet long – and the waving of short sticks which appeared to be machines for launching the spears with greater power and accuracy. The captain and the scientist tried throwing nails and beads ashore, which occasioned, they thought, a certain pleasure but when they followed this up by approaching yet closer, the spears were raised again. Cook fired a musket in the air and the natives backed off, though whether they knew what the thing was, apart from loud, was not ascertained. When one of them grabbed a pile of spears and everyone began throwing them at the boat, it became clear that they did not understand the power of black powder and lead shot. Cook fired once more, peppering one man in the shoulder with pellets. All retreated up the beach. Cook, a Yorkshireman to his boot-soles, told his young midshipman Isaac Smith that he might have the honour of being first ashore. The natives faded away into the trees and left the explorers to their explorations.

No one aboard the *Supply* wants to test the power of those eight-foot spears and, after the boats are hoisted out and rowed to various points around the bay, they proceed with extreme caution, though the natives are not at once in evidence. Phillip and Lieutenants King and Dawes, a young man of a scientific bent, and some of the *Supply*'s sailors, land on the northern shore. Their first objective is to find fresh water, without which there can be no colony. They find nothing on the beach and venture inland, where the ground is covered with grass, scrub and small trees but there is no sign of the fine meadows that Cook rhapsodised about in his journals; obviously a great navigator but no farmer, Phillip reflects, from the depths of his own knowledge of the land. And there is still no water.

They head back to the ship, which is tugging at its anchor chain now, the plaything of a nasty east wind that blows through the heads of the bay. It could, Phillips thinks, be another problem; then he reflects that if it can, it will, particularly if, as it appears, the sea bottom is gently sloping all round; there will be nowhere that vessels with any kind of draft can tie up close to shore and if they moor in the centre of the bay there will be a constant east wind buffeting them. It'll mean that all the unloading will have to done by tender, not unusual in itself, but over long distances and with tricky winds (and light-fingered everyone) it's asking for loss and accident; a most unsatisfactory prospect. Phillip tells King that Captain Cook saw the bay as a temporary anchorage and not as a permanent home and that simply isn't good enough for them.

As they row back to the ship a party of natives appears on shore and they turn about and head back, landing beside a couple of canoes. The owners, suspecting theft, brandish their spears – and they are very long – and advance in a menacing manner; Phillip hangs some beads over the stern of one of the canoes and makes signs of drinking. One of the natives points inland and Phillip fearlessly follows the direction of the finger. King and others follow Phillip with considerable trepidation, worried about ambush. They find a stream with clear, clean, fresh tasting water. A small stream, with muddy banks, but nonetheless, fresh water.

The two parties stand facing one another and King begins to feel uncomfortably burdened by the heavy clothing he is wearing; the natives' nakedness and grace is somehow far more natural here and, for a moment, he sees himself as they must see him: a ridiculous scarecrow loaded down with cloth and objects, sweating and stumbling over unfamiliar ground. Flies buzz loudly in the hot afternoon. No one moves until Phillip unbuckles his sword belt and walks forward. One man advances to meet him. The two stand facing each other, just out of reach. King notices that the governor is missing the same tooth, on the upper right side of his jaw, as the native: it could be a mirror image. Phillip offers beads; the other indicates that they should be laid on the ground. This is done and the beads are picked up and examined, as are some looking glasses. The two groups decide that enough has been achieved for today and back off.

Over the next two days, whilst the rest of the advance guard arrive and anchor, there are more contacts between natives and newcomers. Major Ross, still annoyed that he was not asked to accompany the governor in *Supply*, issues an order to the marines that guard duty must be stepped up and that one officer will be upon deck at all times during the evening and night. It is clear to King and Phillip that this soldier has little or no sympathy with country, colony or convicts but, so far, Ross keeps his feelings pretty much to himself and that evening, joins his fellow officers on the beach for food and beer, during which toasts are drink to absent friends in England.

Concerns about fresh water are growing. The streams that have been found will not supply anything near the colony's needs and none are wide enough to allow passage inland by boat; then there are the areas of marshland that Cook overlooked which seem to lie everywhere and would preclude any substantial building.

The arrival of the rest of the fleet, on 19th January, emphasizes the urgency of the matter. Phillip's orders specifically state that the convicts are to remain locked in their quarters aboard for as little time as possible once the fleet has anchored. This isn't humanity on the part of government; the colony is paying for the hire of the ships and the sooner they are empty, the sooner they are off the payroll.

The only hope of finding good land seems to lie on the unexplored south side of the bay, where there are two inlets and it is to these that Phillip and King, taking a boat each, set off on the following morning. The boats separate and King leads his party around some shoals, almost dry at low tide, treacherous at anything else, and up the first inlet. They find themselves running between the highest hills they've seen so far and spot a dog fox scurrying away into the scrub. Still no decent land, but a party of natives appear on the shore and King takes the boat in. Beads are presented; one of the natives demonstrates his ability with the spear, sending it forty yards and causing it to sink so deeply into the ground on landing that it is all King can do to pull it out. He decides this is a warning not to overstep the mark or more spears will be thrown. The atmosphere begins to turn nasty and King orders his men back to the boat. They have muskets but he doesn't want to use them; far better to retreat with dignity. It doesn't work; this is not a country for dignity, King concludes, just for survival. The natives whoop and shout and, in the excitement, a spear is launched. King orders a marine to shoot with powder only and the crack gives pause to the natives' celebrations and allows the boat to back off and head downstream.

Later, they meet another group of natives who appear less warlike, more curious. King offers wine which is tasted but spat out. The colonists ask the names of various articles and receive answers which they write down in journals and notebooks; the natives gently request various articles, laying their fingers upon them. Some are given, others refused. Despite the earlier encounters, King has no apprehensions about these people; they are, he believes, absolutely honest; what he worries about is the affect of a thousand absolutely dishonest men and women who are shortly to flood ashore. He exchanges greetings and more gifts and asks about the throwing stick, which is demonstrated. In return, the natives indicate their curiosity about the sex of the newcomers. Since none of them have beards, can it be that they are women? King orders one of the marines to drop his breeches so as to make the matter quite clear; it isn't the kind of order the men expect and there is a certain reluctance to air the old belly ruffian in this situation. King insists, the breeches drop and a great shout follows; the natives know where they are now with these fellows. One of them proudly indicates a spot along the shore where a group of young women and girls make their appearance, all as bare as pins. An offer is made, perhaps the newcomers would care to demonstrate their manhood? A few of the marines are thinking about it and are firmly ordered to 'stand down'. King, politely, declines the kind offer but offers a new, white handkerchief to one of the maidens, tying it about her where 'Eve did wear the fig leaf'.

Back at the ships Phillip holds an impromptu meeting of his senior staff: everyone (except Major Ross, who thinks they ought to dump the convicts and go home) agrees that the dampness of the soil (a breeding ground for diseases), the paucity of fresh water, the prevailing east wind and the difficulty of gaining a safe anchorage all make Botany Bay unsuitable. Phillip tells them that he intends to seek out another situation. He is resolved to explore Port Jackson, which Captain Cook named but did not investigate. It is just along the coast and will, he hopes, prove a fitter home for his new government.

Bennelong

he land is full of sounds.

~ *birds and animals.*

~ *the sounds of children laughing as they play, making lizard tracks in the sand with their feet, looking back over their shoulders to see if the lizard men are really following or if, perhaps, they passed through this place in another time.*

~ *the sound of women talking quietly amongst themselves whilst they wander along the shore, flicking up stones with their toes to see what is underneath, bending and scooping oysters into baskets, looking out across the water, some of them feeling the twinge where their little finger used to be that tells them the fish are hungry and waiting to be called into the nets.*

~ *the sound of young men hunting, which is no sound at all as they pass amongst the trees and the scrub, appearing and disappearing in dapple, sun and shade, approaching the river where the ducks swim contentedly until, with a splashing and crashing, they burst from the trees along the banks and the ducks flap furious wings and fly, squawking, along the river away from the annoyance. And as the lead bird begins to rise and bank away from the water, a dark shape comes swooping out from the bush, with the unmistakable cry of a hawk. The ducks swing back to the river's course and fly low, wingtips flicking the water as they skim around a bend and into the net hung across their path. Bodies crash and collide, feathers fly, a terrible squawking arises as the hunters run out from the bank and pull the net to shore and in moments there is quiet again and food for all.*

~ the sound of the old men talking, telling stories that were told to them and have been told for as long as men have been men in this place; stories of the great ancestors, the journeys they made and the things they did and where those journeys and things can be seen now and what they teach. Stories of the great serpent who lived in a pool on the top of a mountain and used to come out of the dark, cold water in the depths and lie in the sunlight so his scales glittered all the colours of the rainbow; of how he looked down from the mountain at all the land stretching out around and how he saw it was green and brown and stretched away as far as the sea but he saw no people at all and he was worried. He waited and he listened but no sounds came except for the birds and the animals. At last he thought 'I shall make the people who will live in this green and brown land' and he took a tree that the ants had bored and made hollow and he blew through it and the sound was deep and a boy and a girl emerged. The serpent was pleased and, so as not to frighten the children, he changed himself into an old man and sat on the rock in the sunlight with them. And all around insects and birds flickered through the bright air.

The old men nod, and say amongst themselves this is the way it is and way it will always be. They blow on the smouldering ends of branches and clouds of sparks fly into the air. They talk and they fall silent as the sparks fall to the ground and they listen ... to the quiet sound of the end of their world.

Metal squeaks against metal, the lock of a musket is pulled back, presses against the spring and clicks into place. Steel locked on steel. Canvas cracks in the wind, the sun catches the lens of a telescope and there is a sudden blinding star; wood works against wood, rope runs through metal pulleys, boot heels hit decking, parchment pages flicker in the wind, pens scratch lines across their flat, worked surfaces and, above and beyond all, a dozen, two dozen watches tick away furiously in waistcoat pockets, each hour, minute and second hand slicing into the timeless land, dicing it into ever smaller moments.

Looking down from the wooded slopes, across the waters he knows so well, Bennelong sees a boat gliding past the headland, turning in towards the shore. Inside it are figures – men or women, who knows – but decidedly different from any man or woman he has ever seen in this world. Because they are, each and every one of them, the colour of the dead and they come from across the sea where the dead go, and yet here they are, back again. It's a puzzle but since they are here, and he can see them, hear them and smell them (and he doesn't like the smell at all) then they must be men of some kind with the same needs that other men have to hunt and live and take wives and walk the paths of the ancestors. Unless they are the ancestors? Maybe it would be best to kill them all and have done with it? It would certainly be wise to be careful. He moves back into the shadow of the trees and is lost ...

Captain David Collins

isappointment is the first emotion felt by Collins as the three boats pass through the forbidding bare cliffs that form the heads of Port Jackson and he sees parties of natives waving their spears and shouting 'Warra warra warra', but as they continue under a mild sky, the water calm and serene around them, a most wonderful prospect opens up: a natural harbour so commodious that a thousand ships of the line might easily anchor there. Governor Phillip fixes on a cove which has several clear, fast-flowing springs and the three boats land their passengers.

The anchorage close to shore looks promising; the ground, gently sloping away from the cove, though covered with trees, will make a fine site for the beginnings of a settlement. Phillip decides there and then to name the cove after Lord Sydney, knowing quite well that, despite their distance from the old world, this new world is going to need a powerful friend at court.

The party re-embarks and heads back to Botany Bay where Phillip informs all captains and marine officers that the expedition will move on to Port Jackson and disembark their passengers and stores at Sydney Cove. Phillip returns to the cove with an advance party of skilled men, the rest are to follow on the next tide. However, what the next tide brings is not departure but the appearance of three strange ships standing in – it looks very much as if the French have arrived.

La Perouse

'The moment I made my appearance in the entrance of the Bay, a lieutenant and midshipman were sent aboard my vessel by Captain Hunter, the captain of the British ships. They offered on his behalf any service it was in his power to render me, adding that, as it was his intention that very moment to get under way, circumstances were not such that would enable him to supply sails, ammunition or provisions. I concluded that, in effect, his offer was limited to good wishes for the remainder of our voyage of exploration. I sent an officer to return my thanks to the captain, who by now had his anchor up and his topsails set.

'From the English lieutenant, we learned that the squadron was commanded by Captain Phillip. The Lieutenant made a great mystery of Captain Phillip's plans and we did not take the liberty of questioning him on the subject. The crew of the English longboat were, however, less discreet than their officer and informed our people that they were going only north a few leagues along the coast to a place where Captain Phillip had discovered a very fine harbour where ships might anchor within a pistol shot of the land in water as smooth as that of a basin.

'The wisdom of the English decision to quit the Bay was amply demonstrated by the difficulty many of their ships experienced in working out against the wind and tide, with booms carried away, sail and yards damaged by collision or near collision, stern works destroyed and tempers exacerbated as vessel after vessel negotiated the narrows and their attendant rocks with little room to spare.'[7]

William Bryant

Below decks on the *Charlotte* they can hear the anchor chain rattling out and feel the motion of the ship changing as the sails are backed and they lose way and come to a stop in the calm waters of the cove. Most of the men are ready to move; some have already been ashore at Botany Bay, Will Bryant amongst them, and have no very great opinion of the place. Too swampy, too many trees, too hot; not that anyone can do much about the heat or the flies or the natives, though a few of the fellows are already thinking about maybe joining up with them and getting over the mountains to China – not that they look Chinese; they don't look much of anything: even the girls, who strut around naked as the day they were born, aren't exactly worth coming half the way round the world to see, not when they've got a couple of shiploads of their own women ready and waiting.

Of course there's going to be trouble about that: there always is with smocks. The fellows have seen the way the marines and the sailors look at the mutton, how they are always offering rum and extra food and cloth and anything else they could get their hands on just to get their hands on the women. The officers too, pretty high and mighty with their airs and graces but in the breeches they're all the same: its been the corporal and four for all these months but once ashore they're going to cream off the best of the bunch because of what they can offer. Not much the convicts can do about that but they've made up their minds about the marines and sailors: 'Keep your breeches on, Lobsterback! No hairy-pie for you, Jackie Tarr.'

Hatches are pulled back and the sharp light floods in; shouts and curses as the marines roust them out and on to the deck for their first sight of their new home. Will wanders over to the rail and gives the coastline a glance, then peers at the sea running alongside the raked sides of the *Charlotte*. The sea that separates him from his home – the sea that will give him the lever he needs to make enough to get back to Cornwall one day.

It's his home, it's what he wants and what he misses. It's what has made him notice, when the men and women have been exercised together, the Cornishwoman who has always looked a little better dressed than the other green geese and holds herself with a certain pride; since Rio, she's been holding a baby too and the gab has that it was an officer back in Devonport who wound up her clock and left her with the brat. That's no problem for Will, he's been keeping his ears open and has a shrewd idea that the new governor wants settled families and smiling faces and Will is happy to oblige the man, as long as it can be turned to his advantage. And the woman, no great looker but young and fit – and he knows from the tattle that spreads through the ship worse than the fleas and rats, that she can turn a trick or two herself and isn't afraid to face it out with any one.

Parson Johnson, who dipped the kid at the Cape, wants to see her settled and will be a good friend to the man who takes her in. He's talked it over with a couple of the lads he's got to know and trust during the long voyage, Jimmy Martin and Jim Cox: it's a smugglers bargain, particularly since everyone – except the parson – knows that Botany Bay marriages won't be legal and once Will's sentence is served, he'll be free to work or buy his passage home. He and the other two have an agreement, they've spoken the oath together:

Hand to hand,
On Earth, in Hell,
Sick or well,
On Sea or Land,
On the Square, ever.

Stiff or in Breath,
Lag or Free,
You and me
In Life and Death,
On the Cross, never.

Will knows they'll keep their mouths shut about his plans, so long as it doesn't become more profitable to sell him out; he'll just have to make sure it doesn't, and he has a few ideas about that already.

Boats nudge the *Charlotte*, painters are slung and made secure; the convicts are told off in groups and clamber down. The sailors and masters are glad to get rid of them: they're no more than annoying freight and once they're unloaded, the ships can sail on to their final destinations in the east and take on more valuable – and less troublesome – cargo.

When the convicts are in the boats, stores and equipment are handed down and the men, well fed but out of condition after months squatting between decks no higher than a ten-year-old child, begin to sweat in the close, damp heat.

Most of the transports have got boats out in the cove with sailors hauling the seine. Will can see that they don't know what they're doing; sailors hate fish and dislike being close to the water and they're getting caught up with their nets, losing half the catch, keeping what looks to him useless and throwing back the good stuff. He's got no problem with this: he's the only fisherman in the whole damn fleet and once the ships have gone and the colony is on its own, he is going to be able to write his own ticket, he will be the Fishmonger of Botany Bay!

Across the calm water, their shouts echoing off the gently sloping hills all around, a navy party is slinging the lead and surveying the bay; ashore the clatter of axes can already be heard hacking against the trees, followed by bellowed curses as blades are turned or blunted; it looks like the wood here is harder than back home and, for men who don't have the muscle and swing of the axe to heart, the felling is proving a hard task.

The cutter grounds, the convicts step out and hardly have their feet touched new ground but axes, saws, iron bars for grubbing roots are thrust into their hands and they are sent off to clear the land. In most cases this means taking no more than a couple of steps before a tree presents itself for the chopping and soon more axe blows and yet more curses join those already tenanting this once quiet country.

Under the direction of a surveyor, marines are marking out where their barracks will stand, the area for the officers' tents, the canvas hospital, the portable house that, so the scuttle has it, Captain Phillip has brought from London; others are setting up a piquet line around the proposed boundary of the camp and already marines with fixed bayonets are walking its length. It isn't to stop the convicts getting away – they've all been told there's nowhere to get away to (except China, some still say, though Will knows they're all noodles and flats) and if they wander off inland they'll simply starve or be eaten by wild beasts. No, the piquet is there to protect the natives and the strictest cautions have already been issued to every man: don't talk, don't touch, especially don't try anything with the women or you'll be dancing in eternity tonight.

A rumour passes through the straining, sweating workers: the women's quarters are to be laid out on the east side of the cove, near the hospital and the officers' tents and the men are to be housed on the west with the marines. An angry growl rises and half-hearted efforts become even less enthusiastic. They've been dragged halfway round the word to this godforsaken hole and now their women are to be taken away. Sullen resentment sits on every brow and a determination not to cooperate is born amongst the hard-barked trees; axe heads, hammers and spikes are being slipped under shirts and into breeches for later use as weapons or trade goods. This may be a new world but, as Will Bryant and every other convict in the place can see, it's the same old government and the same old privilege and the some old bastards at the top and at the bottom of the pile.

By evening a good area of land has – resentfully – been cleared and kitchen tents set up; the cooks are breaking up the slabs of portable soup, each stamped with its government-issue arrow, stirring them into the cauldrons of local fresh water and piling up the fires to bring them to the boil. Lines form, food is eaten and the convicts, exhausted after a day's unaccustomed exercise, watch with only mild curiosity as the officers gather round a newly erected flagpole and toast the King and the Royal Family and the success of the new colony with glasses of wine, whilst a guard of marines blast away at the cloudy sky with their muskets and strange birds in the bush howl and cackle.

Its all the barber's cat, wind and piss, Will Bryant reckons, as they get back to work putting up tents against the hot wind rising and the growl of distant thunder. Flags and muskets, kings and wine, it don't mean a thing to man who is not free and can, any time he's caught putting a foot wrong, be flogged or put in irons. Such a man has only one duty in this world: to himself and what he can get out of it.

Lieutenant Watkin Tench

usiness, and Tench begs to differ from the general resentment, is set on every brow – though some are more businesslike than others. Lieutenant Clark complains that it is so hot that he managed no more than half a biscuit and glass of water for breakfast. It is possible that these latitudes will not suit Clark, but Watkin Tench is quite content as he hurries about the settlement, past the kitchens, the marines and convicts struggling once more with the trees and roots. As he later writes in his journal, he thinks it would be, 'to the indifferent spectator,' a highly diverting spectacle to observe in one place 'a party cutting down the woods, a second setting up a blacksmith's forge', (it was brought ashore yesterday with some difficulty) 'a third dragging along a load of stones or provisions, here an officer pitching his marquee with a detachment of soldiers on one side of him and a cook's fire blazing on the other,' – and there a little group of convicts sneaking off into the bush in the colony's first escape attempt. Mindful of his future readership, though, Tench reminds himself to be astute with the criticism: booksellers like a good positive story with heroic or comical characters, noble villains and lovelorn maidens. Well, none of the latter here and the villains are all pretty died-in-the-wool bully-bucks and sneeze lurkers, not a Captain McHeath amongst them, so it'll have to be the heroic marines who overcome the obstacles of nature and encourage the convicts to greater efforts.

Officers patrol the busy scene reminding the convicts that good behaviour and hard work will earn privileges in the weeks and months to come, once huts have been built and gardens dug. Their future is in their own hands – in fact, everybody's future is in their hands since they make up most of the workforce and by far the greater percentage of those on shore. The operation of the colony is, in a way, a magician's mirror, fooling those people into obedience who, could they but see clearly, might mutiny and take over the whole place and operate it to their own satisfaction. Perhaps a plan exists and they are merely waiting until the ships and the sailors have left before carrying it out?

Over the next few days the colony begins to take shape, the lines and shading becoming clearer, like a picture emerging on an artist's block. The hospital tents go up and receive their first patients; there are a few early, ominous signs, Dr White says, of scurvy; the long haul from the Cape and the reduced rations have not improved the health of the convicts, though, on the whole, most of them are in far better fettle than ever before in their lives.

Tench and a party of fellow officers and men set off to visit the French explorers at Botany Bay and are received civilly. M. La Perouse informs them that a number of convicts have, more by luck than navigation, found their way through the trees and scrub to Botany Bay where they have offered themselves as hands. They were given a day's rations and sent back overland to Sydney Cove, where security is tightened.

Back at Sydney Cove, Phillip orders the ships' masters to fire upon any convicts who attempt to swim out and board their vessels; in addition, no seaman will be allowed to mix with the convicts without express permission and the loss, through concealment or carelessness, of any tools will be punished severely. No one (except the convicts who've already hidden a few away) likes the idea of an axe or a hammer being used as a weapon, particularly when there's such a shortage of the things.

The convict William Bryant is instructed to gather together such boats and equipment as he will need to start fishing for the good of the colony. Bryant is agreeable; the matter has been discussed during the latter part of the voyage, since he is known to have followed the trade of fisherman in the western part of England from his youth. He makes some demands of his own: that he be allowed a hut separate from the general convict quarters for himself and such family as he will have, that he has the choice of those men he will employ as his assistants and that an agreed quantity of the fish he catches will be his, for his own use. So vital are his skills, and so important is it considered to keep him honest and straight and place him above temptation, that Major Ross swallows his desire to give the man a damn good flogging to teach him manners and the requests are agreed without exception.

First Lieutenant Bradley of the *Sirius* continues mapping the harbour, heading inland to find extensive lands fit for cultivation and a wide river. The Reverend Richard Johnson, a man without the least taint of irony in his soul, preaches the first sermon and baptises the first child; his text is: 'What shall I render unto the Lord for all His benefits towards me?'

Lieutenant Clark breaks the first wine glass; more convicts sneak off to Botany Bay and are returned and two marines have a fight over a fish. Tench believes that food may be a problem in the months to come; the commisary, Mr Miller, goes aboard the transports *Lady Penrhyn* and *Charlotte* to issue the new clothing bought on the journey to the women who will be coming ashore tomorrow. One of them, Ann Smith, when reminded by Mr Miller of her 'very indifferent character', as Arthur Bowes notes, throws the whole pile back in his face. Five of the best behaved women are landed early and given quarters near Phillip's canvas house, out of the way of the rest of the camp.

The weather is heavy – airless – it is as if the sky, the whole world and every man in the convict camp, and a good few others, is holding his breath, waiting ...

Mary Broad

Throughout the morning of 6th February the rocking motion of the ship gets worse; some of the women are starting to feel sick and others have headaches brought on by the closeness of the air below. The sound of thunder echoes all around and yet when they go up on deck, they can see hardly a cloud overhead – it is like those storms they've experienced on the passage, impossible storms, lowering on the horizon like billowing black smoke, flickering inside with lightning and yet surrounded by blue sky.

There is something in the air and it isn't just the weather. As they climb down into the boats, keeping their new skirts from billowing in the rising wind, clutching their few possessions or their children, they can smell it coming off the land: the stink of maleness – there are too many men here. The balance is all wrong and they are being rowed surely, inexorably, towards that stink, and every man jack at sea or on land has a wall-eyed look about him, like he knows something bad is going to happen and just so long as each is part of it, then no one will have to feel shame or guilt for what they are about to do.

Mary clutches Charlotte close; she knows that good intentions won't save her tonight, she needs protection and in this place that means a man: William Bryant, smuggler and now, so she has heard and as they have planned, fisherman for the colony. Their agreement has been forged during the voyage – she will do for him and he will do for her. They understand each other as only those who come from the same part of the world can: the way they speak, the things they remember when they're not trying to remember, the taste of saffron cake and salted fish, the sea and the knotting of nets, the high cliffs and the little coves, the pathways folded into the hills, the brambles and the churches and the villages and the smell of dry grass in the summer; the place where they don't care where you've been or what you've done, only that you are one of theirs. Perhaps these things were never true but out here on the edge of the world where nothing is quite familiar, they are the same things, and that makes a difference.

The blue sky is gone, the clouds are churning, low and dark, crackling with enough electricity to raise the fine hair on baby Charlotte's head, though the wind doesn't get any cooler, blowing like the draft from a bread oven; it's as if the day wants to get itself over and done with, as if it wants to weep over what will happen once it is dark.

When the boat lands, William is waiting for her and they hurry off towards the tent he is using whilst he builds their hut. The rest of the women, those without protectors, are led off to the tents that have been put up for their reception, except that none of the tents have actually been put up since the convicts told off for the task have been walking around with their hands on their cocks and cocks like tent poles all afternoon.

Surgeon Arthur Bowes

Before anyone can reprove the convicts for their dereliction – which is no surprise at all to Surgeon Bowes – the darkness descending over Sydney Cove is split by a cat-o'-nine-tails of lightning that burns into the eyeballs of convicts and marines alike and is followed by a vast roar of thunder that keeps on getting louder and louder until surely eardrums will be split. And then, in the silence, the sound of raindrops on the still-folded canvas, drops as heavy as a blacksmith's fingertips, tapping, drumming and then crashing as rain falls like a freshwater wave and turns the world upside down and air into water.

The women are soaked in seconds, their dresses, good and not so good, clinging to their bodies, their hair plastered across shocked faces; around their feet the grass turns to mud and the mud to a stream flowing down towards the cove. Rain hits the ground so hard that it bounces back and forms a thick mist as high as your waist; lightning snakes down again and fastens onto the top of a tree, twisting and hissing as it splits the wood that blunts axes and sends the two huge halves crashing to earth.

The male convicts feel as if time has been called on the first round of a boxing match that has a thousand rounds to go and will leave the milling coves bruised and bloody if not dead, but for now, whatever happens in the future, there is illicit brandy and the prize to be grabbed and torn away and taken in the mud and be damned to what's right or wrong, sometimes a man has to drop his breeches and get out the beard splitter and go facemaking ...

On board the *Lady Penrhyn*, rocking at anchor in the hot high winds, they can hear the terrified screams of women through the storm. The general feeling is one of relief that their cargo is gone and that they can go too, in a couple of days, to China. The men petition the captain to broach a cask of rum in celebration. He agrees; he's been labouring under a penalty system of forty pounds for every missing convict and is heartily glad the bitches have gone ashore at last. The rum flows, faces get redder under the swinging deck lamps, memories turn back to the women as they walked the decks these last months and the efforts they made, as the end of the voyage approached, to clean themselves up and regain something of the looks and spirit they had when they were free. Then resentment is born: why should the convicts have it all when honest sailors are denied? Even drunk, the average sailor can launch a boat without drowning and before long, oars are splashing unnoticed in the turmoil and dozens more are ready to join the band and play the blue-veined piccolo.

Arthur Bowes, wary of losing another pair of trousers to a female shark, keeps his distance but uses his eyes and scurries back aboard to make notes in the feverish, yellow light of a lantern, safe in his cabin: 'The scene beggars every description; some swearing, others quarrelling, others singing, not in the least regarding the tempest, tho' so violent that the thunder shook the ships. I never before experienced so uncomfortable a night, expecting every moment to be struck by lightning and the sailors all drunk and incapable and the heat almost suffocating.'

The next day, everyone who can leave the ships in safety is summoned ashore. The colony steams in the glaring sun like a wet rag that's been used to wipe up after a murder. Red-eyed men drag themselves out from under temporary coverings; bruised and often weeping women drag themselves out from under red-eyed men. Marines stare resentfully as they parade and drive the sodden, sullen convicts before their rigid lines, sweeping them to the largest area of cleared land the colony can yet offer, where beneath flying colours the marine band breaks into a deafening medley of patriotic and sentimental tunes.

Captain Phillip, followed by his officials and officers, emerges from his canvas house and marches smartly – as smartly as a sailor can, Major Ross of the marines puts a real snap into his step – to a pre-arranged spot. He takes off his hat and bows to his staff. The colours are lowered and raised as a mark of respect to the new governor of the English Colony at Sydney Cove. Major Ross cracks out an order: the marines shoulder arms and march in a circle until they completely surround the increasingly nervous convicts swaying in the clear light of the morning. They are counted and it is found that Ann Smith, who threw her clothes back in the commissary's face, is missing.

A table is placed in front of Phillip and two red boxes are laid upon it: they contain all the instruments of government necessary to take, hold and administer the land on which they are standing. The judge advocate, Captain David Collins, reads them out; Bowes is amazed at the extent of the new governor's powers, they are, he reckons, greater than any ever granted to a British governor before.

The marines fire three volleys, the hungover convicts flinch; the sound echoes away into a cacophony of bird calls. The new governor steps forward and begins to harangue his audience, telling them they have proved themselves to be the most deprav'd, incorrigible ...

Captain Watkin Fench

The governor addresses himself to the convicts in a pointed and judicious speech, informing them of his future intentions, which are inevitably to cherish and render happy those who show a disposition to amendment ...

Lieutenant Ralph Clark

e has never heard of any one man having so much power vested in himself.

Surgeon John White

The governor's speech is extremely well adapted to the people he has to govern and who stand before him. He recommends marriage, assuring them that this will tend to their future happiness and comfort.

Arthur Phillip

He steps forward and looks at his charges: pale-faced, leaning on each other for support, apprehensive, hurt, lost; he tells them to sit down. They do so, with a collective sigh of relief. He runs his eyes around the marines, standing with bayonets fixed; over their wives and children in a little group under the shade of some of those intractable trees; at the sailors from the ships in the bay; at the band with their pipeclay catching the sun; at his officers and officials, some in uniform, some wearing heavy, uncomfortable broadcloth coats and he knows that getting them this far, half way round the world, with so few deaths and without losing a single ship out of a fleet with several bad sailers, is a feat of seamanship equal to any in history. It is a quiet triumph, because he also knows that there will be no victory bells for this set of convicts, no celebration sword worth a hundred guineas presented to the commander of this squadron: it is a job well done, the kind of thing the navy expects. And it is, of course, only the beginning and the elements he has to deal with now make the average hurricano look like the ripples spreading from a stone tossed into a millpond.

He tells them he will encourage all those who show an inclination to improve by obeying orders and conducting themselves decently; he adds that marriage is the best way to formalise relations between the sexes and warns that any man seen trying to enter a woman's tent after curfew will be fired upon by the marine sentries. He urges them to forget their old habits and their old way of life, which has generally been indolent, dishonest, immoral and violent, and turn to honesty amongst themselves and in their relations with overseers and officials. He tells them to work hard because if they don't, everyone will starve; here they must build and grow crops or perish and anyone who does not work will not eat, it is that simple: good men will not be slaves of bad men's laziness and cynicism. Bad men and women will be punished with severity; it is not something he enjoys or wants to do but he will do it, if it is necessary. He finishes by saying that for those who work, the future can lead to success, wealth and respect. He announces that the rest of the day will be free of any labour.

The marines fire three more volleys and the parade is dismissed. Phillip invites his new staff to a cold buffet. Toasts are drunk and maggots carefully removed from the mutton – slaughtered only last night – before it is offered to Mrs Johnson, the parson's wife.

Writing to Lord Sydney, Phillip puts down some of his feelings about the colony:

> 'The necks of land that form the different coves are so rocky that it is surprising such large trees as there are should find any nourishment. The whole country round us is covered by trees, most of which are so large that the removing them off the ground after they are cut down is the greatest part of the labour, and the convicts, naturally indolent, having none to attend them but overseers drawn from amongst themselves, and who fear to exert any authority, makes this work go very slowly.
>
> 'Our situation, tho' so very different from what might have been expected, is nevertheless the best that offered. My instructions do not permit me to detain the transports a sufficient time to explore the coast and it was absolutely necessary to be sure of a sufficient quantity of fresh water, in a situation that was healthy.'

He knows, sitting in his canvas house while the work goes on all around him, that the stores they have brought will not last long. The colony must begin to grow its own food: already, Dr White informs him, the first signs of scurvy are beginning to appear amongst marines and convicts. He needs a settled society with men and women who are prepared to work not only for themselves but also for the common good but he knows that the whole way of life of the majority of his charges has led them away from self-sufficiency. Put to work as labourers on the land or in service, stitching shirts or hats or boots, they have been continually told to do this or that, their lives controlled by orders from above, by the paucity of their wages, by their lack of education. Those that could get away have risen in the world or turned to crime rather more successful than the housebreaking and private stealing that have sent the majority of them to this place. There are exceptions, men who have already shown an aptitude for gardening, the far-sighted who begin, dimly, to see a possible future in this new land; but most are resentful at being taken from their prisons and put down half a world away, and this does not apply to the convicts alone: Major Ross is already creating an atmosphere of resentment and discontent which is affecting not only his marine corps but the officers and officials as well. Where Major Ross is, disputes and argument, quarrels and petty jealousies are sure to follow. The man is bad news in a new country where everyone has to do his best.

It is particularly unfortunate that Phillip Gidley King will have to leave the settlement any day in the *Supply* with a small party of convicts and marines to settle Norfolk Island, a tiny dot of land in the vast Southern Ocean, where Captain Cook saw fine pines for masts and flax for sails and government saw a possible base for the French or Spanish in these waters. King has a talent for organisation and getting men to do his bidding that would have been invaluable at Sydney Cove. Phillip only hopes that the great navigator was more accurate about Norfolk Island than he was about Botany Bay, and that his protégé will be able to make a success of the tiny colony.

Phillip's greater concerns are nearer his canvas home: he needs to find or implant a sense of purpose here, a future towards which men and women might work. He has great hopes for marriage and one or two surprises up his sleeve for those who reckon that Sydney Cove weddings aren't legal; he also has the Reverend Richard Johnson, a man of an enthusiastic bent, something of an evangelist who already sees his life in terms of a ministry in New South Wales, where, he says, he may stay many years and even end his days. Phillip is no believer –

though he swears he would be if only Mr Johnson could work a miracle and turn all the convicts into just fifty good farmers. That isn't going to happen and all Phillip can do is encourage marriage and a sober way of life, and that's a start.

Will and Mary

A stormy Sunday, the clouds shot through with the occasional brilliance of sunlight. In a commodious tent, sometimes almost inaudible as the raindrops thunder against drum-tight canvas, the Reverend Johnson conducts the most hopeful of services: that of christening and marriage.

Three children have been received into the church, two of convict parents, one of a marine and his wife. Will and Mary stand at the end of the short line of those waiting to be wed. Three other couples are before them: Henry Cable and Susannah Holmes, who have a love story of their own to tell; William Haynes and Hannah Green; Simon Burn and Francis Anderson – then it is the turn of William Bryant and Mary Broad.

Mr Johnson does not ask any of them whether they are using real names or aliases, he's happy to marry them with the names they were convicted under; he just wants lots of families who will begin to build up a new society and a generation untainted by the sins of the old world. Will signs the register with his name, Mary with a cross. Now there are two of them and their individual strength is more than doubled. Will has the skills necessary to gain power in the colony, Mary has the will to use that power; neither of them has a whit of care or concern for Governor Phillip's dreams of a place that will, one day, become the most valuable acquisition that Britain ever made.

James Boswell

he *LIFE* is nearly finished, he hopes to have the first draft wrapped up by the end of the year and go into 1789 with a hopeful heart, pulling in, from here and there, all those little extras which will make it the perfect thing and knock the opposition out of the ring. It has not been a good few months and he could do with an improvement in his material circumstances and general condition.

His wife Margaret is home at Auchinleck, her health getting worse by the day. He writes to her constantly, assuring her of his love and support and he does feel for her dreadfully. She is terrified of dying, of the dark passage, just as he is: but for her the reaper is already in the near meadow and will, she knows, shortly be coming for his wages. James is doing his best: he no longer sees Mrs Rudd and apologises constantly, by letter, for the affair and boasts, just a little, of his present constancy but there it is, as it has been throughout their marriage, the feared and fascinating Death.

It is, he thinks, quite proper to be frightened of the thing itself because of what must come after. Even Dr Johnson felt a very great terror when he thought of that and, when questioned by a pious man what it might mean to damned, had roared: 'Sent to hell, Sir, and punished everlastingly!' And yet there have been men who Boswell respects who have smiled in the face of the old adversary.

David Hume, the wonder of the age, the great philosopher, died in seeming unconcern of what, if anything, might be lurking outside the door of life. Boswell visited during the sage's last days, hoping to find the old insouciance withering in the face of the wind that chills to the 'bare bane'. Hume was lean and ghastly and quite different from the plump figure he used to present but when Boswell asked, not without a hidden, self-satisfied smirk, what he thought of religion now, the dying man told him that having given it up early in life, after reading Locke, he had managed quite well without it ever since.

Boswell was thunderstruck – what about morality and religion, he demanded.

'What about them?' Hume asked; as far as ever he could see, the morality of every religion was equally bad and when he heard of a religious man, he reckoned he'd probably be a rascal. Though he had, he owned, met some decent men who were religious.

Boswell, who would have been gibbering with terror had he been in Hume's position rather than in a tact-free zone of his own, pressed on: what about an afterlife? Surely there must be a future life. 'Mustn't there?'

It might be possible that a piece of coal put on the fire wouldn't burn, but it wasn't likely, Hume said. It was, in any case, a most unreasonable fancy that human beings should go on forever.

Did not the thought of total annihilation produce any uneasiness at all?

None.

Boswell said that when they met in the afterlife, he hoped then to prove his point. Hume laughed, as well as a dying man was able, and said that Boswell would live for years yet, so that even if they did meet, Hume would be well used to having been proved wrong by then. By this time even Boswell was having qualms about the nature of this conversation but if Hume really didn't care, then why should he. He said that despite the philosopher's words, he maintained his faith and that he believed in the Christian religion as he believed in history itself. Hume said that he did not believe it as he believed in the fact of the Glorious Revolution – saying, as it were, that if Boswell's faith were a bridge, he would not care to ride his horse across it.

For a man who dearly loves a good scene, this was all wrong: not dour and dismal at all, Hume spoke with his habitual good-humoured smile and refused to play the craven, even to oblige Boswell, who left in something of a snit. He explained his worries away by maintaining that Hume had, for so long, looked so closely at the earth that he could no longer look up to heaven and that it was a right and proper thing for a man to feel the fear and the trembling and the dread as the scythe approached him or his loved ones.

Worse, far worse than death, though, is ridicule and Boswell is still courting that. Earlier in the year he'd tried his luck as barrister on the northern circuit; as the oldest junior in the business he once again found himself the butt of many jokes but managed to turn most of them aside without causing offence, but he was, as usual, his own worst enemy. On the night before the session at Carlisle, where he is still Recorder, he joined his colleagues in the local custom of sinking a quart of strong ale. It was no problem for a man of his experience but then, thinking, absurdly, that the beer would act as a protective breastplate against the barb of more alcohol, he started on the port and finished with the brandy and went for a ride through town with the young fellows and fell off his horse.

Fortunately a kind friend helped him to his lodgings where he was able to sleep it off, rather than lie in the gutter all night. He wasn't even earning much on the circuit either and what little he did get, he lost at whist; but he stuck it out to the end before hurrying back to London and the real work, whilst feeling guilty about abandoning his wife to suffer alone.

He moves out of the family home into a small house near Thomas Malone, who is regularly badgering him to get on with the *LIFE*, and get on he does, working day after long day, going out to dine with others, principally Sir Joshua Reynolds, an old friend from the Johnson days to whom he intends to dedicate his biography, or to occasions like the dinner of the Humane Society, where he appears a great man in a suit of imperial blue lined with rose-coloured silk, with rich, gold-wrought buttons. And all the time Margaret is getting worse – a friend who drops in to see her writes to Boswell that she can not expect to live many months more.

This is too much; he takes his daughter Veronica out of her boarding school in Soho and heads north, arriving back at Auchinleck in April 1789. The problem is that there's nothing to do; he comforts Margaret, he's there when she calls, though some of the time, he's also out drinking and falling off his horse – again – and getting up a pamphlet in support of the political ambitions of the Prince of Wales during his father's madness (a bad idea since Prime Minister Pitt and Henry Dundas, his old enemy, are both anti-Prince) and feeling bored and restless. He wants to be back working on his book in London but he cannot bring himself to desert Margaret. At last, after a summons from the eccentric Lord Lonsdale, who is facing a law suit in London and needs Boswell in his capacity as Recorder of Carlisle, it is Margaret herself who encourages him to go so she can at least get some peace and quiet. And Boswell does it, he goes, though missing the coach on the first attempt and feeling pierced to heart when Margaret whispers, 'have a good journey.'

Back in London, he consoles himself with the thought that though Lonsdale is utterly mad, he will, surely, still get his good adviser Boswell into parliament. His old university friend Temple, now a vicar in the West Country, writes a chiding letter: how could Boswell leave his wife at such a time? The next post brings a letter from his second daughter Euphemia writing that her mother is sinking rapidly. Boswell pulls his sons out of school and boards a coach for Scotland. He arrives too late: Euphemia meets the coach in front of the house, her face wet with tears.

When he looks at Margaret she seems younger, untouched by time or disease. He simply can't believe she's not warm and lively and full of sense and sensibility; she can't be lying there cold, insensible, above all, lifeless. He kneels by her and talks quietly for hours to his Peggie and then, at last, they take her away and the bed is empty.

It is a fine funeral, though Boswell may not, according to custom, attend. There are nineteen carriages following the hearse, a large body of horsemen and all the tenants of Auchinleck. Afterwards, Boswell reads the funeral service privately with his sons, over the coffin; he is relieved a great deal but knows very well that there is a lot of grieving and guilt to come. There's also a deal of work, now that Margaret's not there to do it any more. He has to decide about his children: Sandy, the eldest boy at fourteen, is sent to Eton, his eleven-year-old brother Jamie goes back to the day school in Soho Square, Victoria, sixteen, headstrong and rather too Scottish for Boswell's taste, is sent to board at Cheltenham, fifteen-year-old Euphemia, something of a hoyden and always squabbling with her big sister, stays in Scotland but under the directing hand of Boswell's mother, who can be relied upon to keep her on the straightest and narrowest of paths. Little Betsey, twelve, is to keep Euphemia company until a boarding school can be found for her.

He, himself, is inconsolable, shocked by the emptiness; for years he's known Margaret will die, he's almost come to expect it but now she's gone it's worse than anything he ever imagined, and goodness knows, he's got a lively imagination and he's practiced enough with the condemned men and women at Newgate. None of it helps the present pain. He writes to Temple that he's avid for death, wants nothing more than to be laid by her side, finds the prospect of years more life insupportable, can't face the struggle, is constitutionally unfit for employment, must return to London, only his book can save him now, the world has nothing more to offer his grief-stricken soul ...

He writes in his journal. Thursday 14th November 1789: 'By chance met C. Walked in Oxford Road. Spoke with Kemble. Went to Smyth's and got C. lavender. C. asked to make a call before going to City. Followed to Conduit Street. Walked above an hour, waiting. At last she came and took hackney coach to Bond Street. I followed and was a little while at her lodgings. To Sir Joshua's with Malone, Kemble etc. Cards and I supped. Kemble sly wink. I asked him how he knew C. to be ——? He: from extreme beauty, as fine a woman as I ever saw.'

A few nights later he dines at Malone's with Sir Joseph Banks; the talk is of the monument to Johnson to be put up in Westminster Abbey. There had been a little spat with C. but they meet and all is forgiven and Boswell finds he admires her still and is all mildness; he gives her his address and says she might call on him at home. His main work is still the *LIFE*, which is being revised and revised as the prodigious multiplicity of material continues to accumulate. Will he ever finish? Malone comes round and they set-to yet again and he begins to feel better about the enterprise; perhaps one day it will be in the bookshops and that'll be that.

By February 1790 the book is more than half done and Boswell can start delivering pages to the printer. Publishers are beginning to smell a success and notes arrive hinting at substantial amounts for the rights: George Robinson offers a cool thousand; other notes arrive from acquaintances of Johnson who are getting worried about the kind of appearance they might be making in the biography. Boswell and Malone resist all pressure, they are beginning to feel that the juggernaut is at last on the move and picking up momentum with every day that passes. Boswell is in spirits again – good ones and fiery ones; he's everyone's friend and feeling on top of the world until, in May, he starts feeling dreadful as the horrid hypochondria strikes. It's his demon and has been chasing him many a year.

When he was writing a weekly column for the London Magazine during the 70s, he called it the 'hypochondriack' and devoted four of the seventy articles to the syndrome (he wrote as many on drinking, three on love, three on marriage, one on a new invention for freezing wives and one on conscience). The hypochondriac, he writes, has a low opinion of himself, and reckons that everyone else thinks meanly of him too and sees a cloud of dejection extending over all his days. He's distracted between indolence and shame, any kind of work is impossible and yet he doesn't have the courage to stop doing those mechanical tasks that drive him to distraction. He's indifferent to everything around him, he begins to believe that nothing exists apart from his own mind and because his mind is thrown down, so the world appears. He can't fix his mind on any object but has a thousand different ideas flying around his head; he is irritable and irritated by all he meets and is constantly whining, even though he knows this makes him unmanly and pitiful and, knowing it, he hates himself even more, thereby becoming angry at himself and everyone else. He is either afraid of everything or of nothing; he thinks of all the evils and misfortunes that can happen to mankind and wonders how humanity has ever had a moment's peace. Even though his reason still functions and he knows his mind is sick, his gloomy imagination is so strong that he cannot do anything about it. In all other distress there is hope, however pale a glimmer it be; it is the particular woe of melancholy, that hope hides itself in the dark cloud.

There are distractions: his old friend Temple arrives with his daughter Nancy on a visit to London. Unfortunately Temple hates the rush and noise and vulgarity of London whilst his daughter hates the rush and noise and vulgarity of Boswell's daughter Veronica; the Temples retreat back to Cornwall, leaving Boswell all on his own to worry about the approaching general election.

The mad Lord Lonsdale has – so Boswell reckons – promised him one of the parliamentary seats he controls; within weeks, he hopes, his lifelong ambition to sit in the House of Commons will be achieved, though there is a slight worry evoked by Lonsdale's muttered remark that if Boswell stands for election he'll only get drunk and make a silly speech. On the other hand, Lonsdale has helped a number of prominent men, including Pitt, get a start in politics and Boswell has put in a long apprenticeship under the eccentric earl. He feels he's owed the seat because he's certainly earned it; then he receives news through one of Lonsdale's friends that the seats have been given to others but that the earl will keep Boswell in mind if a gap occurs.

This is simply not acceptable. The Boswells have never been stopgaps, James rages, and offers his resignation as Recorder of Carlisle. Lonsdale shows his other side and apologises and says that had he offered the seat to Boswell, as he wanted to, he would have been criticised for nepotism. He asks Boswell, in the politest terms, if he will be so kind as to accompany him to Carlisle and put through some matters connected with the old court case and deal, as Recorder, with the legal side of the coming election, and only then, if he is still adamant about leaving, hand in his resignation. It is, Boswell agrees, the gentlemanly way to do things.

He arrives early in the morning at Lonsdale's London house ready to board the coach. No coach. He waits two hours and goes home and returns later in the day to find Lonsdale fuming with impatience. Boswell says that it is far from convenient for him to leave the printing of the *LIFE* at this time and that he is doing so purely to oblige Lonsdale.

'No, sir,' Lonsdale snaps back, 'you have some sinister motive.'

'How can your lordship say so?'

'Because I know the man of whom I speak, I suppose you want to have a large fee?'

Boswell protests. 'Did your lordship ever see anything in my conduct to make you think so?'

'You asked the recordership of me. I did not wish you to be Recorder. But you were so earnest I granted it. And now, when duty is required, you would give it up. What have you done for your salary? I will ask the corporation not to accept your resignation till you have attended the midsummer sessions as well as the election. I suppose you think we're fond of your company? You are mistaken, we don't care for it. I suppose you thought I was to bring you into parliament? I never had any such intention. It would do you harm to be in parliament.'

With a lordly wave, Lonsdale says the coach will leave in two hours and dismisses the fuming Boswell, who has nowhere to go and so hurries over to Malone's. Malone advises him to get away from Lonsdale as soon as and by whatever means he can; Boswell agrees as he walks back to Lonsdale's house, where Lonsdale greets him cheerily, takes his arms and walks him round the corner to where the coach is waiting.

They set off at a cracking pace and lulled by his good temper, Boswell who never can resist walking closer to the chasm, reopens the parliamentary conversation. Lonsdale repeats his remark about drink and silly speeches and adds that Mr Boswell is a deal too ready with liberal and independent views. Boswell, who is no friend to republicanism and has spoken out against the Revolution in France and the fall of the Bastille, disagrees.

Lonsdale appears to think that Boswell has offered a challenge. He says: 'I am ready to give you satisfaction.'

'My lord,' says Boswell, raising his voice above the rattle and clatter of the coach, 'you have said enough.' He is stunned and shaken and not a little worried about being in a small carriage with a murderous lunatic.

Lonsdale turns upon him and shouts: 'You have kept low company all your life. What are you, sir?'

'I am a gentleman, a man of honour and I hope to show myself as such.'

With cold cruelty, Lonsdale says: 'You will be settled when you have a bullet in your belly.'

They have reached Barnet and stop at an inn. Lonsdale jumps out, Boswell follows him: 'You have treated me ill and used me unjustly, my lord.'

'Then I will give you satisfaction now. I have pistols here!'

'If you please, my lord; and I will be obliged to you for pistols.'

Faced with an opponent who appears more than ready to stand up and exchange fire, the bullying Lonsdale changes tack: 'What, sir, my own pistols against myself? Certainly not.'

Boswell turns on his heel and hurries away into the town to see if he can find a soldier who might lend him a weapon; there is none to be had and he goes back to the inn and tells Lonsdale he'll return to London, find pistols and a second, and return as soon as possible. Lonsdale spends the next few hours soft-soaping Boswell and getting out of the duel without seeming to be in the wrong. Boswell, not wanting to fight against a madman and not being that keen on duelling, agrees with the convoluted sentiments; peace breaks out before night falls and is celebrated with a glass of wine. The rest of the journey is spent in pointless small talk that takes great care never to stray too near contention.

In Carlisle he dreams that his daughter Veronica has got consumption; he wakes in a cold sweat. He decides to remove his other daughter Euphemia from her Edinburgh academy and bring her down to London before she becomes a total barbarian.

He realises, in the end, that Lonsdale was his last and only hope of achieving a position in the world and of gaining distinction in the eyes of men and that as far as his ambitions go, he is the one who has the mortal disease and as for cutting a brilliant figure in town, he is the barbarian.

Now the *LIFE* is the only thing he has left.

Arthur Phillip

alking the colony in July 1788, starting at the west head of the cove, where a small canvas observatory has been erected, Governor Phillip sees the future spread out before him; it's all a question of hope and the belief that something will be made out of this tiny, insecure handhold.

There have been advances. As he walks along the shoreline the first thing he passes is the hospital, placed to catch the freshest breezes. Dr White has twenty-four convict patients in residence and forty-two outpatients, the majority of them male. As the supplies get shorter, the old enemy scurvy is making a return appearance, causing a general lowering in the health of the colony, which in turn results in more accidents, more illness, more theft and lawlessness as food becomes more valuable. In the six months since landing twenty men, eight women and eight children have died. All things considered, and out here Phillip does have to consider all things, it's not a bad record and the governor is determined to prevent it becoming any worse.

Dr White and his team are doing their very best to fight disease; however, Phillip has a suspicion that they are not working so hard to avoid fighting each other. As he pauses outside the thin, wooden walls of the structure, he can hear raised voices; Dr White's fiery temperament is creating tensions which may, sooner or later, Phillip fears, result in violence being offered. A shriek confirms his suspicions: horrid murder at least must be loose within but he is reassured a moment later, on hearing the faint clatter of a tooth in a bowl and Lieutenant Ralph

Clark's voice protesting thickly: 'Oh my God, I thought half my head would come off!'

He walks on and approaches a party of convicts hacking away at the hard ground, turning the soil, digging-in what manure and compost the colony can produce. They stop and raise their hats. The overseer, one of themselves, knuckles his forehead and offers a mumbled apology for the slow progress. This is an area set aside for future cultivation, ropes mark out the extent of the plots; it is vital to get every seed and seedling they've brought with them into the earth as soon as possible. Phillip knows this and one or two of the convicts realise it too; James Ruse, a Cornishman, has a real feel for the land and planting, as does Phillip's secretary, Henry Dodd, who is being pressed into service as an agriculturalist. The rest of them appear to think that manna will appear from heaven or from supply ships arriving in the cove from England. It is a frustrating attitude and the governor does everything he can to encourage the workmen, promising them plots of their own to cultivate if only they'll work with a will rather than grudgingly.

He nods to the overseer, compliments a couple of the men for the rows they've dug and moves on to the clatter of hammers and adzes, the smell of newly planed wood, the grunt of amateur carpenters missing iron nails and hitting their own. Here store rooms are going up and carpenters are in short supply so, once more, he has to make do with what he can find: if a man can wield a hammer and saw with reasonable accuracy, then he's on the building detail. What's more problematic is the skilled work of making and fitting joints and pegs to construct buildings strong enough to resist the assault of hungry, devious and desperate men which will, Phillip knows, become a nightly occurrence once the rest of the stores are brought ashore from the ships left in the cove. He's paying ten shillings a day for their rental and desperately needs to get them away and off his hands before the colony is impoverished and unable to buy stores from passing ships – they should be so lucky – or send their own vessels to the Cape for more supplies.

The transport *Lady Penrhyn* is unloading as he walks and he can see the cutters rowing back and forth and the goods being swung or hoisted over the ships side. Later today he'll have to sign a receipt for: 135 casks of beef, 165 casks of pork, 50 puncheons of bread, 448 barrels of flour, 116 casks of pease, 110 firkins of butter (Major Ross is not pleased that he is to have the same butter ration as the convicts), 8 brams of rice, one complete loom for weaving canvas, mill spindles with 4 crosses, 2 cases of mill bills and picks, a cask of mill brushes, 10 pairs of handcuffs, 589 petticoats, 606 jackets, 121 caps, 327 pairs of stockings (140 damaged), 381 shifts, 250 handkerchiefs, 305 pairs of shoes, 140 hats, 6 bundles of ridge poles, 11 bundles of stand poles, 2 chests of pins and mallets, a transport jack, ventilators for water and wine, hoses, windsails, packs of materials for erecting cabins, bulkheads, beds, hammocks and marines' uniforms. Phillip reflects that if all of that ends up where it is meant to be and in the right hands, then the world really will have turned upside down!

He has a word or two with James Cox, the overseer, a convict but also a skilled carpenter who seems to have the knack of getting his mates to work with reasonable efficiency and without resentment. Cox is exactly the kind of man Phillip hopes to inspire to find a better future in New South Wales but it is impossible to know if his encouraging words are getting through the barrier of subservience. He walks on.

A more pleasing sight awaits him now: the Reverend and Mrs Johnson, standing by the site set aside for the first church to be built in this land. Mrs Johnson is a pleasant-enough woman by most standards but out here, thirteen thousand miles from the nearest drawing room, she is the very paragon of gentility, the peak of her sex, a benchmark for behaviour and gallantry and a future in which such women will walk the streets of a town or even a great southern city. The governor is no enthusiast for religion but is greatly drawn to the standards it sets and the stability it can impose on a frontier society; the wrath to come may not be as immediately effective as the wrath of the governor but in the long term self-imposed discipline is always more efficacious than coercion, and legal cohabitation better than concubinage. Mr Johnson has already celebrated a host of marriages and will soon, he opines, become a deft hand at the christening game, as new citizens begin to arrive. Phillip tips his hat and makes his bow to Mrs Johnson, who returns it prettily, and has a few words with the Reverend; the building work is going slowly (Johnson, no slouch at the flattery, has promised to call the church St Philip's) but then, everything is going slowly.

The governor passes on along the main street – so far entirely a thing of the mind – and the imaginary buildings that line either side; he looks inland, at the imaginary new fields and the actual road that runs beside the stream. Phillip's canvas house stands here with the shape of Government House appearing slowly out of the ground beside it. They have only lately found a source of lime for mortar (parties of women are down at the bay crushing oyster shells) and up to now their bricks have been bound with clay, which washes away every time it rains.

The marines' barracks are still wooden and Phillip is determined that they will be pulled down as soon as something more permanent is in place. He wants, at all costs, to avoid a shanty town, with its attendant evils of squalor and hidden crime, growing up along the cove; rather, he plans spacious, elegantly laid-out streets lined with fine houses, presenting a prospect of the hills that will please and elevate the mind. However, as long as they're still getting their lime from crushed oyster shells, the prospect will have to remain in the mind.

The huts of the convicts are still a mix of canvas, large leaves, whatever wood they've been able to scrounge, although some, like the fisherman Bryant, have made more permanent dwellings for themselves. As always, it's a case of those who want to make an effort and those who don't, and the nay-sayers are by no means all in the convict ranks. Major Ross, the deputy governor, who should be setting an example to all, is caught up in a rigid code of military pride and precedence and can't see beyond the honour of the marine corps, as pretty a collection of scoundrels as you are likely to meet outside of a gaol. Only recently Ross made his views quite plain, stating, though not to Phillip's face:

> *'A settlement on this coast never can be made to answer the purposes or wish of government. The country appears destitute of everything that can be an object for a commercial nation. This is, of course, a private opinion.*

The governor's opinion I am unacquainted with, as he has never done me the honour of informing me of his or asking me for mine.'[8]

This is arrant rubbish: Phillip has made no secret of his plans and hopes – true, he no longer shares them, man to man, with Ross, having become exasperated with his inevitable response – but the general orders are plain for all to read or hear. However, if Major Ross has one great talent, it is for fermenting discontent and, like all experts in the field, he has a hundred stratagems for sullen, sour, carping, niggling, eye-rolling, sneering, snorting disagreement, none of which ever raises its head far enough above the parapet to be sighted on and shot down. Whilst Phillip complains about the constant pilfering, the sexual assaults against convict women and the total lack of commitment on the part of the marines, Ross fulminates about the lack of respect being paid to England's finest. It is a frustrating situation and all Phillip can do is remind the marines – and particularly their officers – that a young colony requires something more than mere garrison duty. He tries to work around his deputy.

His attention is caught by an explosion. Earth and rock flies through the air; convicts cheers and hope that at least one marine will have gone to blazes. Phillip hurries over to find that a iron-hard stump has just been blown out of the ground and that work is now well in hand for sinking an impregnable cellar for the safekeeping of the colony's store of spirits. Beer is brewed daily and, of course, the barm is used for baking bread, but the brandy and rum are a different matter and they will require stout locks, iron bars, an oak lining and a double guard if they are to remain safe from convict and marine thirsts.

It is a worrying indication of the way things may be going that alcohol is becoming a form of currency. There's not much you can't buy for a quart of rum, as the sailors still in the cove have discovered. Not that their attentions are always welcome; no sooner had the colonists landed than patterns of power and precedent began to crystallise amongst the convicts. The men regard the women as their rightful possessions, even though they are forbidden to enter the women's quarters and relations, unless regularised, are not allowed.

They are determined to protect their territory, beating any sailors who venture near the women, unless proper tollage is paid – in rum – which thereby enters the economy and passes round from convicts to marines and back again.

The marines, seeing themselves as the power in the land, expect to exercise their lordship and take what they want; one man, annoyed at being bilked over some transaction, entered the women's camp and beat his supplier to within an inch of her life. He was incredulous to find himself hauled up before the court and sentenced by Judge Advocate David Collins to two hundred lashes. Surgeon William Bowes, still waiting to depart for China aboard *Lady Penrhyn*, makes his opinion on the matter clear in his journal: the severity shown to the marines and lenity to the convicts has excited great murmuring amongst the corps and where it will end, only time will discover.

There is, in fact, no need to wait for time; the kind of seething stew produced by the marines, particularly when the peppery Major Ross is added to the pot, is well known to Phillip. Back in March, a marine called William Dempsey was chatting to a convict woman, Jane Fitzgerald, whilst she was tending a cooking pot outside a tent. Joseph Hunt, a fellow marine, passed by and, noticing the conversation, told Dempsey that he had no right to talk to a woman who had travelled out on Hunt's transport, she was off limits. Dempsey said this was nonsense and Hunt called him a bloody bugger and hit him. A court martial was convened with the fastidious Captain Watkin Tench as president. Hunt was found guilty as charged – he admitted the offence – and was sentenced to apologise to Dempsey in front of the battalion and to receive one hundred lashes.

Major Ross, hearing of the verdict, thought that two sentences had, in effect, been imposed upon Hunt and told the court to reconsider its verdict. They did so and Tench informed his commander that it would stand as delivered. Ross disagreed and told the court to sit yet again and impose only a single sentence.

Tench replied that, legally, only one revision of the court's verdict could be considered and that, anyway, he and his fellow officers were content with the verdict as it stood.

Ross responded within the hour that it was wrong to impose two sentences and that the court must reconsider.

Tench replied that they would not.

Ross, by return post – actually a sweating adjutant rushing back and forth across the colony – ordered them to consider themselves removed from duty and under arrest. They wrote to Phillip, protesting about Ross's actions and stating their wish to go back to England at the soonest opportunity.

The marines, seeing their commander at loggerheads with their officers, paraded and refused to do any more labouring work without being paid for it.

Ross wrote to Phillip, stating that his command was being threatened and demanding that Phillip do something about it before discipline broke and anarchy reigned.

Phillip wrote back, laying out the facts of the case, pointing out that under military law the officers of the court really didn't have any choice and that, above all, since there were only four captains and twelve lieutenants in the colony, two of whom were ill, arresting five of the rest was not a very good idea. He suggested that Ross and his officers work it out between themselves since the only alternative would be a full-scale court martial, which would be disastrous for everyone.

Ross considered the matter for two days and then opted for the court martial as the method most likely to restore harmony.

Phillip pointed put that with five officers arrested and two sick, there weren't enough officers left to sit on a court martial. The matter was left upon the books, the judge advocate holding the various documents. Punishment for Marine Hunt was suspended until the matter could be sorted out and the five officers returned to duty.

This is only one of dozens of disputes – often with Ross at their epicentre – that take Phillip's attention away from the vital business of establishing the colony and when he looks into the future, at the next year, 1789, he wonders how, on this strange earth, they will be coping then.

Mary Bryant

She stands by the shore, looking out over the choppy, blue waters of the cove at the fishing boat. Will is hauling in the net, his mates helping; their voices, laughing, occasionally shouting insults or encouragement at each other, can easily be heard across the flat expanse of the bay.

He's a big, easy man, is Will Bryant, often content to let things go on in their own way; and that's where she's made a difference. It's now March 1789, and that means Will has only a couple of years left to serve; it's important to her that when his time is up there's enough to keep him here at the cove, until her time, too, is done and they can travel back to Cornwall together.

He's not a bad man but he is a man and that's both good and bad. He wants a woman: she's his woman; he wants, any man wants a child of his own: well, there will be a child, she'll make sure of that. And money – he's an old smuggler and does love the yellow boys – and together they've begun to put away a george or two in a place under the wooden floor of the hut. It's no problem, this squirreling away: Will can see clear to the horizon but he's never been able to see eye to eye with anyone who has the smack of authority about them. Show him a wall and he wants to jump over it, tell him he can't and he'll tell you he can and he will. But he does need to be set at the jumps, otherwise that easy nature will tempt him to loosen the sail and coast without a care in the world. He'll fish the cove rather than going down the harbour towards the sea, where the catch is richer but then, as he says, you don't want to deliver everything at once to them as wants it; best to keep 'em waiting, keep 'em hungry.

On the water canoes are lancing out from the shore, each with its load of natives. For some reason they have taken to Will and the other fishermen, far more than to any of the officers, with their beads and looking glasses. Will offers nothing except the odd fish and they seldom take these except to be companionable; they catch as much as they need with ease. Will says their nets are as fine as his and they've got a bit of magic too: from what he's been able to understand, the girls have the top of their little finger cut off and thrown into the sea; when they're grown up this means that all the fishes have a part of them inside and when they call, the fish must come into their baskets and nets. Will sees no reason to disagree with this; fish have a way of their own and back in Cornwall he's seen men, and women too, who can call them or send them away.

Mostly the natives just like to sit in the boat and watch whilst the men fish together. It's something they all understand and no one needs to be chattering or showing off and what's more, they're generous, they'll show where the best fish swarm and where the juiciest oysters cling on the mangrove roots. Will reckons that if you didn't mind walking bare-naked most of your life, you could do a lot worse than live as they do. Except for the flies and the handkerchiefs. Too many of one and none of the other.

Charlotte starts crying, she's hungry, and Mary turns and walks back towards their hut. Jealous glances follow her as she goes but she shrugs them off; she lost any conscience a long time back; it's a bitch-eat-bitch life and she's been at the top for most of the time since she first arrived on the hulks to those mocking cries of 'new chums, new chums'. But she's nobody's chum because nobody cares like you do; let the rest of them go to the devil, with never a petticoat tail to grab hold of.

Back at the hut there are fish to gut and salt and carry on the barrow to where they are wanted; there are also the other fish to sell from under the cart, one here, two there, a promise for something tomorrow or the day after. They may hate her and Will, but they have to buy because there's nowhere else to go.

The wind comes up, catching her shawl; this upside-down summer is coming to an end, grey clouds billow and the rain blows in, sometimes for days on end and even the natives slip away to their caves and fires. She begins to hurry, anxious not to get wet. In everything, she has learnt, there are layers and levels and here the fisherman's wife is sitting right at the front of the church with the mayor and corporation. Such a simple thing, buyers and sellers: on the hulks, a clean and willing girl; on the other side of the world, food.

She has never imagined that night could come down so fast as it does at Sydney Cove. Those long, long evenings in the west, when sometimes it seemed as if you could see the gold of the sun gleaming just beyond the horizon at midnight, are just a dream out here where the dark rushes in with the chatter of insects and huge, white fluttering moths that burn up in the buttery light of the lamps.

Later, Will arrives back, bringing the smell of tar and the sea and fish and sweat and Mary serves up tea. There's not a lot to go round but more than for most, and with the fish Will is allowed to keep as payment for his services to the colony, it makes enough for the three of them. The other fish, given in kind or sold, have vanished long before Will reaches home but that makes no difference when the marines come calling.

They don't bother to knock, they take delight in barging in and collaring Will, dragging him off without a word of explanation. The bugger has been coming it the flash cove of Sydney a while too long and now a squeaker's peached and he's for the long drop. What possessions Mary has got in the hut leave along with the marines as evidence. Without the fisherman she's just another bitch on the beach. It's a lesson in how things can change in a moment.

She's left in the hut all night alone with Charlotte. Will is banged up in the guardroom of the marine barracks. The money under the floor is still safe and she makes sure it's going to stay that way; then, because she can't do anything else, she goes to sleep, holding her daughter tight.

Under the authority of His Majesty King George, the magistrate's court
is convened next morning, with David Collins and the colony surveyor
Augustus Alp sitting as magistrates. Will has asked Dr White to speak
on his behalf and the doctor is happy to do so: stating that he has
always found Bryant to be honest and trustworthy. Then Joe Paget,
that low dog, is called, and delivers his evidence: Will Bryant habitually
sells fish privately and he, Paget, has acted for Bryant on numerous
occasions. The man Paget is an informer, no one denies it, but then
there is little doubt in anyone's mind that Will Bryant has been selling
on the side. Collins and Alp confer – it could be a hanging offence,
Governor Phillip has made it clear that theft of food is not to be
tolerated. On the other, more pragmatic, hand is the fact that no one
else in the colony has Bryant's skills; he delivers the catch.

At last judgement is handed down: guilty – the sentence: a hundred
lashes. Bryant is also to be deprived of the direction of the fishing, but
will go in the boat as an ordinary man and will be turned out of the hut
he is now in. Well, he's been a fool to get caught and so he'll take his
lashes like a man; as for losing direction of the fishing but going in the
boat, it's just a form of words. He'll be back in charge soon enough and
he'll be back in his hut, though that may take a little longer.

Another day, another flogging; it doesn't really make much of a splash,
there have been so many, but the marines are paraded and a crowd
gathers because this is Will Bryant and he's getting his comeuppance.

Mary stands apart from the crowd and Will is led to the wooden
triangle, has his shirt taken off, a leather strap pushed between his
teeth and his hands fastened above his head. A desultory drum
roll, the sentence mumbled through and the flogger steps forward,
shakes the cat to free up the knots and starts to lay it on. Any half-
experienced flogger knows how to make it look good and also, should
he please, make it hurt like the devil. Will's luck has not made him
popular with the marines and the cat goes to work with a will.

The first few strokes just warm up the flesh on the back; the next
begin to cut. Then the lashes start curling and collecting little pieces
of flesh. It's a windy day and though Mary is standing at least fifteen

yards away, blood, skin and red flesh blow in her face as the marine corporal flicks them off his whip. The blows are laid on the shoulder and then lower, to avoid exposing the bone. The flesh around Will's waist begins to turn into something like a jelly before it too starts flying through the air. Time passes – a stroke every half minute ensures that; underneath and around the triangle, ants and cockroaches are drawn by the smell and begin to carry the fresh lumps of flesh away.

By the time it ends, Will is only half-conscious but he knows he must walk away from the triangle on his own legs. To be flogged is just another thing that can happen to a man when he isn't free, but to fall or weep or crawl is a disgrace. So he walks to a place Mary has chosen, where she can clean his back with salt water and cover the bloody mess to keep off the flies.

As the year turns, the colony begins to grow into the countryside around; a farm inland at Rose Hill is started, more land around the cove is put under cultivation and fields of corn can now be seen. Major Ross still maintains it will take a hundred years or more before the country is able to maintain a population; it'll be cheaper, he says, to feed the convicts on turtle soup from the London Tavern than be at the expense of sending them to New South Wales.

Food is still a problem, Phillip has reduced the convicts' weekly ration to seven pounds of biscuit, one of flour, seven of beef or four of pork; three pints of pease and six ounces of butter. The women are to get two thirds of this amount. An outbreak of theft follows the order; three convicts are caught and it turns out that they have often robbed the stores on the same day they were issued their rations. The three are condemned to hang but the colony has no hangman. One of the thieves, John Freeman, is offered a free pardon on condition he acts as public hangman; he takes the job and, after downing a quart of brandy, turns off his confederates, including seventeen-year-old James Barrat, who has been a convict since the age of eleven.

Phillip uses the occasion to make it quite clear to everyone that the transports have all left – look at the cove, it's empty; we are on our own and if we don't conserve our food and grow more, we will starve. The message falls on deaf ears.

A key is found, broken, in the lock of the public store. When the commissary manages to gain entry it's quite clear that provisions have been pilfered. No keys are missing so it's plain that the broken one has been fabricated for the purpose of robbery. David Collins teases the broken key out of the lock and takes it to the blacksmith, the only man in the colony with the skills and tools to work metal; he identifies the key as one he made for a marine, Joseph Hunt, who is arrested and questioned. Hunt offers to turn King's evidence and peach on his mates. Six marines are arrested and charged with theft over a period of months. They are sentenced to hang for it and they do, whilst Joseph Hunt, who planned the whole operation, walks free. There is, it is muttered, a good deal more honour amongst the thieves than among their gaolers. Phillip is disgusted but can do nothing; the gallows is a deterrent only if it is used and if it is used, then it must be for all, without favour. Major Ross begs to differ and laments the loss of the flower of the regiment.

It sometimes seems as if everyone in the place is hell-bent on committing suicide. The convicts have been warned again and again not to interfere with the natives or try and steal their possessions. So sixteen convicts who are sent off to cut rushes at Rushcutters Bay mount a private expedition to rob a body of natives and teach them a lesson but the convicts receive the lesson: one killed and seven wounded during an ignominious flight back to Sydney.

Phillip has always been fascinated by the natives and concerned about their relations with the settlers. In this incident he is 'persuaded that the natives are not the aggressors and, though I do not wish to punish any of them for killing the man, which I'm sure they did in their own defence, I wish to see them.'

Contact is made and he comes to the conclusion that placing confidence in the natives rather than in his own people is the best means of avoiding disputes. In an attempt to get to know how and what they are thinking in this changed world, he arranges for a native to be taken by force; it is far from ideal, almost self-defeating, but he realises that real contact is only going to be possible when two can speak with one understanding. A man of about thirty, Arabanoo, is captured and brought back to Sydney where he settles down to colony life with greater skill than the colonists have so far shown in coming to terms with his country.

Captain Tench is particularly struck by Arabanoo's manly bearing and sensibility. He picks up European manners remarkably quickly and is a brilliant mimic; however, he is never able to come to terms with the nature of European punishment. Even when floggings are inflicted for attacks upon his own people, he finds it impossible to contemplate the slow, cold-blooded infliction of pain. If compelled to watch, he covers his eyes and keens for the victim's agony.

Though at first he is confined with a leg iron, it is soon taken off and he is allowed to come and go as he pleases; he is offered presents but wants very little from his new friends. What he does get is a hidden and terrible gift; those colonists whose work calls them to the beach are finding native bodies, sometimes buried under little mounds, sometimes lying in the open. Dr White diagnoses smallpox. Arabanoo confirms that a strange sickness has come out of nowhere and fallen upon his people. Some have fled inland, others are sick, many are dead. Arabanoo too succumbs, though not before bringing an orphaned girl and boy into the settlement where their lives are saved after inoculation. The Johnsons adopt them and Tench mourns for the manly Arabanoo. He writes of him: 'His fidelity, particularly to his friend the governor, was constant and, although of a gentle temper, we early discovered that he was impatient of indignity and allowed of no superiority on our part.'

The governor comes to the conclusion that there is no reason for the colonists to fear attack by the natives, not because they lack courage; they certainly do not, but because they are quite clever enough to recognise the deadly nature of the newcomers' weapons, not to mention their diseases. As for the skirmishes, in which marauding convicts or even marines are wounded or killed, Phillip reckons that the white man is getting no more than he deserves.

As the year 1790 approaches its end and the beginning of the southern summer, there are more christenings including a child, Emmanuel, born to the reinstated fisherman William Bryant and his wife. Yet more mouths to fill. Everybody who can is cultivating their own garden, but at nights everybody who can is stealing from their neighbour's patch.

Phillip institutes a night watch composed of the most trustworthy convicts and warns them against having any disputes with marines or sailors: if any occur, the offenders should be delivered to the guard house till morning and then handed over to their officers. Major Ross isn't pleased and when a marine is stopped for questioning he explodes with indignation. It is, he bellows, 'an insult to the corps. We will not suffer ourselves to be treated in this manner or to be controlled by convicts whilst we have bayonets in our hands!'

Phillip points out that the marines are not above theft, after all, it's not long since six of them were hanged for it. Major Ross decides to write a long letter of complaint to be sent home with the next ship that calls at Sydney Cove, whenever that might be. 'In the whole world there is not a worse country. It may with truth be said that here nature is reversed, and if not so, nearly worn out. Almost all the seeds put in the ground have rotted. There is not one article which can ever be necessary, but which must be imported into this vile country. All but two of those coming out with me now want to get away!'

The farm at Rose Hill is doing well under the care of Phillip's ex-servant Henry Dodd and the harvest at the main settlement promises a reasonable return; however, Phillip is well aware that most of the harvest must be put aside as seed for the new season and only garden produce will be going into the public store. Judge Advocate David Collins discusses the problem with Phillip and both agree. The stores are running down rapidly – the butter runs out entirely in September – and what is being grown is simply not sufficient for the colony's continued survival. And, as if this is not enough, a plague of rats appears, rapacious, not caring about fences and walls, concerned only with their own appetites. The store rooms are overrun, the gardens stripped; caterpillars and parrots follow on with appetites just as vast. Calculating the losses, the governor works out that there will have to be a further reduction in rations for all. He ensures that no more food appears on his table than on any other in the colony.

Christmas brings little celebration and less food. On two nights a week every boat in the colony sets out to fish for the public good.

Will Bryant has become more vital than ever and has regained all his privileges. His friendship with the natives stands him in good stead as he directs the boats to one or other of the coves and bays along the coastline. When the boats fail to bring in enough, the seine is thrown by shore parties, composed of convicts, marines and officers alike. Even the fastidious Tench joins in, and is happy to offer a dinner he has caught himself to a friend, adding the now common rider, 'bring your own bread.'

Hunters set out into the bush every day looking for kangaroos and emu but more often than not their blundering progress scares off any game long before it is in range. What they do manage to bring down is often indigestible and a receipt for cooking the toughest birds is produced: place the bird in a pot with a marine's boot; cook for two days, when the boot is soft, throw away the bird and eat the boot. On one such expedition a piece of cotton is found caught in a tree; taken back to the settlement, it is identified as belonging to Ann Smith, the convict woman who escaped during the first days after landing. She had always said she would never submit to being a captive in this place.

A piece of good news is the establishing of James Ruse, a convict who has served his time, as the first settler. Phillip has two acres of ground cleared and a small hut built at Rose Hill, where the land seems better adapted to farming. Given seeds and tools and few animals, Ruse resolves to overcome whatever difficulties might lie in his way and make a success of the venture. He is the only one amongst the time-expired men who chooses to settle; the general opinion being that he is bound to fail.

The *Supply* returns from Norfolk Island with good news from Phillip Gidley King: the tiny daughter colony has established itself and the first harvests are good. The governor decides to send King back to England to report on the desperate position at Sydney Cove. He replaces him with Ross and sends the fulminating Major, together with Lieutenant Ralph Clark (who stumps up two guineas for a pregnant sow) off on the *Supply* with orders for King. He is uneasily aware that his gain will be a loss for the Norfolk settlers but almost any price is worth paying to get rid of a deputy who sews nothing but dissention and doubt.

Phillip needs belief in a future that is free and successful; what he gets is rumour, springing up overnight – the livestock will be called into public ownership! It isn't true but, as a result, nearly all the livestock in the settlement is slaughtered in a few days by owners intent on eating their own meat rather than surrendering it for the common good.

Lieutenant Maxwell of the marines gets up early one morning, launches a small boat and rows himself around the cove for three days and nights. He has long been suffering a decline of the intellectuals and has been relieved from duty; he is now confined to the hospital though has hopes of escaping, using the guineas he planted months ago in the hospital garden, which will by now have produced a fine yellow crop.

A listlessness settles over everything – Watkin Tench notices that the marines are running out of useable shoes and boots and some are parading in bare feet; an elderly convict collapses without reason and when Dr White performs an autopsy, his stomach is found to be completely empty. It is death by starvation.

Captain Watkin Tench

'I was sitting in my hut, musing on our fate, when a confused clamour in the street drew my attention. I opened my door, and saw several women with children in their arms running to and fro with distracted looks, congratulating each other, and kissing their infants with the most passionate and extravagant marks of fondness. I needed no more; but instantly started out and ran to a hill, where with the assistance of a pocket glass, my hopes were realised. A brother officer was with me; but we could not speak; we wrung each other by the hands with eyes and hearts overflowing.

'Finding the governor intended to go immediately down the harbour, I begged to be one of his party.

'As we proceeded, the object of our hope soon appeared: – a large ship, with English colours flying, working in between the heads which form the entrance of the harbour. We pushed through wind and rain, the anxiety of our sensations every moment redoubling. At last we read the word 'London' on her stern. "Pull away, my lads! She is from old England! A few strokes more, and we shall be aboard! Hurrah for England, and news from our friends!" '[9]

Arthur Phillip

The ship is the *Juliana*, a transport loaded with two hundred and fifty female convicts and their provisions for two years, almost the last thing Phillip needs. His disappointment only increases on hearing that a store ship, *Guardian*, should have reached them weeks ago; either she has sunk, been blown off course or has been damaged and gone back to the Cape. It is bad news indeed but more is to come in the shape of four more transports, due any day, delivering nine hundred extra convicts.

There is news from the world: of the French Revolution, of the illness and recovery of the King, and that a new corps is being sent out, specially raised for duty in New South Wales, and that many of them will be bringing their wives, who can only prove a civilising influence. There are letters too, hundreds of letters and for the isolated colonists, these are almost better than supplies. And then, as if the gods are finally smiling along with the sun, another ship beats into the cove, the *Justinian*, crowded with enough stores to put the colonists back on their feet and a portable hospital and medicines to enable Dr White to keep them there. Full rations are restored immediately and the old lags get ready to welcome their new chums.

When the ships of the Second Fleet arrive, it becomes clear what happens when apathy and profit, rather than skill and reason, rule an enterprise. The wind is coming off the sea and even as the transports warp into the cove, the smell is almost unbearable; for everyone ashore it brings back the worst moments of their own confinement back on the hulks but this is somehow worse: human filth and effluent, bilge water and the hot, maggoty stench of rotting flesh. Hard men and women, both marines and convicts, have never seen anything like it before. When Phillip reads the manifests, he finds that of nine hundred convicts embarked, two hundred and sixty-one have died on the voyage and almost five hundred are sick and in need of immediate attention.

Dr White and his colleagues simply can't cope with the boatloads of sick being ferried ashore; thirty tents are put up around the hospital and convicts drafted in as temporary nurses. White diagnoses dysentery complicated by scurvy and fevers of various kinds. Fires are lit and green wood burnt and what can be done, is done; for many, there is no hope, they die even as they are coming ashore or have died – as Phillip discovers – on the voyage and are still lying, shrivelled corpses, in their irons. It appears that their fellows still alive were so desperate for any scrap of food that they concealed the deaths in the hope of consuming the extra rations.

They die at the rate of ten or twelve a day when they first land but gradually White's regime of antiscorbutics – parties are sent into the bush to gather acid berries – together with regular and sustaining food produces an improvement. Bread is baked and delivered, wine and spirits administered, though care needs to be taken to spot the old lags who creep into the hospital and lie groaning in the hope of sucking the monkey at the rum cask.

A mark has been passed. As the sick recover and are absorbed into the colony and the increase in rations produces an increase in morale and greater enthusiasm and energy for growing and building, Phillip can at last begin to make out the shape of the settlement, as he has always envisaged it, emerging from the shades of starvation and failure.

As the numbers grow, Phillip's personal influence matters less and he is able to give more of his time to the natives. After the death of Arabanoo, a second man, Bennelong, had been enticed into the camp and captured. He had appeared to settle but at the height of the famine escaped back into the bush.

In September 1790 word reaches Phillip that a dead whale – a tremendous monster which had caused mayhem in Sydney Cove a few weeks before – has been washed ashore along the coast and that a group of natives, including Bennelong, are cutting meat from the body.

Phillip takes his cutter across to the whale site and, on landing a little along the coast, calls for Bennelong, who is indeed with the group. There is suspicion: the last time Bennelong answered such a summons he ended up with a chain on his leg. This time the conversation takes place at a distance until, finally, everyone begins to relax. Bennelong walks forward and names some of his friends; Phillip steps forward, holding out his hands in greeting. A spear is raised, Phillip throws down a dagger he carries to show his intentions are peaceful. The action is misinterpreted and the lance is slipped into the throwing stick. Phillip says 'Wee-ree, wee-ree – this is wrong!' Bennelong attempts to calm his friend but too late, the spear shoots out of its launcher like a bolt of lightning and goes into and through the governor's shoulder. As he falls, the natives run. One of the marines breaks off the protruding end of the eight-foot shaft and Phillip is laid in the boat and rowed back five miles across the water, to Sydney, where Dr Balmain, one of White's assistants, extracts the lance and cauterizes the wound.

David Collins, making his usual meticulous notes on the affair, adds his own opinion that the governor has long been too trusting of 'these people' and has now been taught a lesson which, it might be presumed, he will not forget. But he is wrong. Within ten days Phillip is up and about and making new contacts with the natives; soon, Bennelong and his whole family have become a familiar sight in the colony and particularly along the cove, where Will Bryant is happy to take them out in the fishing boat.

Public buildings advance; an excellent storehouse built of brick and covered with new tiles is completed and another planned. A permanent hospital and barracks for the troops may be expected to rise soon. The governor's wound is quite healed and the colonists are hand-in-glove with the natives. At Rose Hill, Mr Dodd estimates that two hundred acres are now under cultivation. The governor has a house of lath and plaster; there is a new barn, a granary, a blacksmith's shop and brick kilns. In himself, Phillip is feeling a sense of completion, though his health – that old enemy – has been playing up and, aboard one of the returning transports from the second fleet, goes a letter from the governor requesting retirement on the grounds of ill health: 'A complaint in the side from which I have seldom been free, has impaired my health and at times puts it out of my power to attend to my charge in the manner the state of the colony requires.'

Whatever the response, it will be a year or nearly two before it arrives, but for Arthur Phillip the work is done, the colony is established and it will grow. Even when Henry Dodd dies of a heart attack at Rose Hill, after chasing garden thieves off his land in a rainstorm, Phillip is not downhearted. There may be, will surely be, hard times ahead but the future is assured.

Which is why there is general puzzlement when, on the morning of Tuesday 29th March 1791 it is discovered that the governor's launch is missing, along with the fisherman Bryant, his wife Mary, their two children and seven others.

Judge Advocate David Collins

ollins waits by the shore as the search boat comes back round the point; there's no shouting or waving to indicate that any trace or sight of the runaways has been found. He turns on his heel and marches back to the fisherman's hut. A small detachment of marines is waiting: he gives the order and they go in and take the place apart. There's nothing of value left – but they do find a compartment under the floorboards. A bit of cloth and a small coin are there; it's clear the space has been used to hide money and that the money had been used to facilitate an escape.

Outside, the day is dawning; it'll be a fair-weather day and give them a start. Collins notices grains of rice on the ground as if spilled from a sack by someone in a hurry. He follows the trail and picks up a dropped saw, a scale and more rice as he tracks the escapers round the cove and along towards the point, where many of the smaller boats used by officials and others are moored. Here he confirms that the governor's cutter is missing.

At twenty-four feet, fore and aft rigged, with three sets of sails and oars, it is a serviceable craft and almost certainly the best that could have been taken for the purpose. A large net has been discarded; Collins can see it would be too bulky to be handled easily on the cutter, and yet they will need to fish. He sends a man to check if any other nets are missing.

It doesn't take long to work out their destination: the only possible landfall – given the recent departure of a Dutch snow with a disreputable captain, hired by the governor after endless negotiations as a supply ship – would have to be Timor in the Dutch East Indies. Bryant and the master of the Dutch ship, Detmar Smith, have been seen much in company and it's clear enough that more than good conversation has passed between them. It's a long voyage, something like 3500 miles, but if Bryant has managed to get hold of compass, sextant and charts, he certainly knows how to use them as well as any man in the colony and, with luck, a lot of luck, they might make it. Collins stands for a while, looking out across the calm waters of Port Jackson and wonders why.

Back at the settlement there is a definite feeling of excitement in the air; not much happens here and when something does, the public imagination loves to feed off it. Roll calls are taken: apart from the Bryants, seven men are missing. James Martin, James Cox and Samuel Bird: all from the First Fleet. Martin and Bird had a year each to serve and Bird knows something of the sea and sailing, whilst Cox was transported for life. From the Second Fleet, William Allan and Nathaniel Lilley were lifers, Sam Butcher and William Morton had four and five years respectively.

Going through the documentation – his forte, rather – Collins notices that Martin, Cox and Bird all served their time on the *Dunkirk* hulk at Plymouth and travelled out on the *Charlotte*, with the Bryants; it stands to reason that they would have become friends. The others are new men, with no established loyalties and no network of friends and influence. What did they offer: the threat of force, or blackmail or perhaps money fresh from England? The settlement does have a cash economy but, truth to tell, there's little use for it out here; rum, as all spirits are now known (the colony is developing its own argot, Collins notes), goods, labour, sex, all of these are far more viable currency as those who arrive with a full purse soon discover. Perhaps the new men were the bankers? Though since Allen's records mention his long service in the navy, it's quite likely his talents as sailor and navigator would have written his ticket in the boat without necessity of cash.

Over the course of the next two days, the women who had contact or lived with any of the escapers are questioned and one, Sarah Young, eventually admits that she has a letter from her man, James Cox, the lifer who is also a cabinetmaker. It was at his little workshop that he left the note. Cox begs Sarah to stay clear of the worst sort and give up the vices that prevail in the colony. He leaves her his property and says that he has only taken this desperate step because of the severity of his situation, being transported for life without the prospect of any mitigation or hope of ever quitting the country, but by these means that he is compelled to adopt. It is very like the last will and confession of a condemned man.

Collins contents himself with the thought that even if they do succeed, they will have considerable difficulty inventing a story plausible enough to disguise their real character from the Dutch authorities at Timor. Recalling the terrible instruments of judicial examination they saw at the Cape, where the Dutch have had far less time to build up their implacable systems, he cannot hold out much hope for the escapers.

William Bryant

 squall appears out of nowhere, the sea boiling as the wind whips it up into hundreds of wavecaps and sends it racing towards the cutter. Will leans hard on the tiller to bring the boat about but too late; they gybe, the boom swings dangerously out to port and the wind is on them, buffeting the sail with extreme force, putting so much pressure on the mast you can see it bend before a shroud parts, the sail hooks rip free and the boat, under the weight of the loose, whipping canvas, begins to capsize. People sprawl, there are screams as bodies are thrown from one side to the other; the load begins to shift, the heel increases and water begins to boil over the gunwales, filling the bottom of the boat.

Pulling out his gutting knife, Will starts to hack at the shrouds, trying to free the mast before they go right over; the woman leaps gracefully overboard, holding both her children, and begins to swim towards the shore, keeping the babies' heads clear of the choppy water. Those of the crew who can also swim jump in after her, though not for them the easy strokes of the woman; they flounder and splash and spit as they struggle against the current and the unreasoning waves breaking in their faces.

Will stays with the boat; he knows he can't let it go down, otherwise their whole plan will have to be abandoned. He's been over it a hundred times with Cox and Bird: the governor's cutter is the only small boat in the colony built to carry sail and big enough to take the whole gang of them and their provisions. Besides, he knows its sailing qualities backwards; it is Bryant's boat far more than Captain Phillip's.

He's said as much to the Dutchman and Detmar agrees with his friend Willem.

The wind doesn't abate but Will manages to cut the sail free. Even so, there's no way of steering the boat to shore; she is being driven steadily towards the rocks that straggled down, all sharp angles, towards the boiling sea. He bellows at the others, telling them to bail. They grab hats, buckets, anything that'll hold water, and start working. Will wants to howl with frustration; in moments the boat will be smashed against the rocks, its planks matchwood and its keel broken.

A sleek head breaks the surface alongside. Bennelong hauls himself up on the gunwales and points at the oars: 'give me'. Will recalls that the woman with the children is his friend Bennelong's sister. He checks she has made the shore and sees her, a child on each shoulder, emerging from the surf. Other heads appear, natives who have seen the boat founder. They reach out hands and take boathooks, thwarts, lobster pots, nets, duckboards, everything that weighs heavy and keeps the cutter wallowing in the grip of the tide and wind. Then, one by one, the remaining non-swimmers slip over and buoyed up, each of them, by two or three natives, they are carried to the shore.

Will stays aboard, hanging on for dear life, as the empty boat is spun and whipped this way and that by the squall. Bennelong and three or four others swim out, diving under the big breakers, emerging like porpoises to slip through the waves and grab the warps and trailing ropes and pull the cutter, by physical force, away from the rocks and onto the shore where it is safe to land. Will clambers out and walks with unsteady legs across the wet, shining sand to the little knot of soaking survivors who are huddled around a fire. The woman is calmly wiping the children's faces and she offers him a dazzling smile. Bennelong and the others bring the various bits and pieces they've saved from the boat and pile them up. Will offers Bennelong his thanks, not just for saving the cutter but for keeping the plan alive.

Mary Bryant

ad news travels fast in the colony. Mary is down by the government dock as Bennelong and his companions tow the damaged cutter around the point. It's clear things will have to be put back but how long can they wait? Winter will be here by the end of March and the conditions, so Will reckons, will make sailing along the coast impossible. Mary reckons that sailing anywhere at all in the cutter is going to be impossible. The seams are sprung, the mast is broken off near the top, the bowsprit all askew and a large mass of canvas and cordage is humped in a pile along with oars and gaffs and who knows what else.

Bennelong gives her a wave and indicates that her husband will be coming overland with the rest of the crew. As the canoes with their tow pass the ships moored in the cove, Captain Smith emerges from the round house on the snow *Waaksamheyd* and follows their progress. He catches Mary's eye and grins and then shrugs, as if to say: we shall see what we shall see. Mary smiles back. Detmar Smith is almost as important to them as the cutter; without him, their problems will be tenfold and it is worth anything, anything at all, to keep the little Hollander sweet.

She's like an Indian juggler, Mary Bryant, keeping a dozen clubs in the air at the same time, supporting this person and then that one, all the time holding in her grasp the thing itself, the great plan of escape, making the others believe in it.

For some, it's no problem. Two of the new boys are here for the term of their natural lives; they'll do anything to get away. Butcher and Morton are each looking at four years or more and from where they stand, as new chums, that seems a lot; Jim Cox has been one of the gang since they landed and also has his natural life to serve; Jim Martin, a blue pigeon flyer, and Sam Bird are in the way of being family from back in the *Dunkirk* days, and loyalty counts even though they have less time than she does to get through. And Will, William Bryant, what's in his head as he squats under a storm lantern in Detmar Smith's cabin going over and over the charts that'll take them to Timor?

Things are hard in the colony – the drought, the bats that darken the sky at sunset when they stream out of the woods – but things have been harder and now he is a free man, only he's not. That big mouth of his: bragging around the place about how once his time is out, he's off and be damned to the woman and her kids. Did he think the governor would just sit up there in his white house with that long old face of his and not notice a thing? There's no doubt that in many ways Will Bryant is a fool. Spreading it around too much back in the first days when they were selling the fish privately; what did that get him but a hundred lashes and thrown out of his hut? Yes, he got it back but it was her advice and her good sense that steered that particular boat into harbour. Keep your mouth shut, show a respectful face, don't go stepping as proud as Satan.

But he couldn't keep it up, he had to start boasting about how Sydney marriages didn't count back home. God love him, but it was as stupid as the Irish fellows buying the compasses drawn on paper and wandering off over the hills to China. Because sooner or later the governor was going to hear about it, because the governor hears about everything, and that big face would turn slowly round until it was looking right down on Will Bryant and one of those eyes would open and out of his mouth would fly, just like a bat at twilight, another law: Sydney marriages are legal; no convict who enters into marriage with another convict will be allowed to leave the colony until both are free.

Well, who was supposed to be the fisherman? It looked like Will was in the net for sure and if he wanted to run when he heard the news, she made him think better of it; showed how the thing could be done if only they could reach a port where they could pass themselves off as shipwrecked mariners. Beyond that, they hadn't thought; where they'll go to afterwards, where in the world there isn't a British ship and British marines, because Mary knows where she is going and Will knows too – back home to Cornwall.

Anyway, he can't leave her and the children, even if he wants to, because he knows she'll peach; they're in it together, for better for worse.

She stands waiting beside the cutter whilst damp, depressed William Bryant trudges round the curve of the bay; she reads his concern as he comes closer but there's something else in his eyes and when she whispers to find out how bad it is, will they be able to go; he nods and tells her they'll go late but in better style than they hoped. The governor's cutter will need refitting but just because it is the governor's – and the colony's only fishing boat to boot – the work will be done fast and well; no dockyard capabarre here, they'll be using the best materials Sydney can provide and he'll be keeping a close eye on the work.

Mary reminds him to have a care. When he was shooting his mouth off about running from the colony and leaving her and Charlotte and Emmanuel behind, the governor wasn't the only one who noticed. Major Grose, the new deputy governor who arrived in the Second Fleet with the New South Wales Corps, is no fool like Ranting Ross; his men have been keeping a weather eye on the fisherman, just in case he decides to honour his boasts.

Will protests; he's done his time, he's a free man. Mary tells him to look around: no one here is free; for the sake of the common good, the governor can make day night if he wants and by the time the authorities back home can do anything about it (as if they cared) two years will have gone by, the bell will have rung a thousand times and no one will even think of unringing it. Will nods, he may not be able to take a hint but if you shout good and clear in his face the message generally gets through. He goes off to report the boat accident to the commissary, the judge advocate and the governor; she goes back to their hut and begins to prepare a dinner for Captain Smith.

Mary doesn't know a lot about men but she knows enough to feed Captain Smith and make sure his washing and mending is done, to smile at him and listen to his stories and soothe his hurt vanity. And there's a lot of it for so little a man. His ship, the *Waaksamheyd*, arrived just after Christmas with supplies from the Cape; it was due to unload and depart in quick order, carrying Captain Hunter and other officials who were ill or fed up with life at the cove. The problem was that nobody seemed to like Captain Smith; they didn't like his greedy ways or his easy manner, they just didn't like the cut of his jib so they didn't invite him to their tents for supper or to their offices to discuss the contracts. He would be going, certainly, but in the governor's time and not his own and on the governor's terms and all this condescension is making Detmar Smith really angry.

He thinks that if the gentlemen won't receive him at the soirées they attend with the newly arrived corps wives (who already despise Mrs Johnson as a Methodist), where they sing sentimental songs around a piano, then he'll consort with those who do value his company. And Mary knows she can give good value in the company line and Will has no objection as far as that goes: it's just buying and selling, what's up and what's down.

Tonight, compass and sextant are up; charts already lie folded under the floorboards and, as the rum and water goes around and Detmar and Willem get red in the face and Mary serves and smiles, the yellow boys come out and slide across the rough wooden table until enough of them have made the passage to tip the balance and send the instruments of navigation back. Detmar says he'll throw in a couple of muskets and some powder and shot, they'll need them when they land to keep off the natives. Will reckons that they'll make friends the way they have here at the Cove. After all, didn't Bennelong save his life today when the boat almost went on the rocks?

Detmar tells Willem not to be a fool. Down here they're used to you, up along the east coast, it's different. Most of them won't ever have seen white men, and what do you do when something that looks like a dead body – because that, my friend, is how they see us – comes dragging itself up through the surf? You don't invite it to supper, that's for sure. In the far north: well, maybe they're more friendly, us Hollanders have been landing there for years and you'll see natives with little pointy beards, like in the old paintings. And the Chinese, they come fishing for their sea slugs, but mostly, Willem, stay clear of those blackfellows or they'll put a spear through you and that pretty wife of yours.

The drink goes round and the charts come out. The ones of the eastern seaboard of New South Wales are pretty vague but Detmar knows something of these waters and warns again of the great reef and the Torres Strait and the Arafura Sea; it is, he says, a mad undertaking in a small boat but maybe, maybe, it might be done. And the drink goes round and the children are asleep and Will has to slip away to attend to something or another and Detmar and Mary are left alone in the candlelight, shadows dancing over their faces.

Throughout March they gather in supplies; there's too much for their hut so each member of the gang must find a hiding place of their own and everything will be brought together on the night. However, it isn't easy getting the right things together, government has put out an edict forbidding the exchange or sale of any goods from the public store (offering a reward of thirty pounds of flour to peachers) and building up enough flour and pork, not to mention finding a secure cask big enough to hold ten gallons of drinking water – for no one knows how long it will be between landfalls and whether fresh water will be found when they do go ashore.

Every extra day increases the risk of discovery. One of the new chums might blurt something out to his woman, or promise her a place in the boat (and there's no more room) or the movement of supplies might be noticed and a sudden search ordered. Then there's the weather: Captain Smith makes it clear that by April storms will start coming up from the Southern Ocean and the winds along the coast will be untrustworthy. If they don't go by the end of March, they may have to wait until September and Mary knows that lips won't stay closed that long. If nobody else gives them away, Will's big mouth is bound to do the job.

Every morning Will hurries down to the government wharf where they are reconditioning the cutter. As the planking is replaced and paid with pitch, Will realises that they must take something to seal the seams during the voyage or they'll be springing leaks by the dozen. They'll need a net for fishing as well, but nothing as big as the colony seine; with nine aboard as well as the stores, the boat is going to be very near overloaded; he'll have to look around for something smaller.

The work proceeds apace; everyone wants the fisherman back in the bay but there are rumours going round that an escape is about to happen. Nothing certain and Will's name is not yet connected to the supposed plan but the word is in the air and soon enough someone will bring it down. They are all living on borrowed time: seven men and a woman cannot keep a secret for long in a place where gossip and information are part of the currency.

The last plank is caulked, the mast stepped, the shrouds secured, a lick of paint applied and the cutter is ready for service and still they cannot go whilst Detmar Smith's ship bobs at anchor in the cove. Once the escape is discovered, the governor might hire or commandeer any vessel capable of catching up with the cutter to ensure that the escapers are caught and taken, if only to show that there is no way home except by serving out your sentence and waiting for your dependants to serve theirs.

At last, on Sunday 27th March 1791, the *Waaksamheyd* raises her anchor and heads out of the cove. On board as passengers are Captain Hunter, who is without a command since the *Sirius* went down whilst trying to land Major Ross on Norfolk Island – the Major survived – as well as the officers and men from the ship; letters from Dr White requesting his immediate recall are also aboard as are many other letters and packets containing journals and accounts of life in the colony.

The governor and his staff accompany the leave-takers to the heads of Port Jackson, before wishing them a happy return.

Will and Mary watch the Dutch ship as she sails out of the cove; Detmar Smith stands at the stern and raises his hat. After the *Waaksamheyd* is out of sight, there is the sound of gunfire, nine shots and well spaced, a salute offered by Captain Smith to Governor Phillip and his staff or, perhaps, a last goodbye to the only people in the colony who had offered Detmar Smith a welcome and a bed. Either way, it leaves the sea clear for them now. The *Supply* tender is still somewhere in the area but Will is convinced the governor will never risk his only sea-going ship, and his only contact with outside world, just to chase convicts; Smith's ship might be risked, the *Supply* cannot. Mary hopes he is right; if they are caught their sentences will certainly be increased and though this won't make any difference to the lifers, it will to her.

Monday is a fair day with variable winds. Will takes the cutter out fishing with his usual crew; he arranges to meet the new chums at the east point of the cove at eleven o'clock that night. The catch is unloaded and ferried ashore in rowing boats. He pronounces the repairs to be good, though he is far from sure about the caulking, the boat is leaking already but he dare not return her the workmen. The cutter is, as usual moored out in the deeper channels of the cove and it will need to be towed ashore tonight but Will has already thought of that. As he walks back home he passes by the others and lets them know where and what time to meet – only a few will start from the hut, as any large group spotted by the guard will arouse immediate suspicion – and what to bring with them. A smaller net has been found and James Cox has removed his carpenter's tools from the general store; rice and flour and the water cask will be loaded at the point, the last land they will touch before heading along the channel to the heads of Port Jackson and, they hope and pray, freedom.

Mary is keeping the baby awake, to ensure he sleeps later. Three-year-old Charlotte smells something in the wind but she's a convict's child and knows to keep it to herself. Will is calm; this is work he knows in his bones; handling boats in the dark, muffling the rowlocks, waiting for the clouds to cross over the moon, keeping in shadow, keeping their powder dry and the muskets primed. He doesn't want trouble but if they are stopped, trouble will be there. He has no intention of facing another flogging and this time, no matter what he says about his time being up, it'll be a good three or four hundred. Better death than that, he tells Mary and she says better death than here another day.

Night falls under a curtain of bats' wings and the oil lamps begin to glitter in the glassy darkness, some glimmering from windows, some hanging eerily amongst the leaves and branches reflecting animals' eyes; others on the move, as the night watch patrol the gardens with their swinging storm lanterns and the soldiers of the corps mount guard over the store huts. Signs and counter signs are called and answered; snatches of laughter carry across from the governor's house, where he is giving a dinner. A piano plays, insects chatter and birds laugh from the greater darkness beyond the colony.

No one has a watch but they can tell the time from the movement of the stars and the changing of the guard. They need to go between nine and midnight, when, despite the curfew, there are still people about and the watch is getting a little tired and careless. The hut lamp is put out early as it is most nights: the fisherman gets up early and goes to bed early.

They sit in the dark as the moments pass; there's a tap at the door, those told to carry the biggest loads are ready. The rice, flour and muskets are passed out and the figures slip away. After giving them time to get clear, Will stows the sextant and compass and picks up Charlotte – he doesn't have to warn her to keep quiet – and Mary takes the baby, still asleep. She picks up a bag of the dried leaves that make do for tea out here; they aren't the real thing but she has the feeling that if they need a hot drink, they'll be a lot better than nothing.

After a last look round a place they never want to see again, they slip out into the night and realise that not until you really listen do you know how silent it is here, despite the noise of animals, insects and man; a silence as big and unwelcoming as the vast sky and the rocks that make your whole life seem no more permanent than the shadow of a lizard crossing their old, old faces. Mary realises just how much she doesn't want to be in this place; not just because it isn't Cornwall but somehow because it isn't even human.

They pause as an officer comes past whistling *Lillibullero*, a tune that, for some reason, the natives seem to like. He goes by, leaving a trail of brandy and pork and hair oil in the air; definitely one of the newcomers. They move on down towards the cove, pausing at the pre-arranged places to collect the others. They hug the shadows and keep away from the gardens – no point in being taken for a thief; everything is muffled with cloth except the baby but he sleeps on. No one speaks, they know what to do and there's nothing they can add now: it's a good plan, a simple plan: get to the boat, get in the boat, get out of Port Jackson, get away.

The clouds are banking and there's only an occasional glimpse of moonlight silvering the water; a good dark night but even so they won't raise the sail until they're well clear of the settlement. Sound carries over water and if anyone's attention is caught, the glimmer of the white canvas would be as clear as a signal lamp.

They slip and slide down to the shoreline. The cutter is still moored out in the channel. Will whistles and a dark shape moves through the water, barely disturbing it; there is a splash – it sounds like a crash to the little party waiting on shore – as the painter is untied and drops into the water and the prow begins to turn towards them. They wade out to the point that Will has reckoned will allow them to board without the weight grounding the keel in mud. He holds the boat steady and nods his thanks; an arm is raised from the water in a wave and then the shape is gone.

One by one they climb aboard, every splash, creak of wood or rasp of metal on metal booming out across the cove to echo, in their minds, like thunder around the settlement. How is it that no one can hear or see them? They seem massive out here, crouching in the cutter. But no one does and Will swings himself into the stern and takes the tiller whilst others take the oars, fit them in the muffled rowlocks and begin to pull, trying to balance their desperation to get clear with the need to slip the oar blades into the water as quietly and deftly as nimming a guinea out of a purse.

At the eastern point they close the shore to pick up the last of the party, the new chums who bring the net aboard. The cutter wobbles as they clamber across the others and find a space; curses are muttered under the breath. There's no love lost between the old hands and the new; their money and an unspoken threat to peach has ensured they are here. Will would rather there were fewer people in the boat; they're not overcrowded but he knows that after a few days at sea, it's going to seem like they are.

At his nod, the rowers begin again and the cutter backs away and turns to face the open water of Port Jackson. There are no parties out tonight but there will be a lookout at the heads and it's vital they keep as close to the land as possible, using its shadow to mask their passage. The third set of oars is slipped into the rowlocks and their pace increases. Will needs to keep his wits about him; getting out is no easy matter, there are more roads and shallows and false horizons than any port he's ever seen and it'll be a good long pull before they are through the middle cape and past the north head.

Mary sits by the mast, on the folded sails, cradling Emmanuel and holding Charlotte who has no intention of going to sleep: she's caught her mother's tension and grips her tight because she knows by now that they are doing something wrong. The clouds part and for a moment the moonlight catches the great fan of ripples spreading out from the cutter's prow, then the night closes in again and apart from the rhythmic splash of the oars and a dark shadow darting across dark water, there is nothing to be heard or seen.

Shortly after midnight they come round the inner head and there, opening up before them, is the whole wide ocean. A storm is flickering just beyond the horizon – they can see the lighting on the water – but it won't affect them. Will, Cox and Bird raise the sail. For a moment it hangs limp but then draws and bellies out as it catches the wind and the cutter jerks forward, pressing backs against wood, tautening shrouds. Will has the tiller and needs no instrument or compass to tell him what to do now: turn left, head north for Timor and freedom.

It's a long time before they even dare to breath loudly but at last it's clear to all that they are out and away and there are a few shouts, a fragment of song or sighs of relief but mostly they are too wrung out to do anything except look about themselves in the milky dawn light and wonder at what they have achieved and worry about pursuit. Will the governor send *Supply* after them? Likely not, Will has always said, but you can't be sure.

One day out. They go through their provisions; a hundredweight of flour and rice, fourteen pounds of pork and the water. It's clear to Mary that they are going to have to make up their food from what they can gather when they land along the coast. Some of the others aren't so sure about this but Will tells them they will be; after sitting on their arses in an open boat for a few days they'll be praying to get a bit of dry land under their feet and, often enough, even when they want to get ashore it won't be possible. He luffs up and brings the boat closer inshore so they can hear the pounding of the surf and see the constant white unwinding of the waves crashing onto the beach; trying to get though breakers like that – ten, twelve or more feet high – will smash the boat and break her back as easy as black your eye. His plan is to land pretty much wherever and whenever they can in safety.

The others agree, reluctantly, but they've no choice, what're they going to do, mutiny like those fellows they've heard about on the *Bounty*? No chance, not one of them could sail the cutter half as well as Will even on a day like this, with calm seas; as to what it's going to be like once the weather gets up and the water gets angry, nobody even wants to think about. Better to play games with Charlotte or start trailing the net. Will nods to himself, to the others; a couple of them have some sailing skills but there's only one captain on this cutter, and Will Bryant is the man and they'd all better remember it.

Two days out. The wind has been kind up to now and they are as certain as they can be that no one is coming after them. By mid-morning the wind is beginning to turn and Will decides to take the cutter into a cove where the surf doesn't look too rough. They land on a stony beach and haul the boat up as far as they can manage. As Will promised, they are all glad to be standing on solid land.

Mary sets off looking for food and fresh water and some of the men go with her; they don't appear to mind being told what to do by a woman, partly because she's Will's wife and has his authority behind her, but there's something else: she knows what she wants and isn't afraid to say so. She points out the big sea-cabbages with their fleshy leaves; they should be good to eat and, from what she's seen of Dr White's methods, might help against the scurvy. There's also the cask to manhandle out of the boat and roll up to the stream that flows out from the rocks.

Later, they build a fire and put up shelters using the big outer leaves of the cabbage plants. Will reckons the land around here is far better than down at Sydney Cove and, from the luck they've been having with the net, the fishing is better too. The cabbage, though tough, is edible and they cook up some flat bread and a little pork, which they mean to eke out as long as possible. Scattered along the beach are curious dark rocks or stones and when Mary investigates she finds them to be coal which burns well on their fire.

On the morning of their second day ashore, Charlotte wakes her mother with a worried voice. Mary crawls out from under the shelter and sees natives ranged along the tree line. They don't seem angry or dangerous, just curious about who these white people might be. One or two of them walk down the beach, their spears, fragile but deadly, casting long shadows behind them on the stones and sand. Martin and a couple of the others meet them and offer a hat and a waistcoat and a handkerchief which are received politely. After looking round the camp, examining the boat and sniffing the cooking pot, they leave as quietly as they came, fading away into the trees.

For the rest of the day the escapers gather what food they can find, scrub and refill the cask, check the nets and enjoy being totally dry and still. That night they post guards just in case and, in the morning, while the surf is at its lowest, Mary and the children clamber back aboard and the men push the cutter back out into deep water and pull themselves aboard. The sail is set and with Mary at the tiller, because she's a better hand at it than anyone except Will, they sail north.

Five days out. Wind still holding, they come into a fine natural harbour with a wide river running inland. There is fresh water but, more importantly, a flat beach where they can haul the cutter ashore and turn it over so Will can pay the seams with rosin and wax; his concern about the workmanship of the boatwrights back at the Cove is justified. With the extra weight of the passengers the seams are beginning to spring and the leakage is getting worse every day.

Whilst they are unloading the boat, more natives appear and these are not so friendly. Spears are brandished and the wooden throwing swords waved menacingly. Chucking everything, including the children, back in the boat, the escapers relaunch the cutter and take her up the river, standing well clear of the shore, where the natives stalk them. They fire muskets over their heads but it makes no difference and they dare not shoot to wound or kill, for surely then the natives would make far greater efforts to attack, whatever the cost. As it is, they are beginning to wade out towards the boat and after a short conference, with water leaking through the seams and getting deeper and deeper in the bottom, Will decides they must sail upstream, away from the natives, and find somewhere safer to careen the cutter.

The next day they come upon a sandy island in the middle of the river and beach the cutter and empty her. There is fresh water here so they can refill the cask and wash the salt out of their clothes whilst Will, Cox and Allen recaulk the seams as best they can.

Two days later they come sailing downstream and moor off the beach whilst the new chums gather more cabbage leaves. The wind is coming off the shore and there's a scramble to get back aboard as the cutter is driven out to sea; Will reefs the mainsail, leaving only a scrap to give her steerage way, but the weather continues to go down and they are driven out of sight of land for the first time. Throughout the night Will struggles to keep the cutter on a course parallel to the hidden shore and in the morning steers west until land is once again in sight; it has been an experience that no one wants to repeat, being so totally out of touch in this tiny boat.

Will wants to go back ashore to check the caulking but the surf along this section of the coast is too great to risk a landing; they must keep heading north and hope the weather or the surf relent. They do not: day after day the prospect is the same, sheer rocks or open beach fenced off by great walls of surf. There isn't one of them who doesn't remember the reports of the *Sirius*, a well-found ship with a full crew, being driven ashore and wrecked in the surf of Norfolk Island. And there isn't one of them, as the days go by and the water gets lower in the cask and the cabbages begin to run out and their lips get rough and taste of salt, who doesn't begin to wonder if it's not worth chancing it.

Twelve days out. Will takes the boat in close but the roar and the sheer size of the surf smothers any argument for trying to run through it, and once more they stand out to sea.

Sixteen days out. The water is all but gone. The children have stopped crying and lie still in the bottom of the boat. Eyelids, hair, every crevice and crack of their bodies is caked with salt and blistered by the cold winds that batter them day and night. They must have water and Morton and Cox say that if Will can get them close enough, they'll swim through the surf with the cask, refill it ands swim back out.

It's risky, but it's better than the constant thirst. Will takes the cutter in, lowers the sail and uses all three sets of oars to keep her stable as the swimmers lower themselves into the waves, take the cask and surf in to the beach, landing battered and bruised but safe. There are cheers of encouragement from the boat but as they clamber up the slick sands, natives appear and start gesturing with their spears. Morton and Cox try to show they mean no harm, that they only want water but they are driven down the beach and into the surf and have to swim out bringing the cask back empty. Will is devastated; he is not a man able to cope well with frustration and the constant setbacks of these two weeks and more are getting him down. He slumps in the stern and it is Mary who squats beside him and talks quietly, encouraging and coaxing until he takes the tiller and calls for the mainsail to be raised.

They are in a wide bay and Will heads across it towards what appears to be an estuary or creek. They've had luck with rivers before, they might do so again. Approaching, they make out shoals where the water runs shallow – using a man instead of a lead, Will guides the boat through without bottoming, and they land by the creek. There are no natives but it wouldn't make any difference if there were, so desperate is everyone for fresh water. They refill the barrel and look for fish or shellfish but there are none to be found, only a few of the cabbages to cut and take aboard. Of greater concern are the planks of the cutter; the rough weather has worked them so much the rosin and wax have come away. They must repay or sink. James Martin has the answer: soap he bought with him will do the job, not well, but well enough, they hope. They give themselves two days to rest before putting to sea again.

Twenty-eight days out. The first storm has come up, bringing seas that tower above them like mountains fore and aft, so they can see their own track as they race down slopes of dark green water and climb up, up and up until, for a moment, they pause at the peak, white water racing by, before once again they plunge down so fast it seems they will never stop, just go on through the water to the bottom of the sea. Only, somehow, every time, the prow digs in, water bursts over them and they lift, impossibly lift like a cork and sweep up again with stomach-wrenching speed.

There's no talking or even shouting, the wind snatches the words from their mouths and howls and booms around them with a noise which is too great, too loud for men and women and does some kind of terrible violence to their feelings of themselves. Baby Emmanuel clings to Mary like a limpet, Charlotte has left whatever place she lives when she's awake and tries to burrow through the streaming wet

into her mother. The men move slowly, battling against the shock that
threatens to unman them, performing deliberate actions, trying both
to find a meaning in what they are doing and to lighten the cutter,
throwing anything heavy overboard. Tools, clothes, supplies, over they
go as the dizzying ride continues as it has for the last eight days. And
each time the boat fills, it is Mary who struggles, encumbered with baby
and child, through the mayhem to Will, to the others, and puts hats
and bowls into their hands and makes them bail and bail for dear life.

Gradually the weather abates, the wind no longer howls in their
faces, but merely sobs like a ghost and the waves become hills instead
of mountains. Hanging on to the mast, Will can just make out, beyond
the wave peaks, the shore and an open bay. Setting a trysail, no more
than a scrap of canvas, he hauls on the tiller and drives her in. The
closer they get, the more the wind falls and it begins to look like they
might be able to land when they are in the shelter of the bay, but once
through the heads, they find huge surf all around and Will throws out
anchor and grapnel to hold them off shore during the approaching
night, with the hope that in the morning the surf will be down. Instead,
the wind comes up; anchor and grapnel break and the boat is driven
into the breakers. It is the nightmare everybody fears and yet they
have been living in nightmares these eight days and nights, and
with remarkable calm they grab oars and fight to guide themselves
through the surf. White water cascades around them and they jump
forward at terrific speed and find themselves on the beach; the cutter,
miraculously, is still in one piece.

Wrapped in layers of oilcloth, their flint is still dry and they collect
enough wood to get a fire going and heat up some water and Mary is
proved right, the Sydney tea leaves make the best hot drink they've
ever tasted. For the first time in eight days they are warm and, as the
night turns into day, their clothes begin to dry out as well. Around
the cove there are rocks and mangrove branches thick with shellfish;
there is a stream and the natives, when they make their inevitable
visits, are not hostile, merely curious, though perhaps this is because
the escapers are looking less like whites now than seamed wood flung
up by the ocean.

They dry what clothes they have left, eat, drink, refill the cask and after three days decide they have to face the sea again. The cutter is launched through the surf and everyone is slightly surprised that she still swims, but swim she does and Will puts out to sea.

Now the work is of a different kind: slower, more backbreaking, continual baling every hour of the day and night but they are making a good speed and Jim Martin's soap is holding fast.

Thirty-nine days out. Allen, Will and Mary are fashioning a drogue out of canvas. The men hack out an oblong from one of the spare sails and Mary, using her strongest needle, sews it into the shape of a bucket without a bottom; in these racing seas they have to slow themselves down somehow, particularly at night, and the funnel shape, towed astern, should have both a slowing and stabilising effect. When they lower it overboard and stream it out astern, it does seem to make a difference, though the cutter becomes sluggish and difficult to handle and if they meet a sudden squall, they'll need to cut the drogue free.

In the night the sea gets up, and once more everyone is turned-to with bucket and hat bailing for their lives; the drogue holds them back and Will wonders if they'd be easier without it but it's becoming harder for all of them make decisions now and they are inclined to let things be.

In the morning they find they have been driven out of sight of the land, back into that stormy place of everlasting sound and wet without even the chance to make a small fire on board to heat food or drink. They've done this, they've been through the mountainous waves, the roaring and the swooping and the glassy green mountains and the backbreaking baling; they've driven themselves up to and beyond their own limits and having to do it all again is too much. It makes then angry, furious against this stupid mindless sea that batters on and on. They shout and scream at the waves but it only makes their throats sore and they're running out of water again. It is Mary, holding onto the children and the thought of going home, who finds the bloody-mindedness to go on because there's nothing else to do and in the face of her determination there is nothing the rest can do, except go on too.

An island appears out of the dawn and despite the fury of the sea, and whatever the risk, they know they are going to land there. At first it looks like the whole place is ringed by reefs, then they see a way through to a sandy beach where the surf is not impossible – four weeks ago it would have been, but not any more. They take in the drogue and pull for the gap, one man to an oar, so exhausted are they, and finally come to shore and scramble out onto solid land. Water is the first priority as they have only a gallon left, so a party sets of at once to find a stream. The island is small and waterless and they come back disappointed but carrying five large turtles.

This is luxury indeed and soon a fire is blazing and one of the turtles is cooking to make a noble meal. The rain holds off while they cook and dine but if one thing is certain, then it is that it will be raining soon and Will uses the mainsail to rig a rain catcher. For once the weather obliges; it pours all night and they collect more than enough water for their needs. They decide to stay on the island for a week and eat turtle and turtle soup as if they were all living high at the London Tavern.

They explore the island and find vegetables like bell peppers but not so hot and small flightless birds that live in a hole at night and are eaten by the escapers during the day. There are no signs of natives living or visiting the place and for six days they are able to relax more than they have done since the night they left Sydney Cove, making and mending and cooking and drying turtle meat. Will takes sightings and reckons they are close to the point where they will begin to head west toward Timor. There's still a long mile to go, he says, but they're well over half way there.

Forty-two days out. Tiny islands dot the sea like crumbs on turtle soup; they are in the Gulf of Carpentaria and it's hot and getting hotter: fresh water is the most important thing in their lives and they'll take any risk to make sure they don't run out.

The oars creak as they row, the boat cutting a glittering path through the still, hot ocean; on either side canoes filled with natives easily keep pace with the sweating rowers. The canoes pass behind islands, the cutter follows a straight course towards a headland where a stream trickles down the face of the rocks. They want that water but the natives want them dead. Will softly tells the rowers to increase their stroke and the cutter surges forward; two canoes emerge from behind the tiny islets and as if on a command, both start moving faster, curving in towards the cutter. Arrows hiss through the air, one hitting the stern, the barb sinking deep into the worn timbers.

Will and Morton leap up and hoist the mainsail, Mary takes the tiller, the rowers redouble their efforts and the cutter begins to pull ahead, crossing the path of the starboard canoe, receiving more arrows which slither through the heavy air, passing the heads of those in the boat. Will bellows at them to pull harder; the boom swings far to port as it fills with wind and the cutter begins to gather way and pull out to sea. The canoes don't give up, they follow throughout the morning, their paddlers tireless, whilst in the boat the rowers spell each other but still get ever closer to exhaustion. At last the wind lifts and they begin to draw away.

A last few arrows fall in the water behind them before the canoes are lost in the haze. It's five hundred miles across the top of the Gulf and they must have water but they're not going to find any here without fighting a battle that they'll lose. Will looks down at the compass face, the glass glittering in the palm of his hand. It has been more valuable than a diamond and is still true; it points the way west. They'll hope the wind holds and take a chance with the water they have.

Forty-eight days out. The coast swims into view. They've crossed the Gulf: five hundred miles in four and a half days. Will fills in his log as he has done every time they make a landfall. To Mary the letters mean nothing but what they say is that each day brings her closer to home.

There are no canoes filled with warriors waiting for them and they coast into the shore where they fill up with water and food for the last long haul into Timor. Will reckons on two weeks of sailing, touching land occasionally for water and supplies and with any luck the ocean will be kind to them. Charlotte plays on the beach whilst the others talk quietly about who they'll be and where their ship was lost and how; the story needs to be good and clear, forthright with no hint of the lag about it. So far the journey has been all that matters, now they can think about journey's end and beyond. Will doesn't want to wait overnight to be speared in his sleep, he calls them together and they lift the children aboard and push the cutter out.

Sixty-nine days out and they can smell the land – spices and oils, tobacco and meat cooking, bilge water and tropical forest. The smoke of forges and factories and kitchens drifts across the swell, clear to noses which have smelt nothing much but the ocean for ten long weeks, the last two crossing the Timor Sea, out of sight of land, working the stars and the sun for their position every noon and arriving here, off the port of Timor, exactly where they wanted to be. To the yard. It has been a great thing they have done, Will reckons. Three thousand miles in a small cutter crowded with nine people and not a fight, hardly an argument and more than that, not a death amongst them. They look at each other as the port comes into sight, first as a forest of masts, then the white customs buildings and warehouses and beyond them, the town.

There's nothing more to say or do other than go through their story one last time and for Will to take over the tiller and the others to lower the sail as they glide in through water carpeted with wood and straw and paper, dead rats and frayed ropes and all the floating rubbish of a busy dock as it washes against the wooden pilings of the wharf. Faces are turned towards them; big, red Hollanders' faces and beautiful, sharp Timorese faces full of curiosity. Tonight they will either be convicts again and in gaol or shipwrecked travellers and neat as ninepence. Will stands up in the prow and catches the rope that is thrown ...

Captain Edward Edwards

A hard-faced, flint-souled man, the glittering beauties of Tahiti have no effect upon him at all; it's as if he carries a cold mist around that makes men shiver as he draws near. He's a horror, all right, a hard-driving, arrogant, cruel bastard and that's what his crew will tell you; what the prisoners feel, as they are dragged into the boat and rowed out towards the *Pandora*, is sheer dread. If they can hear anything over the heartbroken wailing of their wives, it is the hammering on the ship's deck as the carpenter and armourer complete the timber-walled, windowless box of a roundhouse with its bolts, irons and chains that will become their world for as long as it takes the hunter to track down the rest of his prey. It is, for the *Bounty* sailors who chose not to accompany Fletcher Christian and his mutineers but to wait for rescue on bright Tahiti, a fall from the Paradise Garden to the dark hell of *Pandora*'s Box.

Captain Edwards cares not a jot for their protests and the excuse that they were carried away under compulsion, by accident or because there was not enough room in the long boat with Bligh; he has his instructions and he means to carry them out to the letter. Britain is facing war against Spain and Revolutionary France, her navies control the sea lanes of the world but she is endlessly short of sailors; bribery, the press gang, any means at all must be used to crew the thousands of vessels that make up the Royal Navy. But on every deck of every one lurks the gunpowder of mutiny and the spark of Jacobin notions of freedom and the rights of man. It has occurred to some on board that it is a fine irony that Captain William Bligh's uncle is Duncan Campbell, master of the hulks and the export of criminals and that now, in Bligh's wake, the *Pandora* will be importing criminals for trial, and no doubt, hanging back in London.

Captain Edwards is not a man who appreciates irony and the jest is not communicated to him. He stands, bleak and forbidding, as the mutineers are pulled up the sloping sides of the frigate and stood on the deck. Around the ship a motley flotsam of canoes and rafts and swimmers gather, still howling and weeping for their lost white men. In Edwards' mind is the perpetual dark vision of his own near escape from mutiny off the coast of America. Only floggings of three and five hundred strokes and hanging in chains had kept the hatches battened against the dogs then; this pack of whelps can consider themselves lucky to have so commodious a kennel as *Pandora*'s box. Eleven feet by eighteen, the mutineers are pushed into the suffocating darkness and ironed and stapled to the thick timber walls. The fourteen men, most protesting innocence, will spend every minute of the day and night imprisoned within the box. They will have more than enough time to contemplate the articles of war which are read out on every ship in the fleet on Sundays after divine service, particularly number twenty-four: If any person in or belonging to the fleet shall make or endeavour to make any mutinous assembly upon any pretence whatsoever, every person offending herein, and being convicted thereof by the sentence of the court martial, shall suffer death.

The wailing of their Tahitian wives and friends adds an awful piquancy to their suffering, for each of the prisoners can be certain that that they will never see their island paradise or their families again.

Captain Edwards gives the orders, the bosun's whistles shrill, the waisters trudge around the capstan and the anchor chain rattles into the orlop; the topmen swarm up the ratlines and out along the spars and canvas blooms blindingly in the sun. The *Pandora* begins to gather way, nosing canoes with their heartbroken and angry passengers aside, slowly leaving them behind as she sails out of Matavai Bay and makes westward across the Pacific for the Torres Straights and Timor.

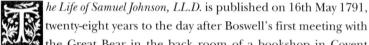

James Boswell

he *Life of Samuel Johnson, LL.D.* is published on 16th May 1791, twenty-eight years to the day after Boswell's first meeting with the Great Bear in the back room of a bookshop in Covent Garden. It is a great success but it is not the only work he issues: he also presents a poem in support of the slave trade, attacking the prominent abolitionists Wilberforce, Burke, Fox and Pitt which, fortunately, passes unnoticed. Everyone is talking about the *LIFE* and the great majority of reviewers ('Peculiarly authentic, very amusing and, in general, very interesting ...') and readers ('Perhaps no man was ever so perfectly painted as you have painted your hero ...') are talking it up.

Even the King has passed generous words, endorsing Burke's judgement: 'Mr Burke told me it was the most entertaining book he ever read'. Boswell plans to include the compliment in the preface to the second edition which is assured now, though Malone warns him against doing so, muttering dark words about hubris.

There are a few criticisms, mostly of the intimate nature of the work, the reportage of Johnson the man in full, conversational tics and all, and of Boswell's habit of noting down private conversations. Basically they are the same complaints that arose after the *Tour to the Hebrides* and Boswell answers them abruptly in the same way. It is not an attitude calculated to win friends but the great biographer is riding high and earning well: over two thousand sets of his *LIFE* – it comes in two volumes – have been sold by the beginning of August, for once he is in the money and heartily glad that he didn't sell the copyright.

He is invited out every single night, which is just as well because much as he loves his daughters, who are at home at the moment, he finds their company tiresome. He dines and drinks with his artistic friends, Reynolds and Malone, who make up the club they call the Gang; he attends great banquets with the Lord Mayor of London (where he sings a song and drinks too much) and a gala dinner given by the Royal Academy to celebrate the King's birthday where he translates and sings a Swedish love song, accompanying himself in the form of a Swedish chorus – and drinks too much; he flicks through the pages of Mr Harris's *Young Ladies of Covent Garden*:

Miss B—lford, Great Titchfield Street. This child of love looks very well when drest. She is rather subject to fits, alias counterfits, very partial to a Pantomime Player at Covent Garden Theatre. She may be about nineteen, very genteel, with a beautiful neck and chest, and most elegantly moulded breasts. Her eyes are wonderfully piercing and expressive. She is always lively, merry and cheerful, and, in bed, would give you such convincing proof of her attachments to love's game, that if you leave one guinea behind, you will certainly be tempted to renew your visit.
Miss B. Number 18 Old Compton Street, Soho. This accomplished nymph has just attained her eighteenth year, and fraught with every perfection, enters a volunteer in the field of Venus. She plays pianoforte, sings, dances, and is the mistress of every manoeuvre in the amorous contest that can enhance the coming pleasure. She is of middle stature, fair auburn hair, dark eyes and very inviting countenance, which ever seems to beam delight and love. In bed she is all the heart can wish, or eyes admire. Every limb is symmetry, ever action under cover truly amorous, her price, two pounds.

In the end he meets a lively little Parisienne who leads him quite a dance and thinks of getting married, if he can find £10,000 a year.

In February 1792 Sir Joshua Reynolds dies of a liver complaint and Boswell mourns the passing of a great painter and a good friend: 'this damps the spirits too much', he laments and, some say, tries to counter the dampness with too many glasses of wine or port or brandy. At a city dinner he makes a fool of himself and is upbraided by his own son, Sandy, who writes from school that his father was reported standing upon a stool, descending to gross buffoonery to gain popular applause. It is a humiliating moment; no man wants to appear a buffoon in the eyes of his son.

The trouble is that the *LIFE* is finished and making its own way in the world; his wife is gone, and he still misses her good sense and care with a keenness that continually surprises; his oldest friends like Temple are stuck in Cornwall or dead like Reynolds; his ambitions as a lawyer and MP have come to nothing very much; what is there left except drink and noisy company to keep away the terrible abyss? And he is in demand: he talks up a storm and he's funny and pertinent, at least in the early part of the evening; later, it's often a different matter, but they love him, his friends, his acquaintances, even his enemies can be caught off guard by his desire to please, to be liked. Great good humour is hard to resist but all too easily it can descend into buffoonery and now there is no Johnson to lift an eyelid or wag a finger and call Bozzy to order.

What he needs, and all who love him know it well, is a cause again, a good reason for getting up in the morning and not going to bed drunk.

Captain Edward Edwards

To lose one cutter may be considered a misfortune, to loose two, as Captain Edwards has managed on his long search for mutineers through the Society, Union and Friendly Islands, can only be considered carelessness and the clerks back at the Admiralty hate carelessness because it always costs money. Sudden storms, missed meetings over thousands of sea miles are not an excuse and Edwards' embarrassment is acute; though not quite so acute as that felt by his servant who falls in with a particularly acquisitive group of Friendly Islanders and finds himself on the beach, stripped naked, with only a shoe to cover his privates.

The missing boats have been sent to reconnoitre some of the smaller islands for signs of the *Bounty* men, and have almost certainly been attacked by the natives to rather more deadly effect than Edwards' servant was. It is clear that M. Rousseau's ideas of noble savagery disdaining the weapons of civilisation do not stand up in the face of experience. The Tahitians are a beautiful, peaceful race – on the whole – but the rest of the south seas seethe with warlike and territorial ambition. Edwards will be glad to see the back of the place and, since his orders state that he may sail home if there is no sign of the mutineers by August, he leaves the missing boats and heads west.

His prisoners are wasting away in the box. Their irons have long since begun to bite into the flesh and cause ulcers that expose bones becoming daily more brittle through scurvy. Edwards is adamant that there shall be no contact between mutineers and crew and keeps his prisoners chained in the dark and his men at full stretch, day and night, using any scrap of wind to gain extra way.

The passage through the great barrier reef at Cape Torres is notoriously difficult; Cook himself came to grief here, and as the *Pandora* approaches the tricky waters between Cape York and New Guinea, he orders sails trimmed and speed reduced so one of his lieutenants can go before the ship in the longboat to find the channel and measure the bottom every inch of the way. The coral is sharp and unforgiving and can rip the copper off of a ship and breach the oak in moments.

The *Pandora* comes to a stand, the anchor is let go as the longboat criss-crosses the barely covered reef to search out a channel. It is two days before a way sufficiently deep (no bottom found) is discovered and Edwards is impatient to press on. Experience tells him not to try the passage in the dark; it will be impossible to make out the white water where the waves crash around an almost invisible spur of coral but he is sure of his lieutenant's soundings, though he posts lookouts and stations a trusted hand in the forward chains to throw the lead just to be certain.

The evening breeze lifts and shivers the sails; *Pandora* begins to ease forward into the coral maze. Every eye is straining to catch the least glimpse of surf or of coral rising up out of the ocean. The leadsman's cries become monotonous: one hundred fathoms and no bottom with this line, no bottom with this line, no bottom with this line – then, impossibly, fifty, fifty fathoms and shelving. Edwards bellows orders: 'All aback!' There's no need, every man has heard and races to take in sail and get the headway off her but the coral races faster: thirty fathoms, twenty, twelve, three fathoms and they strike, coming to a shuddering, tearing halt which throws men from their perches aloft and sends the officers sliding along the deck.

For a moment there is silence, then the shouting of orders as men hurry below to check how fast the water is rising in the well of the ship, how big the gash is and if there might be a chance of warping her off in the morning. The prisoners in the *Pandora*, in the utter darkness, have felt the impact and know that the deck is canting under them as they slide in the filthy straw; they shout and plead: 'What's up, mates?' No answer, just the frenzied activity of men trying to stop their ship from going down a thousand miles from anywhere. The carpenter reports: four feet in the well and rising fast; there'll be no saving her. Three of the prisoners, men who Captain Bligh has stated unequivocally are innocent of mutiny but were still kept in the box, are released to help work the pumps, though they won't be much help in their weakened state. The rest are left chained as the *Pandora* begins to settle by the stern. Marines are stationed outside the box and told to shoot if any attempt at escape is made.

Edwards gives his attention to the launching of the boats. The *Pandora*'s armourer's mate goes into the box to open the irons and unlock the chains but, again at Edwards' order, the door is locked shut, trapping him and the prisoners whilst the rest of the crew abandon ship. At the last moment, a master's mate pulls the bolt and opens the door. The mutineers emerge into the moonlight to see surf all around and Edwards sitting in his boat well away from the sinking wreck. They throw themselves overboard and, after a long wait when they have almost given up hope, the circling boats pick them up. Four of the prisoners are still trapped in the box and go down with the ship.

There are four boats and Edwards – this man without irony – realises they will have to take the same route that Captain Bligh was forced to take when he was cast adrift in a long boat by Fletcher Christian and sailed three thousand miles, from the Friendly Islands where the mutiny occurred to the port of Coupang in Timor. Edwards and his flotilla have little more than twelve hundred to make across the Timor Sea before they reach safety.

Mary Bryant

She watches Charlotte playing in the sun in the yard of the house they have been given. Emmanuel staggers round after his big sister, chuckling. They have both filled out after the voyage; everyone has filled out in the weeks they have been here. Most of the gang have found work on the docks loading and unloading the Dutch East India trading ships that call. So far nothing from England and nothing, thank the Lord, from Sydney Cove but Mary knows that sooner or later there will be a vessel from one or the other, since many of the transports that deliver their live cargoes to the colony sail on to China via Timor. Sooner or later they are going to have to face up to the problem of what to do next.

For now, things are fine; Will writes up his log and drinks with the gang and anyone else who'll buy him a rum to hear his version of their adventures, which get wilder with every glass; Mary is a bit of a local character, the young mother and her babies braving the mighty ocean, standing firm by the tiller when all seemed lost and giving the others courage and strength. It isn't untrue; Will has testified to her great spirit and callers come by most afternoons to satisfy their curiosity and leave a gift or two. Everything is found for them, paid by the governor who follows the law of the sea as far as shipwrecked mariners are concerned and accepts that the owners will settle accounts by and by. Will has signed his name and his position aboard the *Neptune* – the brig they have invented and sunk out in the South Pacific – and with their bellies filled, as James Martin says, the men are completely happy.

Mary is not. They can't stay here and the longer they do, the greater the danger their story will be shown up as a lie. She has always been the one with the schemes and the plans but now when she puts them to Will, he shrugs her off. Maybe he'll sign as mate, he says, on a China trader or join a Yankee whaler and go back into the Pacific, there's no Governor Phillip to stop him now; maybe he'll join the pirates or become a smuggler again or just smoke his pipe in a sea-front tavern and yarn with men who understand the sea. Whatever he does, it'll be Will Bryant who decides and not Mary, she had better give her time to the children and forget about all these visitors and presents because if anyone is making too much of themselves, it is her.

They argue, long bitter wrangles that last into the small hours, until Will stops coming back at night, and nothing can be said and nothing decided and Will's drinking gets worse until the day someone taps him on the shoulder and says, 'Good news, matey, your captain and the rest of the crew have arrived.'

Will growls 'What captain? Dam'me. We have no captain!'

Captain Edward Edwards, coming ashore cramped, thirsty (they've been drinking birds' blood and their own piss for some time) and in no very good temper, makes it clear that he is not from the *Neptune*.

Will, deep in drink, is accosted at the tavern and in a torrent of self-justification, frustration and anger, blurts it all out, the whole story, from Sydney Cove to Coupang, three thousand, two hundred and fifty miles and let that infernal bugger who calls himself a captain put that in his pipe and smoke it. Cook himself couldn't have done better. Nor could Will have cooked his own goose more completely.

Coupang is a small town and word spreads fast. Mary grabs the children, a few provisions and runs for the trees. She's come too far, suffered too much to give it all up for Will Bryant's drunken boasting. She doesn't get away; the Dutch have a talent for law and order and the authorities root her out of her hiding place and take her and the children into custody. They are lodged in the castle that overlooks and guards the port and, one by one, questioned.

Captain Edward Edwards

Nobody tries to lie, there isn't much point after Bryant has told the Dutch authorities everything they need to know but, since their grasp of English is slight and they don't appear to have an interpreter, they do no more than note down the generalities and hand the escapers into the custody of Captain Edwards. There is no doubt about either his credentials or his desire to get back home as soon as possible with a little something to offset the embarrassment of losing three ships. The Botany Bay convicts, he thinks, will do very well. He looks them over, has nothing to say to them, sends them back to the castle to wait for their new quarters to be ready.

Edwards inspects the available vessels in Coupang harbour with rather more interest and finds the *Rembang*, which has an extra deck, deep in the belly of the vessel, which is going to be unused on the voyage to Batavia. He reckons he can house the crew of the *Pandora* in the roomy central section, with access to the upper decks; the *Bounty* mutineers will do very well aft, in a cramped, specially strengthened box to remind them, if not fondly, of the *Pandora*; and the Botany Bay escapers can settle forward, in an even more restricted space where the sloping, permanently damp planks squeeze in towards the bow. Irons and chains are stapled securely to the bulkheads, to be attached equally securely to the convicts; and they will need them, some wit points out, here at the sharp end where every pitch and yaw of the *Rembang* will be magnified tenfold.

When they are brought aboard the woman begs for better quarters, for the childrens' sake if not for hers. Edwards reminds her that, had she really wanted better quarters for the children, they were doubtless available at Sydney Cove; it was her choice to leave, she has no one to blame but herself. Besides, the voyage to Batavia is not a long one.

Mary Bryant

Now, after everything that has happened, can she go back into the dark between the decks, into the heat and the filth, to feel the insects crawling over her body again, to reach out blinking in the unaccustomed lamplight for meals, to hold her children and try and tell them what is happening to them, to carry the irons on her legs? It was to escape these things she climbed so high: out of the squalor of the *Dunkirk* in Plymouth, out of the despair of thirteen thousand miles in the *Charlotte*, from starvation at Sydney Cove and the threat of drowning during all those days in the cutter. She has climbed to the stars and now, in irons and shuffling down narrow wooden steps and across oakum-stuffed deck seams, leading her children into the frightful, stinking darkness of the forepeak, she is back where she began and seems to have gone nowhere at all.

Seven adults and two children are crowded into the tiny space. The barred door, built by *Pandora*'s carpenter into the bulkhead, slams shut on their misery. They sit in stunned silence. Yet the children have to be fed and cleaned as well as they can be in these conditions, they have to be talked to, reassured, sung to and rocked to sleep; for Mary the work must be done, there's simply no choice, so she does it.

Outside, in the daylight and warm spicy air of Coupang, the ship is loaded and the decks rumble under the impact of feet and goods being stowed and finally the monotonous rocking of the harbour gives way to a different kind of motion and the shouts of the dockyard mateys and the sailors (somehow the same the world over) and the rattling up of the anchor – loud down here – tells them they are setting out to sea.

Over the following days the all-too-well remembered stink of human beings closely confined builds up, but there is another evil down here which Mary knows is worse than disease and scurvy. She can hear it in their voices and most of all in Will's. He's always been a man for quick thinking and fast action: running a stolen cargo ashore under the moon and pulling a pistol and firing at the revenue men; stepping out from the crowd to make friends with the natives at Sydney Cove and listen to their advice about the fish; deciding to steal the cutter and sail for freedom. He can handle the short haul all right but when the voyage begins to stretch out and the difficulties mount up, he tells himself that it can't be done.

Any number of times on the boat she had to push him and the others to one last effort, another hour's baling and then another and every time they got through but here and now is when she feels it slipping away from Will and some of the others. Whatever she says to encourage them escapes like a fish slithering from a hole in the net; they've given their all and it wasn't enough so they've given in. It's the younger ones who haven't been up and down the hills so many times who feel it most; they still expect something from the world other than hard knocks. They lack the weathering, the sheer stupid refusal to lie down under the pricks and kicks that the older men and Mary have learnt. They may go on moving around, eating, fighting and swearing for weeks to come but the mark is on them and there's only one home they are bound for: their long one. The old lags just grit their teeth and stagger on and Mary cares for the children as best she can.

On the sixth day out the motions of the sea become agitated and their little cell starts to rise and fall alarmingly; they know bad weather is coming and grab hold of whatever they can whilst there is still a chance. Waves start to batter against the wood of the bow, the timbers begin to creak and then scream as they strain and seawater oozes through; the motion gets worse and in the dark all of them are sick, puking up the thin gruel of their rations until their bellies are empty and the deck is swilling with vomit and bile. Mary hangs onto the children, anchored, like the others, directly to the bulkhead by rigid irons. Someone hangs on to her so she isn't thrown about in such a way as to break both her legs. The shaking is enough to shatter the stoutest resolve and the adults howl as loudly as the children, terrified as the power of the storm increases and their tiny cell swoops and plunges until they have no idea what is up and what is down. Then, at the height of one endless rise, the whole ship shudders to a halt and a shock passes through every timber in her, stinging the prisoners with its force, as if the storm wants to smash the *Rembang* to matchwood.

Will knows what it is: she's lost her canvas. There has been a sudden change in the direction of the wind, the sails have been caught aback and, in one unbelievable moment, every shred of canvas she has aloft has been ripped to ribbons, leaving her at the mercy of the storm.

They seem to hang in space forever and then she starts to go down, faster and faster. Surely she must broach and find herself broadside on to the great waves, swamped in a moment by a million tons of water. For the prisoners it's like being dropped in an oak box from a fifty-foot cliff into a whirlpool: their very teeth are shaken lose as the deck comes up and hits them in the face before falling away again. They are going to drown, they must; without any way on her, *Rembang* cannot ride out seas this big. But she does, and in this upside down world of theirs, they learn it is Captain Edwards they have to thank for their lives.

Captain Edward Edwards

he Dutch topmen are hanging onto the spars for dear life, unable to reef the sails before the storm takes them; the *Rembang* is helpless in the face of typhoon winds driving her onto a lee shore. The terrified crew can see the surf breaking over the rocks along the coast of Flores but they can do nothing as the canvas is torn from the eyebolts all around them, taking fingernails and even fingers with it into the night.

It is Edwards' moment. He assumes command and sends *Pandora*'s well-drilled crew into the tops to save what canvas they can and work the ship back out to sea. The *Bounty* mutineers are rousted out of their cell and set, along with the Dutch crew, to the pumps. The fight lasts long and is harder than forty rounds against Mendoza, but in the end, it is the Pandoras, exhausted and bruised, who step up to the mark and the weather which stays down. They may not like their captain but no one wants to drown and their professional pride will not let them lose what would be a fourth ship.

Edwards is determined to get his *Bounty* prisoners back to England and will brook no interference; they are sent, soaking, exhausted and unthanked after a night at the pumps, back to their confinement. The Botany Bay convicts are of less importance; they don't even rate a mention in his report of the incident. The Dutch captain, back in command and thinking of the unimaginable sufferings of a woman with young children in such conditions, offers his cabin for her relief. Edwards will have none of it; they will stay below, locked to the deck by their ankle irons, until the *Rembang* makes Batavia.

No one's reputation is going to suffer as a result of their deaths, whilst Edwards has his career to consider. When the reports are written up for their lordships of the Admiralty and published in the *Gazetteer*, for the instruction of his fellow captains and the general public, he intends to be the hero of the piece. He ends his account of the voyage of HMS *Pandora*: 'should their lordships on the whole think that the voyage will be profitable to our country, it will be a great consolation to your most obedient and humble servant, Edw. Edwards.'

Mary Bryant

Batavia is a city and they've seen nothing like it for years; two fine jetties stretch out into the harbour where ships of every size and nationality are moored, serviced by hundreds of tenders loading and unloading, and with bumboats and boats of pleasure selling their varied wares. Commodious canals run from the harbour through the city and into the country beyond. The streets are laid out in a pattern of squares and fronted by imposing official buildings, tall dwelling-houses, shops and factories; the very air of the place speaks of trade and industry, of elegance and regularity, with wide tree-lined avenues, imposing domes in public places, spacious parks and walks where storied white buildings cast deep black shadows.

There are crowds hurrying to their work or pleasure and the canals are full of lighters conveying trade goods both inward and outward; civil servants crouch over desks in shaded rooms totting up the myriad comings and goings of the Dutch East India Company and filling ledger after ledger with the manifests of its vast fleet. Here, profit is perpetually king and the height of respectability equals the height of the piles of gold hidden in the company vaults. And yet, under it all, beyond the smells of the thousand trades and crafts that are practised, of the kitchens that cook in a dozen different styles and the dens selling dreams in opium, brandy and tobacco, there is something else always present, something disquieting that everybody knows about and nobody seems to mention.

After a while it becomes clear what it is: the smell of death, because Batavia is a city of the dead where citizens drop in the street or into their soup or never wake from their night's sleep, where the funeral carts continually rumble through the midnight streets and bloated bodies float along the canals, gently nudging each other out into the harbour where they bump along ships' fenders before being taken by the tide. For all its sunlight and spices and domes and towers, fever is the master here and it exacts a heavy toll from all travellers.

Mary sits by the cot in the twilight of the hospital looking down at Emmanuel, lying there so serious, older by far than his years; her child, Will's child and now dying. So much a part of her these two years, more the child of the boat journey than of Sydney Cove, because that's where he started to become who he is: curious and brave, rushing off across unknown beaches chasing crabs and grabbing at plants and berries the rest of them dared not eat. She listens to his breath, as she listened in the moments after he was born: in and out, in and out. Then, her fear was that there would be no next breath but there always was and she laughed at her fears or forgot them; now she knows that at any moment the little breath will go out and there will be no more. Just silence.

Mary sits by the cot in the twilight of the hospital looking down at Will, lying there so serious, younger by far than his years; her husband and now dying. His breath is rasping, very different from his son's, but they are both going to the same graveyard, Emmanuel innocent of any crime; Will, knowing that for him there is no going home because, once out of the dark of the forepeak cell he had to face the gaze of the others and their implacable belief that it was his drunken boasting that gave them away and delivered them into Edwards' hands. He knows that as far and fast as he runs, he'll never outrun the brand of being the traitor. He knows that, like so many sailors, his bones will rest in a far country.

Mary wipes the sweat from his forehead, not afraid for herself because she knows she will go home and take Charlotte with her; they will see the bay at Fowey and the fort on the cliff and stand in Readymoney Bay waiting for the sea to throw up Spanish gold. They will walk the cobbled streets and she'll show her daughter the roof beams in the church that open like a mackerel's spine ... and, in that moment, Will is dead and the nuns take over, washing and wrapping the body, taking it and burying it, because if there's one thing they're really good at in Batavia, it's death.

Then it's back to the harbour and the Dutch prison hulk where the rest of the escapers are lodged, at Captain Edwards' pleasure, whilst he books passage for the Cape on three separate ships. After six weeks he finds suitable berths: Mary and Charlotte and William Allen, along with some of the Pandoras, are sent aboard the *Horssen*, where Edwards insists that Mary and Allen are securely ironed and allowed only an hour's airing a day. The rest – Martin, Morton, Bird, James Cox, Nathaniel Lilley and James Butcher – are sent to the *Hoornwey*, put in irons and confined. Captain Edwards travels on yet a third, better-appointed ship, in high comfort and self-regard.

But they do not travel alone: fever, the constant companion ashore, comes too and as the little fleet leaves port, the hectic flush, the swelling of the neck and the supressed cough announce its presence on board.

Walking on deck in the hour allowed before they are locked down for the night, Mary has to hold Charlotte up lest she fall over – her legs keep going from under her, her eyes are glazed and, even in this heat, she is as hot as bonfire. The Dutch master notices the sick child and damning the eyes of the English captain, has Mary released from her irons so she can look after her daughter in a proper cabin.

Able to move more freely around the ship, Mary hears how the others are faring aboard *Hoornwey*: Sam Bird and Will Morton have died of the fever; James Cox, one of the old gang from the days aboard *Dunkirk* in Plymouth harbour before the voyage out, simply walked off the ship's side during evening exercise hour and sank fast and deep under the weight of his irons. He was a lifer, there was no free future that he could see back at Sydney and besides, he was Will Bryant's mate, they had sworn the oath together coming out to New South Wales and now they'll sail their last voyage in company too.

Mary says nothing of this to Charlotte; she wipes a damp cloth across her daughter's forehead and tells her stories about Fowey and the hobby horse and how the saffron bread crackled as it stood cooling on the tiles and of how it was when her mother was a wild girl on the highways.

Captain Watkin Tench

His tour of duty is over and he is going home – more to the point, the promotion point – he is going back to fight the French who killed their king and have every intention of killing King George too, if they can get their nasty republican hands on him.

Before he leaves the settlement – it is December 1791 – he takes a tour of inspection and visits James Ruse, the convict farmer, at Rose Hill. He is one of Governor Phillip's experiments and his land is to be held free of all taxes and quit-rents for ten years, to prove that farming can succeed here. He already has a fine brick-built house and eleven acres under cultivation. He is growing maize and doesn't take to Tench's suggestion that he try vines or tobacco: best stick with what you know, is his credo. He has four breeding sows and thirty fowls and the governor has promised him a convict labourer for Christmas.

There are other farms to examine: Robert Webb, a sailor from the *Sirius*, has set up with his brother to farm sixty acres; Christopher M'Gee is growing wheat, maize and tobacco. When Tench asks how he means to prosper, M'Gee says by industry and hiring all the convicts the governor will allow to work in their free time. Tench thinks that as long as the fellow keeps off the booze, he should succeed; however, that temptation is by now constant as the officers of the New South Wales Corps expand the rule of rum through the fabric of the settlement, to their profit and the ruination of many. Tench is not a moralist, rather a realist, but any fool can see the danger of rum as currency.

On the whole, he agrees with the governor; they must use the talents they have at their disposal, as long as those who possess them show a genuine commitment to reform. In any community like Sydney Cove, there cannot help but be many persons of perverted genius and mechanical ingenuity. He is particularly impressed by Frazer the locksmith, who demonstrated his skills before the governor by opening four unpickable locks with a bent nail in a moment. A little later, when a vital key was lost, Frazer was sent for: he examined the lock, asked for ten minutes to fabricate an instrument to speak to it, and had it open in seconds. A useful man but, like so many, Tench fears, wedded to his villainy even when offered a better and easier path. He once confided that he'd made dies for a gang of forgers, every one of whom had been hanged – except himself.

Tench feels, as he makes his farewell tour, that the convicts are, in many ways, like children: they can be swayed by wonders and tales, by compasses drawn on paper, by a story that gold has been found; they are at one and the same time, brilliant artificers and forgers and astoundingly clumsy; they are noble and self sacrificing and venal and cowardly; they are, in short, pretty much like the rest of humanity. Except, he thinks, for the flash or kiddy language which they use to hide their designs and thoughts from authority. This language has many dialects, each reflecting not only the practice but also the separate legends of the criminal trade. Thus, the footpad operates through brutal ferocity, bludgeoning his victim with his words as much as his club; the pickpocket talks with a dexterity and slight-of-word that reflects his or her gentle touch; the highwayman appears witty and genteel whilst the midnight ruffian is as brief and final as his deadly trade. Tench believes that an abolition of the cant would lead to a better chance of reform, removing the exclusivity and the glamour from the trades of evil.

And yet, being who he is, he cannot resist the chance, whilst visiting Rose Hill for the last time in his life, of seeing the celebrated

Barrington, the prince of pickpockets, who has been in the settlement three months already ... As he writes afterwards, documenting this:

'*I saw him with curiosity. He is tall, approaching six feet, slender, and his gait and manner bespeak liveliness and activity. Of that elegance and fashion, with which my imagination had decked him (I know not why) I could distinguish no trace. His face is thoughtful and intelligent; to a strong cast of countenance he adds a penetrating eye, and a prominent forehead; his whole demeanour is humble but not servile. Both on his passage from England, and since his arrival here, his conduct has been irreproachable. He is appointed High Constable of the settlement of Rose Hill. His knowledge of men, particularly that part of them into whose morals, manners and behaviour he is ordered especially to inspect, eminently fit him for the office. I could not quit him without bearing my testimony that his talents promise to be directed in future, to make reparation to a society, for the offences he has committed against it.*'

Tench boards the *Gorgon* on Sunday 18th December and picks his way through the deck cargo, which bids to recreate the very settlement it is leaving. Kangaroos and opposums, wombats and nondescript birds and snakes and lizards and flying and crawling things and shrubs and plants and trees (eight pine trees) and soils and clay (four casks) are all going back for the amazement of collectors and botanists in Britain. And so is Ralph Clark, back from Norfolk Island. Tench knows, and so does everybody else, that Ralph's non-stop extravagant declarations to his Betsey Alicia back home haven't prevented him taking a convict mistress and leaving her at Sydney with a child, whilst he heads back to his wife and son but nobody criticises: at least, not to his face.

He leans on the rail as they pass through the heads of Port Jackson. It's three years, give or take a month, since he sailed past them first: 'As far from God and the light of heav'n as from the centre thrice to th' upmost pole.' He thinks of the natives, of Bennelong and Aranbanoo and Colby and the others, men he's come to know and respect and concludes that man is basically much the same in Pall Mall as he is in the wilderness of New South Wales and he has no doubt that the progress of reason and the splendour of revelation will one day bring knowledge, virtue and happiness to the land which recedes behind him.

Three months later the flat top of the Cape's mountain guardian come into view and the *Gorgon* lets go its anchor in Table Bay. There is time for visiting and seeing if the same old hands are still nailed to the gallows; for trekking inland to gawp at the animals or strolling amongst the cool gardens and sampling the grapes with Major Ross of the marines, who is a good deal better tempered now he is going home. Lieutenant Clark is overjoyed to find a letter from his wife waiting for him and rushes off to his cabin to write a reply, even though it will be carried home with him on the *Gorgon*.

A couple of days later three Dutch East Indiamen anchor in the bay and a little group of convicts is transferred to *Gorgon* for onward passage to England. Captain Tench finds himself face to face with the escapers: with Mary Bryant, who was in the hulks at Portsmouth, where he was stationed, who went out to Botany Bay on the *Charlotte*, on which he sailed, and now returns with him on the *Gorgon*, though whilst he goes to war and glory, she is surely heading for the gallows and an ignominious end. Not that he can quite believe it so, surely the fates will arrange a different close to this story? In his notes, he writes:

'*I confess I never looked at these people without pity and astonishment. They had miscarried in a heroic struggle for liberty; after having combatted every hardship, and conquered every difficulty. The woman and one of the men had gone out to Port Jackson in the ship which had transported me thither. They had both of them always been distinguished for good behaviour. And I could not but reflect with admiration, at the strange combination of circumstances, which had again brought us together, to baffle human foresight and confound human speculation.*'

It is, he thinks, a fine passage and will set well in his complete account of the English Colony in New South Wales, demonstrating both his sense and his sensibility.

Lieutenant Ralph Clark

 rom his records:

April, Friday 6th	About four o'clock this afternoon got under way – Saluted the fort which the fort returned. NB, this afternoon a child belonging to Cpl Bacon died.
Sunday 8th	Moderate weather a fine breeze – I am in hopes that I shall not be sea-sick as I have not been since we came out this time.
Thursday 12th	Fine weather and a charming trade wind – hope to see St Helena by Sunday afternoon – a few of the small black Pettralss round the ship.
Friday 20th	Fine weather – a great number of flying fish round the ship – Faddy caught a Bonito last night which is the first time that has been caught.
Monday 23rd	Fine Moderate weather – the island of Assention in sight. Made a complaint to Captain Parker of

the Midshipman for being beastly drunk and impertinent – this afternoon the other of the twins of Corporal Bacon died. Several more of the young children I am afraid will die.

May, Tuesday 1st   A light air – the child of Mapp died in the night. Two sharks were caught in the morning – in the belly of one of them was found a prayer book quite fresh not a leaf of it defaced – on one of the leaves was wrote Francis Carthy cast for death in the year 1786 and repreaved the same day at four in the afternoon.

Wednesday 2nd   Fine moderate weather – this morning at a little after six past the line – thank God I am once more in the same hemisphere with my Betsey – at about twelve o'clock the younger boy of Sergeant Devans died – the children are going very fast – the hot weather is the reason of it.

Friday 4th   Squally weather with great deal of rain – last night the youngest child of Jno. Turner died and the body was committed to the deep.

Sunday 6th   Squally weather – last night the child belonging to Mary Broad the convict woman who went away in the fishing boat from P Jackson last year died about four o'clock.

Mary Bryant

harlotte, no less than the rest of them, has been on short rations and water, confined in the dark and eaten by a hundred different insects, and even her child's resilience, recovered in Coupang, is no match for the Batavia fever. She sinks, she falls away from her mother into death and then, wrapped and slid over the side, she slips away into the ocean, a white shape shimmering through the green waves for a moment before being ushered to her deep home by the wings of flying fish. She'll never see the morning sun creep across the harbour now, nor pick up gold in Readymoney Bay, or smell the hot saffron cake fresh from the oven; she'll never watch the mayor and corporation file into the church, nor buy a new bonnet for her wedding.

Mary stands watching, as Captain Parker finishes reading the burial service and his wife looks on, as do some of the officers. Her face is set; she has discovered that there is an end to tears and that in that end, what you do is endure.

She is allowed to stay out of the irons that Captain Edwards recommends for so dangerous a prisoner. The captain on *Gorgon* is no tyrant and he gives her permission to walk the deck, to talk with the other passengers if she, and they, wish. Gradually her health improves as the ship draws nearer England but even when she docks at Portsmouth, Mary is not home by a long mile. She and the other escapers are to be sent to London where they will face justice at the Old Bailey.

It is not a youthful crew that is hustled into the coach by Sir Sampson Wright's police officers on the morning of 11th July 1792. Apart from Mary, who is twenty-three, the rest are getting on, men who have seen a thing or two of life and expect no surprises. William Allen is fifty-five, John Butcher, fifty; Nathaniel Lilley is thirty-nine and James Martin, thirty-two. They have survived so far and have every intention of living a little longer, despite the fact that the penalty for escaping from a sentence of transportation is death. They also know the form, know what is expected of them; they have seen how the passengers on board *Gorgon* have listened to their story, have shed a sentimental tear or two and offered a bumper to their courage. Just as when they were sitting in the cutter approaching Coupang and making up the details of their shipwreck, so now they think about what to say and how to say it because they know, more than most, that in this world it is never a question of guilt or innocence but one of getting away with it or not.

The coach finally clatters over the cobbles into Newgate yard and comes to a swaying halt under the shadow of the forbidding prison walls. The constables swing open the door and escort the prisoners out – into a buzzing, seething crowd of onlookers who utter a collective 'Ahhhh!' when Mary emerges, the little heroine, the convict maid, the courageous young mother who shepherded her infants across the mighty ocean only to lose them in heart-wrenching horror! Hands reach out to touch them, faces push between packed bodies to get a glimpse, their names are called out in supplication, not command. Already, sallow hacks are scribbling copy: 'The resolution displayed by this woman is hardly to be paralleled!!' and 'The men gave themselves up for lost but this Amazon cried "never fear!!"', or 'Her example was followed and the boat prevented from sinking!'.

It is, they are, an event. But they are still in gaol and facing the rope.

James Boswell

I t began with John Reid eighteen years ago, in 1774, back in Scotland when Boswell had seen the power of the establishment at its most unforgiving. In a way, Reid was an old acquaintance: Boswell had first defended him on a charge of sheep stealing in 1766 and finagled a verdict of not proven from the jury, which didn't say Reid was innocent – nobody believed he was for an instant – but that the good men and true couldn't prove it in their own minds to the extent of sending Reid off to eternity. The judges were not pleased and one went so far, whilst giving an opinion on another case, as to say so in court.

And the court doesn't forget. When, eight years later, in '74, Reid faced new charges, the court was determined that this time, and within the law, the law would take its course. Once again Boswell was representing the accused, though the solicitor from the first case had declined to appear in so hopeless a cause: the prosecution lawyers included, amongst others, the Lord Advocate of Scotland, John Montgomery and the Solicitor-General, Boswell's old not-quite-friend,-not-quite-enemy, Henry Dundas. On the bench were Lord Kames and Boswell's strict and terrible father, Lord Auchinleck. It was clear that John Reid, butcher of Hillend, was riding for the long drop.

The prosecution was able to introduce witnesses who testified to the theft and to Reid's habit of rustling sheep. Boswell made it clear that the court was prejudiced against his client on account of the earlier acquittal and that, anyway, the charge of theft was not, strictly, provable. The prosecution accepted the charge of bias, which allowed

them to underline their own conviction that Reid had been guilty in
'66. It was a clear case, Boswell thought, of judges telling a jury what to
think and in his summing up he spoke 'in a very masterly and pathetic
manner which did me great honour as one who wished for free and
impartial trial by jury.' It was a forlorn attempt. The jury didn't need
prompting by the bench to bring in a guilty verdict, after which they
all rushed off to the local pub where they, and Boswell, got drunk at
the court's expense.

The next day the judges sat to pass sentence, which in a case of
sheep stealing (in a nation where sheep were seeing families off the
land) could only be death. Boswell didn't like it; he had always thought
himself able to read men and reading Reid, he was convinced that
though he was a sheep stealer – the man admitted any number of
unaccountable sheep arriving in his shop – on this occasion he really,
truly had been innocent. The actual criminal was one Gardiner, who
had been tried for theft of cloth and transported to America.

It didn't sit well with the judges, who had the feeling that butcher
Reid owed justice a hanging withal and consequently sentenced him
to death. Boswell petitioned the King for mercy, asking that Reid be
transported for life. Whilst they waited for a response, Boswell had
Reid sit for his portrait and, on a number of occasions, sat with him,
chatting about life and death and taking the odd dram. 'I had not
thought how I would drink to John until I had the glass in my hand. I
could not say "Your good health," so I said "Wishing you well," or
some such phrase,' he wrote in his journal.

The portrait sittings proceeded and Boswell hoped any pardon
would arrive after they were finished, which would give the picture the
extra lustre of being done whilst the subject was under sentence of
death. And so it happened: the portrait, a fine likeness, was finished
and no pardon appeared.

Boswell began to wonder if, to save his client, he might have to
resort to reviving Reid after hanging. Could it be done? He had dinner
with Dr Munro, the celebrated professor of anatomy, who gave his
opinion that a man who is hanged suffers a great deal and that,
with the blood being forced up into the brain with great power, it

would prove difficult to recover the victim. Though it might be done, were the neck not broken, as it was in cases of drowning: by heat and rubbing to get the blood moving and blowing air into the lungs by introducing a pipe into the trachea. He also mentioned that a number of his students had, over the last years, tried to revive a number of Boswell's clients *post mortem* but had not, so far, succeeded.

It was not a good omen; it looked like curtains for the butcher, though Boswell was avid to prove to his own satisfaction that the man was innocent and decided to stay by his side up to the final moment, to hear his last words on the subject.

Then a stay of execution of fourteen days arrived and Boswell hurried round to the gaol to present it to Reid: 'The poor fellow was in a dreadful state. He was quite unhinged. His knees knocked against each other, he trembled so; he cried bitterly.' Boswell told him that it was only a stay of execution and that the judges would be sure to speak against it; the gallows still waited, but a little further away. On 7th September 1774, the date originally set for the execution, Boswell confronted Reid with the question of guilt or innocence, recording the details in his journal. 'I had chosen to be with him when two o'clock struck. "John," said I, "You hear that clock strike? You hear that bell? If that does not move you, nothing will. You remember your sentence? This is the day, this is the very time. After this day you are to look upon yourself as a dead man. I think it is your duty to own yourself guilty upon this occasion if you really be so?"'

'Aye, I'm dead in law,' Reid had said, but stuck by his story. He was innocent on that day, in this case. Boswell shot off a quiver full of new petitions but before any hit the target, the King's final decision was through: His Majesty had indeed been inclined to clemency but so strong was the feeling of the Scottish judges in the case, that it could not be done. The original sentence would stand. Boswell got blind drunk, threw candlesticks around the room and shouted at his new wife Margaret. In the morning he apologised and shared his revival-after-death plan with her. She told him to forget it.

On the morning of 17th September Boswell walked down to Grassmarket in Edinburgh and looked at the gallows. He went to the prison at about twelve; Reid had been freed from his irons. His wife was waiting with the white linen clothes – the grave clothes – he would put on before the execution. There was deep settled grief in her face.

Boswell went in to see John Reid who repeated that though he had stolen sheep in his time, he had not stolen these. He then changed into his white clothes. Looking at him, Boswell was struck with a kind of tremor. Reid prayed aloud. 'Grant, O Lord, through the merit of my Saviour, that the day of my death may be the day of my birth into the life eternal.' Then Reid said 'I think I'll be in eternity in about an hour.' He told his wife she was not to be there at his execution. Boswell told him that the executioner was waiting down the hall and that he would tie his arms before he went out.

Reid's wife said 'Aye, to keep him from catching at the tow.'

Boswell agreed. 'Yes, that it may be easier for him.'

Two o'clock struck and Boswell said: 'There's two o'clock.'

A sheriff's officer came in and said: 'Will you come away, now,' and the party went out of the room and down the stairs. Boswell noticed a pretty, well-dressed young woman and her maid standing, watching. Other prisoners formed an audience. There was no sound at all, a dead silence.

The hangman, who was waiting in a small room, came out, took off his hat and bowed to the prisoner. Reid bowed back. The two men stood looking at each other until Boswell told Reid he should feel no resentment against the hangman who was only doing his duty. The hangman then said: 'I only do my duty.'

Reid said 'I have no resentment against him.'

Boswell asked the sheriff's officer to give the man another glass of wine. This was done and Reid drank to his friends and kissed his wife. He seemed deep in thought.

The prison door opened and Reid went outside with the hangman. His wife went to the window and cried, 'Oh let me up,' and watched until her husband was lost to sight.

It was a fine day and the sun shone brightly. Boswell stood amongst the crowd around the scaffold. When the cart arrived, Reid showed great calm but just before climbing the steps, he asked to see his wife and children again. He was told they were not here. He went on up and stood under the rope calmly whilst the black hood was put over his face. Just before the hangman pulled the lever, he seemed about to speak. Someone in the crowd shouted 'Pull up his cap.' The hangman did so.

Reid said 'Take warning. Mine is an unjust sentence.'

The hood was pulled down and he was sent off. For a moment his feet scrabbled for a hold, then he was still. The body hung for three-quarters of an hour. In the crowd Boswell could hear voices arguing: 'He said his sentence was just,' 'No, he said it was unjust.'

Boswell saw Mrs Reid and told her that her husband behaved as well as they could wish. There was a sort of dull grief upon her. He felt a gloom come upon him and he went home but found his wife no comfort. She told him that he had carried his zeal for Reid too far and hurt his own character. She said that she thought Reid was guilty.

The next morning a friend called by and whilst talking of Reid told Boswell, 'Well, God has blessed you with one of the best hearts that ever man had.'

It had begun with John Reid, eighteen years ago, but now, he decides, it will go on with the prisoners from Botany Bay. Their story, as much of it as has spread through gossip and the public prints, intrigues him: it has all the elements of stirring drama and high romance with the chance to break a lance for justice against the powers that have, over the years, frustrated all his efforts to gain a place in the world for himself. And there is the woman, Mary, 'the convict maid', whose courage has inspired the men around her to do great things, to be more than they are. Maybe even now, after all is said and done, maybe she can inspire him to rise to one more challenge. And besides, that old sober-sides Henry Dundas is the secretary of state at the Home Department (succeeding Tommy Townshend) and it will be no end of a hoot to annoy him, particularly since he has just remarried a rich and pretty woman! And it will get Boswell out the house and give him a rest from his daughters Veronica and Euphemia, who are all very well but no company for a man of the world. Then there's his old friend Temple, whose wife has died after a short illness, and Boswell knows how terrible an affliction that can be – though Mrs Temple was a woman of less than pleasant temper, as even her husband had to admit. So Boswell has promised to go and stay with his friend and tour Cornwall in the near future but for now, a cause beckons. He calls for his jacket, picks up his stick and sets off for Newgate, where Mr Kirby the keeper knows him well and will, he's sure, grant him an interview with the escapers.

Mr Kirby welcomes his old friend (and fellow death-aficionado) but is a little surprised as they drink a dish of tea in the drawing room of his quarters – at least, Boswell does, since the keeper never takes tea but once a year – on learning his guest's intent. He is not here to see the aristocrats or the High Tobys waiting for the drop but to meet the Botany Bay escapers. Kirby takes him through to the woman's quadrangle where Mary Bryant has somewhat better quarters due to the small sums collected on her behalf soon after her arrival. Kirby has no doubt that more will be subscribed and tells his guest that the woman considers her lodgings at Newgate a thousand times better than those to which she is used.

Face to face at last. It is clear at once that Mary Bryant has no idea who the corpulent (the drink is catching up with him, though he's not aware of it and still thinks himself the slender Jamie of thirty years past) gentleman might be. He doesn't mind and is happy to explain, with that friendly manner of his, his ability to make it seem that Mary is the one object of all his attention and care at this moment, that he is a lawyer, a man of some distinction in the literary world ('Dr Johnson? No?') and that he has taken an interest in her case.

She tells him that quite a lot of gentlemen have taken an interest in her case and in few other parts too; she has been gazed at, mooned over, propositioned, touched, nudged, nuzzled and interviewed without pause since getting off the boat and she is beginning to feel that her head will soon start spinning like a top. She is, however, polite. Mr Boswell has no need to remind her that the scaffold is no longer built at Tyburn but next door in Newgate Yard, nor that she could easily find herself standing under it in a week or two and end up cold meat in some resurrection man's larder.

She's no beauty, the years between decks and under the sun of the Southern Ocean, the loss of two children and a husband, the world itself, have seen to that: but there is something about her. She has been to lands that few have visited, she has sailed seas that have made men weak and there is, in her calm, grey eyes, an acceptance of things as they are that makes him believe her when she tells him that now she is so near home, she would rather die than go back to Sydney Cove.

All his life, Boswell has been looking for something certain. He thought, once, that the quality may have resided in his father but he was wrong; he came close to finding it in Samuel Johnson but that man was too great ever to succumb to the temptation of omniscience and yet here, in this convict woman, he can glimpse a part of it. He knows he will never attain certainty himself but he can see it and find some comfort in the fact that it does exist in this world.

He says none of this because the woman would not understand, and if she did, then the whole idea would pop like a soap bubble. He says instead that he will help her and that she will not hang and that he will do everything in his power to see that she, and the others, are granted a pardon.

She smiles politely and thanks him for his efforts; she doesn't really believe anything will come of it; he can see that and doesn't press the matter. He leaves her some money to pay the keeper for better conditions and food and takes his leave. Outside he reflects that has just spent an hour with a young woman and not once thought about buying her favours. It won't last, he tells himself as he rings for Mr Kirby and goes through to the men's quad where he interviews the male escapers about their experiences and about Mary. They are no fools either; they know quite well that the convict maid is their best key to the locks on this place and they supply the gentleman with what he needs: 'Ahhh, sir, she showed greater courage and resource than any of us! You should've seen her with the children!'

The next day Boswell attends the hearing before Magistrate Bond. It is going to be quite a show and despite his stick and (he believes) his fame, the great biographer is pinned somewhere near the back of the heaving, sweltering crowd as Mr Bond enters with his various functionaries and seats himself behind his oak desk. The audience falls silent under his professional glance: this, he seems to be saying, is not a circus, it is business, the business of the law. Boswell catches his eye and nods – Bond (a slight acquaintance) nods back and calls for the accused to be brought out. They have been waiting for hours; they were brought across from the prison itself just after dawn. Their comfort is not at question here – only their presence.

Boswell sees the effect this strange young woman has on the crowd and is more than ever determined to do something for her. The men repeat their account of how Mary gave them the courage to go on in the face of impossible seas, and state that they would all rather face the gallows than see Sydney again. Mr Bond says he is not yet ready to send them for trial, and they are to be returned to Newgate and recalled to face further examination next week. Boswell prompts the starting of a collection for the unfortunates and Mr Bond allows it to be taken and the money passed to the prisoners before they leave.

Editorial opinion in the *London Chronicle* is agreed on the case:

> '*It was remarked by every person present, and by the magistrate, that they never saw people who bore stronger marks of sincere repentance, and all joined in the wish that their past sufferings might be considered as a sufficient expiation of their crimes.*'

> '*His Majesty is ever willing to extend his mercy. Surely there have never been objects more worthy of it!*'

At their second appearance, Magistrate Bond sends them to the Old Bailey where they are put to the bar and, in double quick time (no trial necessary) are directed to remain on their former sentence until they should be discharged by due course of law; that is, serve out their original terms, from the time of their escape. It's better than death, and they aren't being sent back – the judge is as quick as anyone at picking up the general sentiment and doesn't want his coach pelted with orange peel, rocks and dead rats on his journey home – but for the lifers, it's not much. Even for Mary, it's hard to think of the years ahead in Newgate or some infinitely worse gaol in the provinces where every month will pass like a year.

Boswell promises she won't go down, he'll work for a free pardon; no one, he tells her, can read the signs of the times better than he and he knows those signs are propitious. She looks at him blankly. 'Good,' he says, 'the signs are good.' She shrugs. She will be free, he says, but she can only look at him and say that she was free in the cutter, sailing unknown seas, but now she is back in prison. It doesn't matter very much to her what might happen one day – all she knows is what is happening today. Boswell tells her not to give up hope and goes away.

He sets to and writes a letter to Secretary Dundas. It's true, they don't like one another: Dundas is not a clubbable man, he represents in Boswell's mind the very structure of authority that bears down upon him and the ordinary folk. He is quite aware that Dundas thinks him a clown, a fool who has wasted his talents, but they are both Scotsmen and went to the same school and if Boswell can swallow his pride to the extent of asking for a meeting, surely Dundas can (not swallow, the man has so much pride he'd choke on it) but at least set aside a corner, a moment, to see the great biographer. And so it is: the secretary of state sends a note of the time and place. It is going to mean Boswell putting back the start of his trip to Cornwall to comfort his old friend Temple and, perhaps, write a new tour of the West Country. However, the cause is good and Temple can be dreary and self-righteous so a few days less of his company can be borne.

Boswell presents himself at the Home Department and a clerk asks him to wait and wait he does, for hours, until it is quite clear that Dundas is not going to see him. It is a blow to the face and leaves Boswell in a fury. He rushes home and scratches out a furious letter.

The next day, Dundas sends round a note saying that he will duly consider the matter of the Botany Bay prisoners but giving no date or undertaking in the matter and leaving little doubt that some time must pass before things can be bought to a head.

Boswell sets off for Cornwall with Veronica and Euphemia, stopping on the way to visit his youngest daughter Betsy who is staying with a Mr Williams, the father of a school friend. He is pleased at the way Betsy's accent has become thoroughly English, as have her manners – she is even a bit frosty; in fact, come to think of it, the general atmosphere has a touch of winter about it. Concerned, he asks Betsy if anything is wrong, if perhaps she'd prefer to leave and come to Cornwall with him.

Indeed she would not, especially so after the exhibition her father put on last time she visited him at home (an evening out from boarding school) in the company of her friend Miss Williams! The cold begins to seep into Boswell's bones as he tries to remember the occasion and can't, which generally means he was a little muddled: that is to say, stewed as a prune. With the chilly disapproval and the long-suffering, narrow-lipped, eye-rolling sense of permanent injury that only a teenage daughter can summon up, Betsy informs him that on that occasion, after dinner, when he had taken too much wine, he had been over fond to her friend Miss Williams. And that Miss Williams complained of the matter to Betsy and to their boarding mistress back at school.

And Miss Williams is how old? Fourteen! Oh, what a sad degradation of character and, almost worst of all is that Betsy makes allowances and assures him that, though she is angry, she did persuade Miss Williams not to mention the matter to her father.

Reflecting that girls are so much more forward in their understanding than boys, he bids Betsy and the Williams' family farewell (Miss W is a remarkably attractive girl, so at least his taste, if not his self-control, is still good) and continues on his way to Cornwall, stopping off at friends and acquaintances on the way.

Cornwall and the Temples are welcoming. Down west, Boswell really is the great biographer and with no buffoonery and standing on chairs to set against his reputation, he is lionised, exhibited, fed and flattered, though the Cornish are perhaps a little tight with both the drink and the witty conversation and his mind does begin to rust in all the damp weather.

Temple, though, is far more relaxed than he had been in London and the two old friends sort through their correspondence and discuss Henry Dundas, who has not, so far, done anything for the Botany Bay convicts. They wonder how the man has done so well, given that back in college he had always seemed so inferior. Boswell is concerned that their old enemy might not bother with the Bryant matter but resolves to keep at the task until some good is produced.

He does not visit Fowey to see Mary Bryant's family though what intelligence he receives – a friend of Temple's says they are sheep rustlers – does not leave him full of confidence; he decides that should Mary get her pardon it might be better if, for a while at least, she stays under his protection in London.

In turn, he also wonders if his daughters might stay under Temple's protection for a while in Cornwall; it would keep them out of trouble and out of his wig. Temple's daughter Nancy has not changed her opinion of the Misses Boswell since her London visit and is not keen for more of their company: can one image anything more absurd, she complains, than a woman almost six feet tall blubbing because the sea is rough, or her silly sister running away from a man on a horse all terrified and alarmed and tearing her dress to tatters on thistles? These town manners will not do for Cornwall and Victoria and Euphemia return the sentiment. Boswell and Temple think the young women dote on each other. Miss Nancy thinks Boswell a curious genius, forever falling in love and wittering on about whichever angelic creature has caught his fancy. In a man of more than fifty, it is folly. She wishes him and his daughters gone almost as much – she thinks – as they themselves want to be away.

Back in London, Boswell calls on Evan Nepean at the Home Department. The old fixer tells him that government does not want to treat the Botany Bay people with harshness; the secretary's opinion inclines towards mercy but mercy tempered with time; let the escapers' story fall out of the headlines and new gossip take its place, so that no one else in New South Wales thinks a jaunt of three thousand miles in an open boat will win them freedom, and then the hand of kindness will be extended.

Boswell keeps up a steady drizzle of notes, just to let the hand of kindness know that someone is watching and waiting.

Arthur Phillip

overnor Phillip takes up his pen to write to Henry Dundas at the Home Department. The letter is dated October 1792. Outside, it is hot, almost impossible to breathe. Inside his study in Government House it is a little cooler though Phillip still sits uncomfortably on his chair; in fact, he hasn't been comfortable or relaxed for as long as he can remember. He has a constant pain in his side and, though he falls into his bed every night on the verge of exhaustion, he never seems to get a good night's sleep or wake refreshed. Over the past two years he has written endless letters asking to be relieved and allowed to return home; no positive answer has been received. He sighs and nods to his secretary and begins to dictate, reviewing in his mind's eye, the colony as it is today, almost five years after the first landing.

Despite the years and the progress, he notes that they are still short of some of the most basic items: iron cooking pots, cross-cut saws, axes; the clothes that are sent out are often worse than useless, falling apart at the first washing and now the colony is clothing thousands rather than hundreds, this is a matter of deep concern. So is the state of much of the flour that arrives: even though it is guaranteed by the merchants as first quality, it arrives as anything but – not that this stops them claiming full payment for the goods.

There are many things the colony still needs, he points out, particularly livestock in a healthy condition to populate the country, and it is vital that government understands the need to supply as efficiently and quickly as possible those articles which are still necessities because –

and he has emphasised this point again and again – the colony, if given a fair chance, will climb to its feet and stand fair as something a great deal more than just a convenient prison.

Going to the window and looking through the flaws in the thick glass he can see a town that is growing: three acres of it by now, with brick-built houses, many with fence-lined gardens; the hospital with its own gardens, six acres growing vegetables and fruit; shops selling trade goods and others selling beer though hard liquor is still forbidden to most but sold to many, under the counter, by the officers of the New South Wales Corps.

At Rose Hill, renamed Parramatta, where conditions are kinder, there is a small village, barracks and hospital, a public hall, almost a thousand acres under official cultivation and, better yet, four hundred acres being worked by settlers, either time-served convicts or marines and sailors who have decided to stay. And the farmers are learning to live with the land and climate rather than fight it by trying to impose the seasons and customs of Britain. Their produce is carted along a newly finished road between Parramatta and Sydney or down the river in boats built in the colony's own yards.

Above all, perhaps, as Phillip looks out at his settlement, it is the children, who now number more than three hundred, who point to the future. Far fewer infants die here than back in Britain; they thrive in the open air and have already begun to colonise the beaches when they are let out of school.

The bay is seldom empty of ships; many are transports arriving from England with more convicts but others are trading vessels, making landfall at what is becoming a convenient staging post on the voyage east. Here they can renew their water, buy in fresh vegetables; soon they will be able to buy livestock and take trade goods on board. There is also a constant trade in knowledge, as new animals, plant species and seeds are sent back to the cold north.

The governor is particularly concerned about the health and fate of the kangaroo he dispatched recently. He has heard that 'Governor Phillip's Kanguroo' has been valued at £500. He protests – he is not a showman, the kangaroo is not be exhibited as a curiosity, it is to be treated well and have a private room with a warm fire in cold weather; he knows the beasts enjoy the heat as he has four of his own which always sleep in front of the kitchen fire. He also has a fruit bat which hangs happily around his study ...

There is still crime in the colony, there always will be. Constant petty theft and minor violence, illegal brewing, escape attempts aboard visiting ships. The master of the transport *Britannia* spent the night ashore and whilst he slept, his watch and knee-buckles were stolen from his bedside and have not been seen since. One or two of the more daring or desperate convicts have escaped to the bush where they range dangerously and prey on the unwary.

And, as always, there are the thousand and one little tasks that keep the system oiled, from the judiciary to the commissary; from the church to the ships in the cove; from the baptismal figures to the burials; from government salaries to pardons and the appointment of trusted convicts to public posts: each one of them requires that the governor consider the matter and give a decision, often in writing. He is exhausted and would have left before now, except that he was determined to leave the colony in the state he has so long and anxiously wished to see it. He awaits conformation – he doesn't ask for permission – of his decision to take leave of his task. He knows the letter will not arrive on the desk of Henry Dundas for months, possibly even after he has presented himself at the Home Department, because he has made up his mind to go home.

At six o'clock on the evening of Monday 10th December, Governor Phillip becomes plain Captain Arthur Phillip when he hands over his charge to Major Francis Grose, Deputy Governor and Commander of the New South Wales Corps. He steps aboard the transport *Atlantic* as the corps parade and a salute is fired. With him are the natives Bennelong and Yemmerrawannie, who are curious about the place beyond the sea from which these new people have come and have accepted his invitation to have a look at it.

As he passes through the heads of Port Jackson, even his supremely controlled and reasonable mind is pray to a storm of emotions;

he knows the colony will flourish but under other men's hands and he's certain that they, and not he, will gain the honour. And he's not dead to the idea of glory, the sudden moment of inspiration or wild courage that drove him to pit his frigate against a Spanish battleship or prompted him to walk along the beach beside the dead whale to reclaim his friendship with Bennelong at the risk of an eight-foot spear. He has always wanted glory. He has never courted it or schemed for it and in his day-to-day life he has always seemed the least glorious, the most prosaic of men, but all the same the spark is there, glowing deep within the wood and one day it will ignite and ... and what?

At home there is war with France, the chance to find a ship and take it into battle, to win a victory that isn't hidden in the secret world of intelligence or behind the seemingly dull task of transporting eight hundred prisoners halfway around the world. Granted, he's not a well man and he's been away, out of the mind's eye of the Lords of the Admiralty. Other, younger men are making their mark as fighting captains whereas his name is linked with organisation and governance; worthy objects, to be sure, but never dashing. But there is still a chance, he is convinced of it; just let him find a command and crew to lead ...

The coast of New South Wales falls away as the *Atlantic* heads west and for home. Bennelong and Yemmerrawannie are fascinated by the working of the ship; they are familiar with the colony's smaller boats but this is on a different scale and they have a thousand questions that Phillip must answer. He promises them that they will meet the King and that they can go home whenever they wish. He also has reports to write and letters and notes on his recommendations, and visits to make at every port of call and dinners to attend and give and time passes, as it does at sea, until, after a voyage a good deal less difficult than the trip out, the *Atlantic* enters the port of Falmouth, Devon on 20th May 1793.

Arthur Phillip clambers carefully down the raked sides of the ship and steps into the tender which takes him on the short, choppy journey to the port steps; as he climbs the wet, seaweedy stone, he looks around: it is a cold day with sea mist still hanging above the hard and in the eves of the dockside taverns and warehouses. There is a smell of tar and bilge water, tobacco and dung, ale and smoke from a hundred fires; it is a world away from Sydney Cove and as he makes his way to the inn where the London coach waits to start its journey (*Deo Volente*), Arthur asks himself, what now ...

Mary Bryant
alias Broad

WHEREAS *Mary Bryant alias Broad, now a prisoner in Newgate, stands charged with escaping from the persons having legal custody of her before the expiration of the term for which she had been ordered to be transported AND WHEREAS some favourable circumstances have been presented unto us on her behalf, inducing us to extend our Grace and Mercy unto her and to grant her our free pardon for her said crimes, OUR Will and pleasure therefore is that you cause the said Mary Bryant alias Broad to be forthwith discharged out of Custody and that she be inserted for her said crime in our first and next general pardon that shall come out for the poor convicts in Newgate without any condition whatsoever; and for so doing this shall be your warrant, GIVEN at our court of Saint James's the Second Day of May 1793 in the Thirty-Third year of our reign,*
By His Majesty's Command
Henry Dundas[10]

Mr Boswell reads it to her and at first she can't take it all in, the words seemed mixed up, like fish in a net, slippery and sliding here and there, looking like one thing and then another. He reads it again, slowly, and tells her she has been pardoned by the King. She may not be able to read but she can count and tells him that her original sentence would have finished six weeks ago. He says that she is, in many ways, better off since she is not in New South Wales and is no longer just another convict woman but has a measure of fame. She tells him she doesn't care for it and asks about the others. He tells her that nothing has been heard yet, their cases are still under consideration. He has high hopes, though and thinks the delay is due to government not wanting to seem too kind to escapers. He is, he tells her, writing a draft of a new petition for the four men. They will, he hopes, be free by and by; but Mary is free now. What does she intend?

She doesn't know what she wants but she does know what she doesn't want: to go back to Cornwall. For any number of reasons she isn't ready to face them yet; all those people who know what she has done. She wants ... she wants to sit in a room and go in and out through the door, which she will open and close. She wants to look out of a window that doesn't have bars on it; she wants to walk in a street that has tall buildings on either side; she wants hustle and bustle, crowds and markets and she wants a room of her own where she can sit quietly and drink real tea.

Mr Boswell tells her she can have all of these things, for the while at least, since he is going to collect some money for her support. There is a room in Little Titchfield Street near to his own house where she can lodge and she will be hardly five minutes from Oxford Street where they have some of the most wonderful shops in the world, and she will be able to entertain herself for months just looking at the wonders in their windows and the high change of the walkers and strollers. He supposes she hasn't had much chance to follow fashions in Sydney, or since, but things are altering rapidly: necklines are down, stomachs are out, it's all a touch provoking for a gentleman but she will, no doubt, find her own way amongst the follies and furbelows and – he adds, emphasising his words – Mrs Bryant will do well to steer the most respectable of courses, so as not to disappoint those who have reposed their confidence in her.

If nothing else, this tells Mary that Mr Boswell probably doesn't want to claim his reward in bed; he is acting out of the goodness of his heart, for no reward other than to do something fine. She has little she can offer in return, since little has been left to her over these months but she does still have a packet of the leaves they used to make tea in the settlement and she gives them to him. Then she asks him not to call her Mrs Bryant, since she would rather not remember her husband Will and all the times they had together: especially the last times, in Batavia, when his words sentenced them to a worse punishment at the hands of Captain Edwards than anything she'd known at Sydney.

He agrees and stands and says nothing, waiting for her. She realises she is free to go, that for the first time in over seven years she can decide to stand up and go out of the room, collect her few belongings and leave the building, climb into a coach and go home. It is for her to say and so she says: it is time to go. Mr Boswell escorts her from the Women's Quadrangle, through the great yard and out into a city alive with the smells and sights and sounds of freedom.

James Boswell

here's something about her. He can't quite put his finger on what it is, though he's thought about her long and hard; perhaps it is her single-minded pursuit of one thing: to get back home.

He's always wanted so much, so many things, most of which have slipped from his fingers or passed him by and those he has – Johnson and the great biography, though bringing renown and fame, second edition now printing; Malone furious at Boswell's new preface puffing himself and his abilities – are somehow, for all their prodigality, in the wrong currency. He's perpetually a traveller in the land of gold with a handful of tin. And yet, what to do with Mary? He knows there'll be gossip, he's waiting for it and, in a way, won't be sorry to see and hear it; he does have a reputation to keep up, even under false pretences.

He reflects that gossip is a shifting thing, it comes and it goes and though Mary must finish her journey and go to Cornwall, she doesn't want to go yet. She's happy with her room in Little Titchfield Street where she can receive visitors and drink her tea and she has confided in him that she does not want to see her people at present. Who can blame her – how will they look at her after all she has been through and done? She was, after all, a highway robber and convicted to the hulks; on the other hand, she is something of a figure now and Boswell is aware how that can change many things, though not the gossip of the village. Sooner or later Mary will have to face it but not just now. She can have her time in the city and Boswell will find the money to pay for it.

Mary Broad

She turns right outside her door, walks a few paces to the end of the road, turns left and walks up to Oxford Street in under a minute. It's everything she always dreamed a city would be. It takes almost an hour to stroll from end to end. She passes brightly shining street lights, under which beautifully lacquered coaches gleam as they wait for custom. There is easily room for two coaches and chairmen to pass one another on the street and on the flagstoned pavement, well away from the mud, whole crowds can stand together gazing into the shop fronts in comfort.

She looks into a watchmaker's window, into a silk and fan store, then a silversmith's and a china and glass shop. Such lovely things to be had here. The spirit booths are particularly wonderful, with crystal flasks of every shape and size lined up in front of lights which glimmer and glitter through the many coloured spirits like a church window in the sun. She thinks Will would have thought he was in heaven here. She likes the confectioners and fruiterers, where, behind the polished glass windows, pyramids of pineapples, figs, grapes, oranges and all manner of fruits are on show. She asks the prices and after the shopkeeper has found his way through her accent, he tells her six shillings for a fine pineapple that comes from 'the other side of the world, my sweet'! But most of all, she loves the shop which sells the Argand and other lamps: it's on a corner with two windows facing out like a lighthouse, each filled with crystal, lacquer and metal lamps and silver and brass in every possible shade, filling dull afternoons and dark evenings with dazzling light.

James Boswell

e's collecting contributions from friends and acquaintances and has a sheet set aside, headed: Mary's money. When he asked former Lord Chancellor Lord Thurlow, his lordship growled: 'Damn her blood, let her go to a day's work!' It was no more than a few minutes work for Boswell to recite the details of the convict maid's story in his most pathetic tones, before sentiment got to work on the crusty old lawyer and produced tears and money. He writes to his friend Temple but gets a less than enthusiastic response; the country vicar brings up the Broad family reputation as sheep stealers as the reason that his local collection is less than might be hoped. Even so, there is money and time for Mary to come, at last, to a halt and recollect herself.

Her companions are still inside the walls of Newgate and Boswell has not forgotten them. In conversation with Lady Hope Dundas, the new wife of his old enemy, he mentions how very helpful it would be if she could, perhaps, prompt Henry to reconsider the official position and give to the poor wretches a glimmer of hope ... She freezes him out, coldly informing Mr Boswell that it is a rule of hers never to mention official matters to her husband.

He turns instead to Governor Arthur Phillip, and pays him a visit to talk over the case. The governor is something of a celebrity himself, being shown in various drawing rooms accompanied by his natives from Botany Bay who, alas, do not appear to society to have the same degree of *bella figura* as Sir Joseph Banks's native, the Tahitian Omai with his tattoos and easy charm. The novelty of the newcomers is not expected to last the season; as for the gentlemen themselves, Bennelong and Yemmerrawannie are less than enchanted with the virtues of London. It seems to them that the way of life of most of the poor souls who labour their days away for gin and pence is far inferior to their own; sometimes the air itself is hardly fit to breathe and they both look forward to going back again, though Yemmerrawannie has the beginnings of a nasty cough.

Captain Phillip is anxious to regain his health and resume his career in the navy but gives a morning to the great biographer. There is not much he can add to the facts as far as they have been presented; he had little to do with the Bryants or any of the other escapers at Sydney Cove, though he did promulgate the law by which no time-served person was to leave dependants upon the charge of the colony. Boswell wonders if this – Will Bryant's often voiced intention of quitting the settlement without his wife – has something to do with Mary's dislike of her married name. Governor Phillip can offer no opinion on the matter, though, as a reasonable person who believes in the power of man to reform himself, he does not oppose Boswell's efforts for those still in Newgate; no doubt their experience will have led them to a better understanding of their place and potential in the world. And certainly, as the two men talk, it becomes clear that both understand that few are better placed than Evan Nepean, to influence the course of policy. Boswell has already penned the draft of a petition concerning the prisoners and recorded it in his journal:

Case of the Convicts who Escaped from Botany Bay

General Observations
Not one of these poor men has been either a highwayman or a housebreaker [not quite true but he hopes no one will check]. Their offences, though justly punishable, have been of a slighter degree of malignity. For this they have atoned: by an imprisonment before trial – by a confinement on board the hulks at Portsmouth – by a severe passage to New South Wales – by servitude and almost starvation there – by a series of the most distressful sufferings in the course of making their escape – by imprisonment since,

in the gaol of Newgate. They did certainly in the impatience of misery subscribe a petition to have their wretched captivity exchanged for a situation on board his Majesty's Fleet. But it is humbly submitted to Government whether they should not have a second chance to be good members of society and be permitted to do the best they can for themselves and their families. It should seem to be of the genius of our constitution to act with mildness and compassion where there is no obvious call for severity.

Particulars

William Allen, born at Kingston-upon-Hull, in his fifty-sixth year, served both the last wars in His Majesty's Fleet under Captain Moutray in the Ramilles _and, after he was broke, Captain Marriot and Admiral Graves. Was in her when she was cast away. 'Water I must follow' are his words but would rather go where he can get most of it, viz, in a merchantman. 'I have the world to begin again.' Has a wife at Beccles in Suffolk, from whom he has heard since he came home._

John Butcher, born in the Parish of Kidderminster, Worcestershire, in his forty-ninth year, was always a husbandman, unmarried. Has heard from Mr Woodward, who keeps the Lion at Kidderminster, Would be kindly received and get his bread in his own country.

Nathaniel Lilley, born at Sudbury in Suffolk, in his thirtieth year, by trade a weaver and fishnet maker. Has a wife and four children (one since his return home). Has an uncle, Richard Wardell, who married his aunt, who is a cabinetmaker and joiner in Gatney Street, Pimlico, no.4, and a brother, Robert Angus, who is a waiter at —— in Old Russell Street, corner of New Hummums, who married his sister who keeps a laundry. By these he would be supported and put in the way of getting a livelihood by means of his own trade. In the meantime he has worked night and day in gaol as a net-maker to support his family, being employed by Mr Mason, Fleet Street.

James Martin, born at Balymenoch, county of Antrim, Ireland, in his thirty-sixth year, by trade a bricklayer and mason. He worked in England *seven years before the misfortune happened to him. Has a wife at Exeter from whom he has heard several times, also one child, a son. Could get a guinea a week, being a very good workman, as he proved when at Botany Bay, where he had worked a great deal for the settlement. Is willing either to return to his own country, where his mother, brother and sister are – and he has heard from them – or he will get work in London.*

All of them would go to sea in any manner that Government thinks fit rather than remain in prison. But it is hoped that in recognition of their extraordinary sufferings, they will be allowed to do the best they can for themselves, in an honest way.

Conclusion

It is therefore earnestly requested that in this extraordinary case the clemency of the Crown may be benignantly exercised.

Once more government is concerned not to appear too clement to escapers but it does seem as if the message is getting through and that, in a few months, the men will be released once the case is well and truly forgotten, so Boswell is less than pleased when a canting, versifying friend brings the case back into the public eye by producing some insolent sentiments on the supposed love between the Convict Maid and the Great Biographer as they meet upon a McHeathian scaffold:

> *Great in our lives, and in our deaths as great,*
> *Embracing and embraced we'll meet our fate:*
> *A happy pair, whom in supreme delight*
> *One love, one cord, one joy, one death unite!*
> *Let crowds behold with tender sympathy*
> *Love's true sublime in our last agony!*
> *First let our weight the trembling scaffold bear,*
> *Till we consummate the last bliss in air!*

Crass but effective, and there are those who say no more than a just repayment for Boswell's verses on Johnson and Mrs Thrale. He doesn't care overmuch – the verses will not last and he has a drink or two to wipe the matter from his mind and decides to visit Mary to reassure her: though since she cannot read, perhaps she needs none.

He weaves his way along Little Titchfield Street towards her door; it's late, he should be home he should be anywhere but here, when a hand taps him on the shoulder – 'Ho, Cully, let me give you a hand, you looks a trifle shaky' – and whack! The pavement comes up to meet him and rough hands go through his pockets as he is expertly rolled and filleted of money and watch and fine linen. Hours later, though it might be minutes to his disordered mind, a passer-by helps him to his feet and walks him the hundred yards or so to his own door.

Inside, to much wailing and moaning, it is found he has a deep cut and bruising to the back of his head and more bruises on his arms, where they were roughly grasped. He can remember nothing except the hate on the face of the man who knocked him down and as he lies in bed, his confusion deepens as the fever rises: what if he'd been killed whilst he was drunk? What sort of state is that to arrive in before the awful judgement of God; and worse, imagine the embarrassment of being unable to answer the charges or make a plea for mercy without slurring the words. And then there are the men in Newgate: were they not robbers, was Mary not a highway robber, knocking down some poor soul for a shawl and a bonnet? But it cannot be, circumstances alter cases and he would do well to consider his own position, trembling like the tiny spider held on the shovel over the roaring fire. He will be a changed man from now on: no more excessive indulgence in wine. This is a crisis in the life of the biographer.

A few days later, when the event is noted in the press, some hack writes: 'Mr Boswell's death would have caused a vacancy in the mirth as well as the instruction of the nation.' He isn't quite sure whether this is affectionate or not, but, on rising from his bed a week later, turns his attention to the second edition of the *LIFE*, which is selling well. Even so, he can't seem to shake off a general feeling of depression – everything he does, he does wearily.

Then, in August, a gentleman – though not quite a gentleman – presents himself at the front door. He says his name is Kestle and that he is a glazier at 12 Cross Street, in Carnaby Market; Mr Boswell has no broken windows but he does have Mary and Kestle says he knows her and has done so from her childhood and that he is an intimate of her family back in Fowey. Boswell's immediate reaction is one of suspicion and he questions Kestle closely. The glazier says that he has had a letter from Fowey, from one of Mary's relations, asking him to see how she is and to arrange a meeting between her and her sister Dolly, who is in service in London; but this is not the half of it: it seems that Mary's father, the fisherman (and sheep stealer?) of Fowey has received, with some others, an inheritance of £300,000.

Boswell is no fool; only the other day he was at the theatre watching a melodrama and he knows a third-act happy ending as well as the next man and also knows that they don't happen in life – though they very well might to a young woman of celebrity. There has already been a story in the press about a mysterious high-ranking army officer who spirited Mary out of Newgate and drove her away in his curtained carriage, his horses' hooves striking sparks from the cobbles.

Kestle has the makings of an impostor or a dreamer and Boswell thinks it best to keep an eye on him: they'll go round to Titchfield Street now and see Mary, he says. Kestle is unaffected by this suspicion and walks happily alongside Boswell, chattering about Cornwall and the Broads.

Mary Broad

She doesn't recognise this man who says he knew her when she was a child. After all, it's hardly a lifetime: fifteen years, so she should remember. And yet he knows her parents, her cousin Puckey that married Edward and he says he knows her sister Dolly and that she's in London, in service as a cook.

Mr Boswell sits quietly in the corner looking in that way of his, seeing everything, listening to each word, considering and thinking and saying nothing. Though he doesn't like it when Mr Kestle tells her about the money, lots of it, due to come to her father through an inheritance. Thousands of pounds he says; the family will be rich and well thought of, she can have anything she wants, a carriage and fine linen and someone to light the fires in the morning. She doesn't feel anything at all. What does it mean, all this money? It means nothing if it isn't in your hand. She looks at this glazier and nods as he goes on and on, getting as excited as a child with all his news. She wonders if he's putting some sort of bite on her or Mr Boswell but can't see what or why. Maybe he's just mad or maybe he's telling the truth.

When he goes, promising to bring Dolly to see her, Mr Boswell agrees: there's something rum about the cove but he can't put his finger on it either. He tells her not to trust the man as far as the end of her nose until he stands in front of her with Dolly and even then not to believe his stories about the huge sum of money. There are hardly that many guineas in the King's Exchequer, never mind in Cornwall. There may be money, he says, but never count on it till it's in your purse, and when it is, then keep it shut.

304

James Boswell

He walks down the narrow staircase, his heels clattering on the bare wood and questions echoing around his head. He's glad she doesn't like this man Kestle; she doesn't need these people, these friends who may be false friends. If the sister is true, then all well and good, maybe there's a chance she can go home but he has a feeling, something he has known since his early twenties, that in London a man or woman can be whatever they want; no one knows them from their childhood years, they are what they say they are. And Mary is discovering this too. She's not the daughter who went to the bad and ran away from Fowey and ended up in prison; she's not even the convict maid who braved the storms: the stories and reports have become so confused and wide-ranging that in London she can pick and choose and be anyone she wants.

He wanders up to Oxford Street and thinks of buying something but doesn't; he wanders down to Whitehall and slips into the afternoon service but the minister is droning on about sin like a chanter with a hole in it – not that he minds a good hellfire sermon, it helps keep a man straight; it's boredom and flatness that finishes him – and he slips out again and walks around, letting chance carry him to the door of a friend where he has dinner and manages, despite his gloom (it seems habitual since the robbery) to amuse the table. Afterwards he walks back to Oxford Street and, on a whim – is it truly a whim or did he mean all along to end up in Little Titchfield Street? – finds himself at Mary's door. He knocks, is taken up and finds her with her sister Dolly.

Kestle may be a dark glass but in this matter he's quite clear. Mary says 'Here is Dolly' and looking at the two of them together, he cannot but believe that this is, truly, Mary's sister. A fine, pretty girl of twenty or so, he reckons, her eyes wet with tears of affection, sentiment, love for her sister. Mary is ... diffident; for the first time since he has known her, unsure of herself; asking what they think of her, what their feelings are, how they might receive her. But it's been a while since Dolly was home and she, like her sister, is no hand at writing or reading. She doesn't know and, anyhow, it's getting late, she must go.

The affecting scene brings the fate of the other escapers once more to Boswell's mind and he decides to visit them in Newgate and reassure them that he is still doing all in his power to win them a reprieve.

He sets off on a bright Monday afternoon and calls in on an old girlfriend for a few amorous moments, carrying on to the prison where he takes tea with the keeper, Mr Kirby, his family and a number of ladies who have been permitted into his drawing room. He feels the strangeness of being in this domestic scene yet confined behind walls of stone.

After tea, the keeper escorts him to the Botany Bay men's quarters and Boswell remarks – to himself – how much respect, awe even, Mr Kirby evokes from those poor souls as he goes amongst them. Where there is usually a clamour of requests, demands, threats and promises for any money the ordinary visitor might have about them, now there is only respectful doffing of hats and silence. It is like going though hell accompanied by Virgil with a club.

Caught in a limbo between punishment and release, the escapers are fraught, nervous, hopeful, despairing and eager for news of any sort. Boswell offers them continued hope: they will be free men, though it may be two or even three months before a pardon comes. He is seeing Mr Nepean again and will also visit Captain Phillip, who is sure – now his governor's pension has been settled – to offer a good word on their behalf. It is, he tells them again, just a matter of letting public interest die away. He gives them some money for their meagre comforts and to buy the good opinion of the keeper and bids them good day.

On the way out he is introduced to Lord William Murray, currently a resident of Newgate, where he keeps a little stone room with his wife. Lord William, who was imprisoned elsewhere for debt, is now in Newgate for plotting, so it is said, to blow down the prison walls. Boswell knows his family well and feels strange chatting so easily to the young radical and his pretty wife.

At the end of the week, on Sunday evening, he visits Mary and meets her pretty sister Dolly again. The two young women appear close, though Dolly is clearly the more sentimental of the pair, still weeping tears of happiness at finding her lost younger, as it turns out, sister. Boswell is much struck by her good nature and neat figure. She tells him a little about her life and career in London, where she now works as a cook for a Mr Morgan in Charlotte Street. She tells Boswell that if she and Mary really are to be rich, she'll give him a thousand pounds for all his kindness. Boswell wonders if he can't find her a better situation, something not too hard for one so young and slender.

The reason for Mary's pensive silence becomes clear when Dolly tells him she is trying to persuade her sister to go home, at least on a visit, to see the family. There is even a letter from Edward, the husband of her cousin Puckey, urging her to return to Fowey where she will be kindly received.

Mary is not so sure but Boswell persuades her: it will be for the best and he will take care that her allowance is paid to her in Cornwall or any other place to which she might move. He suggests that she go by sea – he will pay for her passage; the journey will not be so fast but it will be safer and more comfortable. Dolly adds her pleas and her tears to his words and at last, still anxious, Mary agrees. She will go back home on the first ship to Fowey. It is the right thing to do and as he walks across to Great Portland Street he decides that should the other subscribers to Mary's money not keep up their payments, he will make up the ten pounds a year out of his own pocket. And yet, over the following days, as they wait for a boat to take her home, his spirits sink ever lower.

At the beginning of September he meets an old acquaintance, Lord Inchiquin, in the street and is invited home to an early supper; just Lord and Lady Inchiquin and James Boswell. Together they down a couple of bottles of claret and many glasses over dinner but each glass only brings more painfully to mind those who are no longer here: Johnson, Sir Joshua, clubbable men both and so very much missed. After dinner, the Inchiquins go off to the theatre and Boswell finds himself at odds and ends, wandering the streets. He decides to go home and go to bed and thinks 'strange kind of life ...'

The 11th October is the day set for Mary's departure on the *Ann and Elizabeth*. The master, Job Moyse, sends a note that she must board on the night of the 10th as he wishes to catch the early tide. Boswell hurries round to Little Titchfield Street and warns her to be ready to board this evening, in just a few hours. Whilst she packs her box, he asks her to tell him about the escape from Botany Bay. As she talks, he takes down her words as he has taken down so many tales and conversations in the past; he wonders if this may be the last story of all. When he puts away his pens and paper and gets ready to say goodbye, she is upset, tearful and does not want him to go; she doesn't want to be alone. He promises to come back later and see her to the dockside and into her cabin.

He goes home to dinner and returns later with his son James, who is back from school. He tells Mary that he has a hackney cab waiting to take her and her box to Beal's Wharf in Southwark. Her spirits are still low as they clatter across London; she looks out the cab windows, taking everything in as if she may not see it again. It is as if she is being transported a second time rather than taken home. Boswell is concerned and when they reach Southwark, sits with her in the kitchen and then the bar of the pub on the wharf. She tells him that she is sure her relations will not treat her well. As they drink punch, Boswell says it is her duty to see her mother and father and, after all, if the story of the inheritance is true to any degree, it may be to her advantage. But sitting there, the hot glasses in their hands, the warm, spicy smell of the punch mixing with the tobacco and ale of the pub, they both know, somehow, that the story is just that: a story.

Boswell tells her again that, whatever happens, he will ensure her ten pounds a year, and he teaches her to write the initials of her name, M.B., in such a way that, when inscribed in a letter from a local vicar, found by Temple, or from her cousin Puckey, he will know that she has received the money. She nods and stays silent. He reminds her that, with her money, she will be able to leave Fowey if she wants and even return to London.

Captain Moyse comes rolling in from the foggy hard and joins them for a bumper, then Boswell tells the potboy to shoulder Mary's box and walks with her, out of the pub, across the cobbles, up the gangplank and onto the *Ann and Elizabeth*. The deck moves gently under their feet, the gunwale nudges the dockside; tar and coal smoke, oil lamps and damp canvas and a mist rising off the Thames. He takes her down to her cabin and gives her some money for the trip and an advance on her allowance of five pounds. She puts a match to the wick of the hanging lamp and the cabin fills with buttery yellow light. She looks at him, he looks at her and bids her adieu, with sincere good will; he backs out of the cabin, away from the light and goes up on deck.

Mary Broad

S he stands amidships, stockings and shoes between her feet and the damp planking of the deck. To starboard, cliffs swoop and rise, chalk faced, topped with green grass and trees, their branches whipping in the sharp wind. There's rain in the air, mean drops that sting her face like blown sand, and salt water too, caught up from the whitecaps around the ship. The sun is somewhere beyond the grey overcast, the horizon lost in the misty band between sea and sky. A church clock, carried on the wind, sounds for a moment but she can't tell how many chimes there are; all her attention is forward, to the shape of the cliffs as they come round the headland and there is the fort sliding into view and the sound of the crew, hurrying aloft to take in the mainsails as the deck heels sharply under her. She grasps the rail and the vessel comes about and sails in between the heads of the bay and she realises that at last she has come home and wonders if this is what she wants.

Fowey Haven opens out around her: the houses of the town straggling down the hills towards the sea; fishing boats tying up, unloading their catch and piling their nets, the ferry across to the boatyard; the church spire, Readymoney Bay, the river winding between the hills, the faces watching from the shore. Do they know she's coming home?

Captain Moyse bellows out his orders, the topsails shiver as they are lowered and the way comes off the *Ann and Elizabeth*. The anchor is let go and smashes down, the chain rattling over the hawser. Already boats are putting out from shore and she strains to see if she can recognise anyone. On deck, they are moving the cargo, ready to unload; someone puts her box down with a thump. Her box, her things.

The Bay closes around her.

Arthur Phillip

And he gets married. He's in Bath for the cure, on indefinite leave, with time on his hands. Margaret, his estranged first wife, died last year and he is free to marry again if he wishes. He's in his mid-fifties, has a good pension for his work in New South Wales, a captain's half-pay, good prospects still in the navy, he hopes, and has just joined the local library, as has Miss Isabella Whitehead, a lady in her mid forties, well-read, from a prosperous manufacturing family in the way of linens and weaving in Blackburn, Lancashire. She is in Bath with her father, who is taking the cure, and has time on her hands. The two have enough in common to find each other's company congenial and decide to set up a hedge against loneliness and age. They marry in London on 8th May 1794. It is not, in anyone's estimation, a love match, but rather a marriage of mutual interests.

Shortly after the wedding, Isabella's father dies and they find themselves in a most comfortable position, able to live pretty much as they wish. Their visiting list is extensive and includes, as well as Isabella's commercial contacts, Phillip's many acquaintances and friends picked up during a lifetime of service. There are the Sydney officers when they are in town – Captain Hunter, Philip Gidley King, Dr White; there are his civil service contacts and spymasters like Evan Nepean; and those more celebrated like Sir Joseph Banks, who is always ready to discuss the progress of the colony; then there is an ever-growing circle of acquaintance in Bath, where the captain is something of a local celebrity.

And yet, as his health improves, so does the need to get back to some useful work.

James Boswell

ere comes the great biographer. He's fifty-four years old and drunk again, winding his slow way home; here comes James, here comes Jamie, here comes Jimmy trailing the black dog, here comes Captain Standish looking for a walking mort, some Haymarket ware, a little laced mutton before bed but it's been a while and somehow it never seems to go the way he wants these days. He's a joker and he's a joke at too many dinners and there are too many pretty girls who remember what he did and what he said when he can't remember a thing and fears it was all about shoeing the goose. Here comes James Boswell, here comes fumble-fingers lost in a fog.

All those things he wanted once to be and to do:

~ *A career as a Guards officer: it came to nothing, he was never a man to stand in the line whilst lead shot buzzed around his head – and yet he is not a coward, he's certain of that.*
~ *Social success: well, he has had friends who love him and his stories, his attentions and his jokes. Doctor Johnson once said that sitting in a fine chair in your own club surrounded by your friends with ample food and fine wine was about as good as it gets in this world and he's had all that too.*
~ *Favour of politicians: well, nooooo!*
~ *Adoration of beautiful, rich ladies: not that either, but there have been ladies, beautiful, witty, some willing, some friends, some young, some old, some for sale, some for love.*

~ *Visit stately homes: he's been in and out of a few drawing-rooms in his time, and dining rooms too – and bedrooms, when it comes to it.*

~ *Reading men and their weaknesses: Yes, it's all there in the LIFE.*

~ *Mastery of science and the arts: an interest, a continued curiosity as to how and why the world turns as it does.*

~ *Touring Europe: been there, written about that.*

~ *Being received at foreign courts: all in the diaries.*

~ *Returning to brief the Prime Minister: not Pitt, never Pitt. The man ignores him – and as for Henry Dundas, Lord Melville! He and Temple knew him when he was not so great a man as he styles himself now.*

~ *Becoming a secretary of state: unlikely.*

~ *Raising a regiment: the most he can do is settle £500 on his daughter Veronica, as he promised once because she alone of his children, of his whole family, really did like Johnson. That and paying the household expenses and Mary's money.*

~ *Repelling an invasion: it is not given to many to achieve this.*

~ *Marrying beauty and one hundred thousand pounds: no, but marrying Margaret and loveliness and common sense and true devotion was better.*

~ *Having many children of whom he can be proud: on the whole, yes, though he wishes his two eldest daughters weren't so loud and so out of place wherever they come to rest – but they are, all of his children, good hearted and he loves them deeply.*

~ *Being universally loved and respected: even Samuel Johnson did not achieve this.*

~ *Honoured by all: laughed at by many.*

~ *Painted and sculpted: by some of the best hands too.*

And then there are the Botany Bay men, who were released from Newgate on 2nd November.

It wasn't exactly a pardon, since government did not want to encourage others in the belief that daring escapes and suffering would redeem their crimes – instead, the lawyers found a means whereby the clerk of the court of the Old Bailey issued a proclamation asking whether anyone wished to prosecute the men for any crime. It was a foregone conclusion: no one was expected to, no one did and thus the men were able to go free. Their first act was to hurry round to Mr Boswell's house and thank him for his efforts on their behalf. He reflects that this too was something to have done.

In April 1795 he falls ill whilst spending an evening with friends. He is taken home and goes to bed with chills and a headache; a fever comes on, he feels nauseous. The doctor is called and it becomes clear that he is suffering from kidney failure. He's too weak to write and dictates a letter to his old friend Temple. He says: 'the pain, which continued for so many weeks was very severe indeed, and when it went off I thought myself quite well; but I soon felt a conviction that I was by no means as I should be. All then, that can be said, is that I must wait with patience.'

So he waits and the days and nights go slowly by and something gets closer with each moment. Something vast, full of goodness and humour and learning, full of forgiveness and understanding, a great shape that comes shambling, clumping and mumbling up the stairs, elephant-dancing back and forth over the cracks in the floorboards, twitching and flinging arms and legs all about and uttering a perfect stream, a cataract of words until it stands in the shadow just behind the bedroom door, waiting, impatiently for good company. And at two o'clock on the morning of 19th May 1795 (a time when many a bottle is still to be opened) that great weight leans against the door, it begins to open and James Boswell dies.

Arthur Phillip

In 1796, Arthur Phillip returns to active duty as captain of the *Alexander*, a first-rate with a crew of six hundred; it is, in a manner of speaking, also a homecoming since he served on her as first lieutenant after his Portuguese service. The ship is sent on escort and patrol duty in the channel. Relations with France are deteriorating by the day as Napoleon Bonaparte exercises his military genius and brings more of Europe under his rule. Britain is isolated, despite a policy of buying friends and secretly giving financial support to anyone who will oppose the Corsican Ogre. Phillip is hungry for action but *Alexander* finds no enemies waiting to engage with her seventy-four guns.

He transfers out of *Alexander* and takes over the *Swiftsure*, another first-rate, which is refitting in Portsmouth. By January 1797, the ship is ready to put to sea and Phillip hopes to be posted to the British forces in the Mediterranean, where they are stalking the French and Spanish Fleets blockading Gibraltar. Before the orders come through, news of a great victory arrives: Sir John Jervis and Horatio Nelson have smashed the French and Spanish at Cape St Vincent; Gibraltar is free but short of supplies. *Swiftsure* is assigned as escort to the convoy which relieves the island base.

Phillip, denied glory by chance and time, directs his concern to the state of morale aboard his own ship, where muttering and discontent are growing by the day. *Swiftsure* is not alone in this; the whole fleet is seething with mutinous thoughts; French ideas of liberty and fraternity and the rights of man are in the air and, as the press gang snatches more men from the streets of ports and fishing villages to serve their country as sailors, with neither choice nor limit to the time of their bondage, it is hardly surprising if tempers are rising.

Many on the top deck of the service put the whole thing down to lower-deck lawyers, discontented drunks and republicans but they are wrong. The navy is facing an ever-present threat of invasion or defeat at sea; it has over a hundred thousand men serving in its ships, a good third of them pressed or otherwise unwilling; their meagre pay is generally late or missing; their rations are far from fresh but give them both the energy they need to work their ships and to feel aggrieved by their treatment, an aggravation that is often inflamed by the rum ration.

Arthur Phillip has a better understanding than most of how to recognise a real grievance and set it right; he also knows that, fair or not, to give way and show weakness in this situation will only lead to anarchy. He comes down hard on the crew of *Swiftsure*, handing out floggings for drunkenness, insolence and disobedience but in each case the sentence is no more than a dozen or two dozen lashes, a terrible enough punishment but one that can be seen by all as fair rather than tyrannical.

When Rear-Admiral Nelson inspects the ship he finds it in good order, the sailors fit for action. The same cannot be said for the rest of the fleet: first at Spithead and then at the Floating Republic of the Nore, the Channel and North Sea squadrons refuse to put to sea.

The Admiralty reacts quickly: at Spithead they recognise that the men have real grievances and do their best to improve conditions and cut down the brutality and corruption which so often makes the lower deck a hell afloat; at the Nore they see only French devilry and imagine the guillotine rising from a crowd of Jacobin demons, howling for the head of the King and the middle classes. They respond with brutal ferocity, crushing not only the mutineers but also those who offer any kind of support for their views: a surgeon, John Redfern, who says that the men might have some points in their favour is sentenced to life in New South Wales; there are hangings by the score and floggings without number. Mutiny is crushed – the fleet is safe.

Sir John Jervis, who has been created Lord St Vincent in recognition of his victory, calls on Phillip to transfer out of *Swiftsure* and take over *Blenheim*. Once again, he is being asked to use his diplomatic rather than warlike skills. *Blenheim*'s previous commander, Rear Admiral Thompson, a dour but fair-minded man, has found himself hipped by St Vincent's favouritism towards his protégé Horatio Nelson and has demanded an accounting. It is an unwise move, the service does not, will not, simply cannot support a junior against a senior, particularly one who has just won a famous victory. Thompson is sent home, Phillip arrives aboard *Blenheim* to soothe ruffled feathers amongst his followers and crew.

St Vincent orders Phillip and *Blenheim* to Portugal which is facing invasion by French and Spanish armies. His instructions are to bolster the Portuguese in their defiance of Napoleon and underline Britain's continued military and financial support. Phillip is, as his Admiral recognises, the perfect man for the mission and he is able to renew many old contacts from his South American days.

Then history intervenes. Napoleon has other plans, he goes off and attacks somewhere else, the invasion is postponed and *Blenheim* is recalled to the fleet where Phillip finds his ship has been given to another. She is to be the flag of the newly arrived Rear Admiral Frederick, replacing Admiral Thompson, and Captain Phillip no longer has a command. He is sent home under the most mortifying circumstances: he has done everything asked of him, St Vincent is more than happy with his efforts but Admiral Frederick's friends at the Admiralty are more influential than Captain Phillip's. As he leaves *Blenheim*, he fears that he is also leaving any chance of ending his career with the kind of glorious 'thump-em-again-and-again' sea action that began it.

Back home he is given command of the Hampshire Sea Fencibles, a home guard trained (on the few occasions they bother to turn up) to resist a French invasion force. Phillip divides his time between raising and training men and winkling them out of the clutches of the press gangs. It is unexciting work but at least it is something; he feels useful, part of the national effort against the enemy.

In 1801 the combatants begin tentative peace negotiations and Phillip is posted to Portsmouth to inspect the hulks in which Spanish and French prisoners are being held. He has by now, according to the system that operates in the Royal Navy, risen to the rank of Rear Admiral of the Blue, so his suggestions, humane and sensible, are listened to and the conditions of the prisoners considerably improved.

He has a reputation as a man of sense who can get things done against bureaucratic odds, self-interest and an endemic corruption that would defeat most; he is asked by the Admiralty to prepare a report on the Impress Service, the press gangs which man the navy with whatever bodies come to hand or bludgeon. Though there is an uneasy peace with Napoleon and, at this very moment, thousands of half-pay officers and indigent seamen walking the streets or, in the case of the impressed, hurrying back to their farms and fishing boats, it is clear that it will not last. Napoleon's ambition is limitless and the Sea Lords need to know that when hostilities resume, the press gangs will be able to swing back into action with all their old ferocity and efficiency and that once more the jolly cry of 'Yo ho, matey, you must come with me!' will echo about the coastal towns of Britain.

Phillip is no friend to the rights-of-man brigade and, as a lieutenant he led a press gang himself on any number of dark and drunken nights. He is concerned with removing corruption, bribery and too much violence and in encouraging a general improvement in record keeping. Once more he does a good job. His reward is to become inspector of the Sea Fencibles for the whole country, a not inconsiderable responsibility now that the war is on again. Not inconsiderable – but not active service.

Somewhere deep within the reasonable man there still hankers a Nelson, ready to leap from ship to ship, take outrageous chances, ignore orders and steer to glory. He offers his services to St Vincent who, after all, owes him something – but he can give him nothing. Prime Minister Pitt, out of office in 1801, is back in power and his shadow and sidekick, Henry Dundas (now raised to Lord Melville) is running the Navy Board and has no time for St Vincent and his followers.

Arthur Phillip is sixty-four years old in 1804, and has risen to Rear Admiral of the White and is, despite his achievements, being retired from active service. Evan Nepean, ever careful of the sensibilities of old friends and old agents, softens the official letter of dismissal but, even so, it hurts Admiral Phillip and he ends his last report with the words 'I will not take up their lordships' time with any further observations and remarks.'

In 1806 he and his wife Isabella move to Bath; they buy a property at 19 Bennet Street: three stories, very much an admiral's house, respectable and solid, and the couple become part of local society, attending balls and recitals at the Assembly Rooms, visiting London and Oxford, entertaining old friends and new.

The world is changing around the old admiral – fashions are become loose, it's the only way to describe it, and what's more they are coming from France: whilst the Royal Navy and the British Army are locked in a life and death struggle with the ogre Napoleon, dress patterns cross the channel with impunity. However, though the French and English middle classes may well be wearing the same styles, the *élan*, the flair with which they wear them is certain to be quite different, and that is reassuring to the English admiral.

He retains a lively interest in the colony he helped to found and, on occasion, his advice is still sought by government. He writes many letters in support of Philip Gidley King, who has become the governor of New South Wales but is still trying to get full pay for the time he spent on Norfolk Island.

His health still causes concern and in March 1808 he suffers a stroke which leaves him near death for some weeks. He fights his way back to fitness, but the damage has been done and Philip Gidley King, visiting with news of Sydney, notices that Phillip's right side, arm and leg are badly affected, though his spirits are still good and his mind sharp. Christiana Chapman, who has known him since before the departure of the Botany Bay Fleet, when she was thirteen (she is now in her thirties) finds him more emotional than usual, recalling the past, holding her hand, even shedding a few sentimental tears as he shares his pudding and a glass of Madeira with his young friend.

Ever practical, Phillip has extra handrails fitted on the stairs so he can pull himself up and down with greater ease – always remember: one hand for the ship, one for you. His health gets a little better, he is able to travel, to visit and receive friends, to go away to Oxford and, in 1811, to Clifton in Bristol, where he meets the architect Frances Greenway whose crimes are shortly to deliver his talents to New South Wales.

One August day in 1814, Admiral Phillip – he's now in his seventies – pulls himself up to the top floor of the house on Bennet Street and stands looking out of the window at a clear, blue sky that seems to go on forever, like the oceans he has sailed his whole life long. Is it time now for that one glorious moment of risk, of disobedience, to gain the greatest prize; is it time at last to steer to glory?

It is the general opinion that the fall is accidental, an elderly gentleman unsure of his footing, slipping from an upstairs window. A tragedy and a release. He is buried in Bathampton Church, by now Admiral of the Blue. His wife lives on in Bath, dies in 1824 and is buried beside him.

Mary Broad

he steps ashore and looks at the faces, some full of recognition, others blank. Her mother and father are there, coming forward

She stands in Readymoney Bay watching the sea foam up across the wet sands and into the runnels of the rocks. She searches for gold coins under the fast running water.

the smell of saffron cake

Tar and the twists of the fishing net

Accusation and anger

carefully she makes the marks that she and Mr Boswell practised together before she left London. The M and the B, the pen nib scratching the surface of the paper as she inscribes the lines. Cousin Ned reads out what she has told him to write: her thanks to Mr Boswell for all that he has done for her and for others. She wishes him well. She wishes she could see him again and live in London but

church beams like a fish laid open to show its backbone

Looking back as she crosses the hill and the sea is lost to sight; she turns her head and walks on, along the winding track that leads away from Fowey.

Mr Baron says he has written to Mr Boswell's friend Mr Temple telling him that Mary's conduct has been satisfactory in every respect since her return. He asks her to make her mark in receipt for her allowance. She dips the pen in the ink pot and slowly writes the letters M and B. She tells the Reverend Mr Baron that she is not sorry she left Fowey, she doesn't like it there any more.

He is dead.

Mr Baron does not think the allowance will be paid any more.

She waits by the shore looking at the sea and thinks of Mr Boswell and she is sorry that he has died.

time to move on

A new King ...

Time, so much time, so many years but she can still remember the cutter and Will and Charlotte and Emmanuel and the others as the sea tips them down a mountain of glass green water and she screams at them to bail, bail for their lives. And the last breath leaving Emmanuel's little body and the tiny noise Charlotte makes as she slips beneath the waves.

Sitting, darning clothes by candlelight, the needle like a silver darling darting in and out of the waves

How many miles to Babylon?
Three score miles and ten.
And can I get there by candlelight?
Yes, and back again.
If your feet are nimble and light,
You can get there by candlelight.

A new Queen – a young woman, hardly older than Mary was when

the light is there, then gone ...

she turns her head and sees

The History

It is my practice when I am in want of amusement, to place myself for an hour at Temple Bar and examine one by one the looks of the passengers, and I have commonly found that between the hours of eleven and four every sixth man is an author. They are seldom to be seen early in the morning or late in the evening, but about dinner time, they are all in motion, and have one uniform eagerness about their faces, which gives little opportunity of discerning their hopes or fears, their pleasures or their pains

But in the afternoon, when they have all dined, or composed themselves to pass the day without a dinner, their passions have full play, and I can perceive one man wondering at the stupidity of the public, by which his new book has been totally neglected; another cursing the French, who fright away literary curiosity by their threat of invasion; another swearing at this bookseller, who will advance no money without 'copy'; another determining to write no more to a generation of barbarians; another murmuring at an unanswerable criticism; and another wishing to try once again whether he cannot awaken the drowsy world to a sense of his merit.

Dr Samuel Johnson

Telling Mary

Mary Bryant's story isn't really history. She could neither read nor write and apart from the two pages she dictated to James Boswell before returning to Fowey in 1794, she does not seem to have left any kind of record of her experiences. Everything we know about her is from the recollections and journals of others and from the official records: she appears and disappears like a shoal of fish, leaving an intriguing and, almost certainly, forever unknown trail.

Her life can't escape a succession of 'it mights, it appears, it could have been, it has been suggested, the evidence points towards, it is likely, probable, possible' and so on. Her story recently featured in a radio series about oral history under the title *Voices of the Voiceless* but, in point of fact, she has no voice, since her thoughts and experiences were never recorded. Even James Boswell, that most industrious of scribes, reports her conversation, rather than transcribing it. Virtually everything, beyond the most basic facts, is speculation and extrapolation. There's nothing to translate – with all the problems that implies – from the language of the past into the language of the present; the best we can do is adapt or dramatise events and, in the end, who's to say that J.G Farrell's *Singapore Grip* gives us a worse understanding of the fall of Singapore than any number of histories – and if its truths are partial, then they are also profound; as V.S Naipul once wrote, nothing is more open to misinterpretation than non-fiction whilst fiction is always, cannot but be, true to itself.

If we don't know much about Mary, we do know quite a lot about the circumstances and surroundings in which she lived her life: growing up in a Cornish village, the eighteenth-century criminal world and the hulks, the First Fleet and the settlement at Sydney Cove and the lives of James Boswell and Arthur Phillip.

However, whilst telling, or speculating on, Mary's story from a dramatic point of view it seemed unfair to me to give those around her the weight of history. So, as far as possible, I've related the events of the three main lives, as they touch each other, as drama (which always exists in the present – and is never out of date) with no attempt to speculate on their motives and no second thoughts or guesses. Thus Henry Dundas appears as the jealous James Boswell saw him and not as the brilliant and hard-working politician he undoubtedly was; which is not to say that historical research hasn't opened up the past. Biographers and historians have continually asked why an undistinguished run-of-the-mill naval plodder like Arthur Phillip was chosen to command the First Fleet and establish the colony at Sydney Cove. Only after Alan Frost's seminal study – *Arthur Phillip, His Voyaging* – have we begun to recognise the secret world of intelligence which Phillip inhabited and the contacts he made there. He and his employers knew exactly what he was up to and managed to hide it so well that only after Frost has the catch been slipped and the door opened a crack. The all-pervasive influence of Evan Nepean is likewise only beginning to be understood and explored and a number of studies of eighteenth-century sexualities are throwing new light on hitherto modestly shadowed areas.

I have not hesitated to use new research to illumine the world in which the characters move, just as I have borrowed many scenes from the works of the superlative cartoonists and artists of the period, whilst keeping in mind Carlyle's words: 'in every object there is inexhaustible meaning; the eye sees in it what the eye brings means of seeing.'

James Boswell's attendance at the execution of Hannah Dagoe and Captain Paul Lewis is set in a Tyburn brought brilliantly to life by Hogarth, from the Good and Bad Apprentice series. The paintings and drawings of Thomas Rowlandson, the Deightons and James Gillray have shone a light on worlds as different as the lower deck, the drawing room, the brothel (it is one of Gillray's lovely molls who holds her fingers in a signifying circle behind her back) and street fashions.

The life of James Boswell is almost overly available through his diaries, one of the great serendipitous finds of literary history; Arthur Phillip, though the most private of men, is pretty clearly delineated through the literature of an official life, but what do we really know about Mary?

She was christened at St Fimbarrus's church in Fowey (pronounced Foy) Cornwall, on Sunday 1st May 1765 by the Reverend Nicholas Cory. Her parents were William Broad, mariner, and his wife Grace, both of Fowey. She had a sister two years older, Dolly, and a younger brother and sister, neither of whom survived infancy.

In her study of Mary, *To Brave Every Danger*, Judith Cook gives a wonderful picture of eighteenth-century life and customs of Fowey; this is backed up by I.D. Spreadbury's *Fowey, a Brief History*, which has contributed the meal at the Ship Inn and many other facts about local life, all of which must, in the nature of things, have had some effect upon a growing child who, from the evidence of her later life, was probably (that word again) inquisitive, self-aware, inventive and not afraid to stand up for herself.

She would have attended the church with its unique roof, she would have seen the mayor and corporation enter in procession and watched the major families of the area, the Treffreys and Rashleighs, go into their private pews. Saffron cake was a well-known local food and she must have seen her mother cooking or at least mixing it before taking it along to the baker's to be baked in his ovens. Cornwall was known for the number and venality of its MPs and elections were closely and often viciously fought out, so even though politics would have made little difference to her life, she would have seen the aftermath in broken bottles, torn rosettes and blood in the gutters. Her father was a fisherman, we know that; there was no son in the family, so again it is highly likely that she learnt some of the skills of sailing and, possibly, navigation, from her father.

However, we actually know nothing at all about her life from the moment of christening to the moment she appears before either Sir Beaumont Hotham or Sir James Eyre at the Exeter assizes in March 1786. The charge was that in the January of that year she and two others, Catherine Fryer and Mary Haydon alias Mary Shepherd, violently attacked and robbed Agnes Lakeman, spinster, in Plymouth, stealing a bonnet and other property worth eleven guineas. They were interrupted during the commission of the crime, chased and apprehended. The case was open and shut and the three were sentenced to death. As was common at the time, the death sentence was commuted to seven years transportation beyond the seas – Mary's name, spelled Braund, appears on the document along with Fryer and Haydon and, amongst others, James Martin or Martyn, who would later be amongst the escapers from New South Wales.

She is sent to the prison hulk *Dunkirk* in Plymouth and at some time nearing the end her incarceration on board, she became pregnant; we know this because the next solid record of her life is from Dr White's journal of the First Fleet's voyage to Botany Bay in which he notes, on 8th September 1787, shortly after the fleet had left Rio de Janeiro: 'Mary Broad, a convict, was delivered of a fine girl.'

There is no record of Mary being registered as convict in the First Fleet, she appears out of nowhere in Dr White's account, though it is possible that due to confusion and lax paperwork, her name was either misspelled or she answered, at one or other roll call, to a name similar to her own. Either way, the times involved make it clear that her pregnancy must have originated on the hulk *Dunkirk* before the Botany Bay voyage. This would suggest either that she had become the mistress of an officer or sergeant in the marine detachment guarding the ship (not a lot to be gained from shagging a private) or that (perhaps) she had already met and formed a relationship with William Bryant, who was also confined aboard *Dunkirk*. When the baby was christened at the Cape, she named her Charlotte after the transport on which she was confined, or possibly after Queen Charlotte, and Spence, after, one may presume, the father.

Also aboard the *Charlotte* with Will Bryant, fisherman of Cornwall, were James Martin or Martyn, and James Cox; it is likely that all three were already in a gang since they were to escape together in the cutter.

On 10th February 1788, six days after she landed in Australia, the records show that Mary and William Bryant were married by the Rev. Richard Johnson, the colony chaplain.

The next mention of the Bryants, as they now are, comes in David Collins' *An Account of the English Colony in New South Wales*, in his records for the month of February 1789. He is lauding the good behaviour of many of the convicts and their inclination towards honest industry. He goes on: 'There were others, however, who had no claims to this praise. Among these must be particularised William Bryant, to whom, from his having been bred from his youth to the business of fisherman in the western part of England, was given the direction and management of such boats as were employed in fishing, every encouragement was held out to this man to keep him above temptation; an hut was built for him and his family; he was always presented with a certain part of the fish which he caught; and he wanted for nothing that was necessary to a person of his description and situation. But he was detected in secreting and selling large quantities of fish, and when the necessary enquiry was made, this practice appears to have been of some standing with him. For this offence he was severely punished, and removed from the hut in which he had been placed; yet, as not withstanding his villainy, he was too useful a person to part with and send to a brick cart, he was still retained to fish for the settlement; but a very vigilant eye was kept over him, and such steps taken as appeared likely to prevent him from repeating his offence, if the sense of shame and fear of punishment were not of themselves sufficient to deter him.'

Court records state that Joseph Paget was the convict who peached on Will Bryant. In his evidence he says that the fish was sold to raise money for rum, for which Will Bryant obviously had a penchant. Paget had worked in the boat with Will and also about the fisherman's hut on shore, alongside Mary – it is more than likely that his informing was not a question of public duty. Dr White gave evidence in Will Bryant's favour but it was an open and closed case and Will was sentenced to a hundred lashes.

On 4th April 1790, the Rev. Richard Johnson records that he christened Emmanuel, the child of William and Mary Bryant.

In February 1791, Judge Advocate David Collins records in his *Account* that 'William Bryant, who had been continued in the direction of the fishing-boat after the discovery of his malpractices, was ... over-heard consulting in his hut after dark, with five other convicts, on the practicability of carrying off the boat in which he was employed. This circumstance being reported to the governor, it was determined that all his proceedings should be narrowly watched, and any scheme of that nature counteracted.' Collins goes to say that on the day following this, the governor's cutter which was used as the colony's fishing boat, lost its fore tack and only the intervention of Bennelong and other aboriginals (his sister was in the boat at the time) prevented the total loss of the craft. It is clear that whatever his problems with authority, Will Bryant had no trouble in making friends with the 'natives.'

On 29th March 1791, Collins recorded the news of the escape: 'Their flight was not discovered until they had been some time without the Heads.' Mary is mentioned in the list of 'these desperate adventurers' as Mary Braud. Of Will Bryant, Collins wrote, '... that Bryant had been frequently heard to express, what was indeed the general sentiment on the subject among the people of his description, that he did not consider his marriage in this country as binding.' He writes, however, nothing about any motives Mary may have had for going with him. None of the other women attached to the escapers had chosen to leave, though they were all 'silent on the subject.'

As far as the voyage itself is concerned, there were two accounts: one, a log which Will wrote, later lost, though sections of it were seen by Captain William Bligh when he visited Timor some years after the mutiny on the *Bounty*. The governor of Coupang, Timotheos Wonjon, had possession of the manuscript and showed it to Bligh, amongst others, though no one had the time or inclination to make a complete copy. Bligh wrote that Will Bryant's feat of navigation was of the highest order (though not quite so high as his) and that the fisherman must have been 'a determined and enterprising man'. He notes that Bryant writes of Mary and her two children that 'they bore their sufferings wonderfully well'. Another witness to the journal wrote that 'they bore their suffering with more fortitude than most'.

The second document is a brief memorandum by one of the escapers, Nathaniel Lilley, lost for many years and later discovered amongst the papers of the social philosopher Jeremy Bentham, though how he came by it is unknown. It covers the escape from leaving Port Jackson: 'On the 28 Day of March Made My Escape in Compr. with seven men more and me with One Woman with two childn. – in an open six oar Boat' to their arrival in Timor: 'We ran along the island of Timor till we came to the Dutch Settlements where we went on shore to the Governor's house where he behaved extremely well with us.' It is, on the whole, a laconic record and mentions Mary and the children hardly at all; which is not surprising since none of the escapers saw themselves or her as romantic heroes and their day-to-day concerns were the practical ones of continued survival.

Dutch records note the arrival of a boat with eleven persons on board, 'who professed to have lost their ship, approximately off New South Wales.'

Captain Edwards, late of *Pandora,* was as brusque as his nature would suggest and wastes few words of his official journal on any of the escapers, let alone the woman amongst them. His surgeon, Hamilton, mentions that Will Bryant's drunken, loose tongue gave the escapers away though Bligh, recalling a passage in Bryant's journal, says that the fisherman blamed one of the party who gave the others away through pique at not being accorded as much attention as his companions. If it was Will who gave the game away, he would certainly have wanted to cover it up by blaming another.

The next mention of the escapers comes from Watkin Tench, on his way back from duty in New South Wales, who coincides with the party at the Cape. In his book, *A Complete Account of the Settlement at Port Jackson,* he adds a footnote to his recounting of the escape itself:

'It was my fate to fall in again with this little band of adventurers. In March 1792, when I arrived in the *Gorgon* at the Cape of Good Hope, six of these people, including the woman and one child, were put on board of us, to be carried to England: four had died and one had jumped overboard at Batavia. The particulars of their voyage were briefly as follows. They coasted the shore of New Holland, putting occasionally into different harbours, which they found going along. One of these harbours, in the latitude of 30 south, they described to be of superior excellence and capacity. Here they hauled their bark ashore, paid her seams with tallow, and repaired her. But it was with difficulty they could keep off the attack of the Indians. These people continued to harass them so much they quitted the main land and retreated to a small island in the harbour, where they completed their design. Between the latitude of 26 and 27, they were driven by a current 30 leagues from the shore, among some islands where they found plenty of large turtles. Soon after they closed again with the continent, when the boat got entangled in the surf, and was driven on shore, and they had all well-nigh perished. They passed through the Straits of Endeavour and beyond the Gulf of Carpentaria and found a large fresh water river, which they entered and filled from it their empty casks.

'Until they reached the Gulf of Carpentaria, they saw no natives or canoes, differing from those about Port Jackson. But now they were chased by large canoes, fitted with sails and fighting stages, and capable of holding thirty men each. They escaped by dint of rowing to windward. On 5th June 1791, they reached Timor, and pretended that they had belonged to a ship which, on her passage from Port Jackson to India, had foundered; and that they only had escaped. The Dutch received them with kindness and treated them with hospitality; but their behaviour giving rise to suspicion, they were watched; and one of them at last, in a moment of intoxication, betrayed the secret. They were immediately secured and committed to prison. Soon afterwards, Captain Edwards of the *Pandora*, who had been wrecked near Endeavour straits, arrived at Timor, and they were delivered up to him, by which means they became passengers in the *Gorgon*.

'I confess that I never looked at these people without pity or astonishment. They had miscarried in an heroic struggle for liberty; after having combated every hardship, and conquered every difficulty.

'The woman and one of the men had gone out to Port Jackson in the ship that had transported me thither. They had both of them been always distinguished for good behaviour. And I could not but reflect, with admiration, at the strange combination of circumstances which had again brought us together, to baffle human foresight, and confound human speculation.'

In fact, Watkin Tench had served in the marines at Portsmouth, where Mary had been imprisoned on the *Dunkirk* and there is a school of 'romantic' thought that puts him in the picture as the father of Mary's first child; it is, however, most unlikely. Tench and Phillip appear to have been the only officers who did not take mistresses from amongst the convicts; Phillip, because his position and temperament (his most intense relationships certainly seem to have been with other men) would not allow it; Tench's reasons remain concealed behind the façade of his elegant prose.

Also on the voyage back to England in the *Gorgon* were Ralph Clark, who mentioned Mary only once, when her daughter died, and the Captain's wife, Elizabeth Parker, who wrote an account of the voyage but didn't mention Mary or her daughter Charlotte. In her biography *To Brave Every Danger*, Judith Cook mentions an account of Charlotte's burial at sea that has Mary stony faced and unmoved, but as Cook says, by this time she can have hardly had any tears left to cry.

On her arrival in England, the newspapers take up the story and we can follow her progress from Portsmouth to Newgate and through her various examinations by Magistrate Bond. We can also read her repeated avowals that she would rather die than return to New South Wales, though it is more than possible that the reporters were quoting each other rather than Mary. It is from this time that we have the only description of her person – she was five feet four, with grey eyes, brown hair and a sallow complexion. Obviously, after her ordeal, she was not at her best and when Boswell met her elder sister Dolly, he took her to be the younger of the two by at least a couple of years, reversing the true position.

She appears in Boswell's journals and letters, whilst he was fighting her case, in a manner that makes it unlikely there was any romantic or sexual relationship between them. Had he fancied Mary, her ordeal would not have been a bar to his advances and it seems clear that he found her slender sister Dolly an attractive and likely prospect; however, he never wrote about Mary in the terms he habitually used about women he wanted to have sex with – and he wanted to have sex with most women – nor would he (probably) have introduced his son James to a woman who was either his mistress or a whore. On the other hand, Little Titchfield Street, where Boswell found her lodgings, was a turning off Great Titchfield Street, the address of at least one of Mr Harris's *Ladies of Covent Garden* who offered 'action under the covers,' and a 'clean Venetian Mount at reasonable rates'.

We simply don't know. However, it is quite possible he acted out of the best intentions, since he took care to ensure that the pension he set up would be paid to her alone, going so far as to arrange a private sign between the two of them so she could let him know the money had been delivered.

The glazier Kestel, or Kastel, with his news of an immense fortune inherited by Mary's father, is something of a mystery. Judith Cook has searched out a relative, Peter Broad, a ship's master, who left some three or four thousand pounds to be shared amongst relatives, and some of this might have come to Mary's father. As for the sheep stealing, there seems no reason to make it up but it is just as likely that Temple had the Broads mixed up with some other family.

The last we see of Mary, after she tells Boswell her version of the story – which he writes down on a couple of sheets (subsequently lost) – and gives him the dried tea leaves from Botany Bay, is when she embarks, apprehensive and a little depressed, on the packet back to Fowey. Beyond a couple of letters received by Boswell bearing her initials to signify the safe arrival of her money, there is nothing more. We don't know if she stayed in Fowey or moved somewhere else, if she got married, had children, or even how long she lived. She vanishes from the records completely.

Judith Cook's research reveals mention of a Mary Bryant getting married at a village a few miles along the coast from Fowey, but given that Boswell always refers to Mary as Mary Broad and not Mary Bryant – presumably since it was her wish not to be linked in any way to a man who betrayed the escapers in Timor – it doesn't seem likely that this is the same person, though we cannot be certain; Mary simply fades away like a squall on the water.

Watkin Tench

atkin Tench, that most amiable and intelligent of recorders, went on to pursue a successful career in the Marine Corps. He was promoted to brevet major on his return to England and served aboard *Alexander* in the Channel Fleet. In November 1794, the *Alexander* was involved in an action against three French ships of the line, acquitting herself courageously before the inevitable end, and he found himself a prisoner of war in the port of Toulon. Here he observed the behaviour and customs of the French and wrote a book about Napoleonic Brittany. He was exchanged after six months and served mainly on convoy protection vessels until 1802, at which point he was too senior to serve at sea and continued on land, mainly as a depot commander. He retired in 1827 with the rank of lieutenant colonel. He kept in touch with events in New South Wales and corresponded with John McArthur, who had come out as a lieutenant in the New South Wales Corps with the Second Fleet and stayed on to become the founder of the Australian wool industry and a perpetual thorn in the side of government, inciting a feud which culminated in the mutiny against Governor Bligh (something of a connoisseur of mutinies by that point).

He married Ann Marie Sargent, the daughter of a surgeon, on his return from Australia and the couple adopted the four children of her sister and brother-in-law, who had perished of fever in the West Indies. Watkin Tench died in Devonport on 7th May 1833.

Ralph Clark

Ralph Clark was not to enjoy anything like as long a life as his more sanguine colleague Tench. On his posting to Norfolk Island, along with the disruptive Major Ross, he settled into a relationship with a convict woman, Mary Branham. She is not mentioned in his journals – understandably since he would be showing them to his much missed wife Betsey Alicia – nor is there any note of the daughter, Alicia, born on Norfolk Island in July 1791. When he returned to Sydney in November 1791, he took Mary and Alicia with him, presumably settling them in some way, since they did not accompany him on the voyage back to England. Given his excess of sentiment, it seems unlikely that he would be the man to abandon them totally to chance and fortune, though their story remains unknown.

He was not to spend much time at home in England with his wife Betsey Alicia before he was posted, in 1792, to the *Tartar*, which was bound for the West Indies. His son Ralph was old enough to enlist in the marines – though still frighteningly young by our standards – and accompanied his father. Betsey Alicia was pregnant but died after giving birth to a dead child; before the letter bearing the sad news could reach her husband and son, both were also dead, killed within days of each other, fighting off Haiti.

David Collins

f all the senior officers who went out with the First Fleet, Judge Advocate David Collins served the longest. As the settlement's senior legal official and, after six months, the governor's secretary, he was at the centre of colony life and his book, *An Account of the English Colony in New South Wales*, reflects his closeness to the centre of action. He writes more about the aboriginal inhabitants of Sydney Cove than any of the other chroniclers and is generally sympathetic both to their culture and their ultimately tragic dilemma. He is a gatherer of facts; his writing can become clogged and certainly lacks the elegance and erudition of Watkin Tench, but on the whole his is the most complete account of the early years.

Collins went on to become deputy governor of Hobart in 1804, where his efforts helped the new Tasmanian settlement establish itself. However, when William Bligh arrived from Sydney, after being thrown out by the mutinous colonists, Collins found himself in something of a quandary. Bligh had promised his persecutors that he would take the ship they allowed him, the *Porpoise*, back to England and present his case there; he had not done so and was attempting to gather support to retake Sydney Cove by force of arms. Collins felt he had to support the colonists at Sydney and found himself blockaded by an irate Bligh – and few men did irate better than Bligh.

With support for the colonists and the deposed governor roughly half and half at Hobart, Collins found himself immersed in the kind of bitter in-fighting that Major Ross had specialised in provoking back at Sydney. Collins had never liked Ross, indeed had once wished him dead, and now found himself facing the one man in the hemisphere who could have taken the position of Ross's master. Bligh's intransigence was threatening the very legal basis of the English presence in New South Wales. Collins said he had always wanted to be a priest or an academic rather than a soldier and administrator and tried, without success, to mediate between the various parties.

The situation was resolved, as far as David Collins was concerned, when he suffered a fatal heart attack on 24th March 1810.

Dr White

r John White served the colony as surgeon general for seven years. He was a dedicated and outspoken man who found it impossible to keep his opinions or impatience to himself. He quarrelled with all his assistants and fought a duel with his third assistant, Balmain. The two disagreed over some trivial matter during a dinner party and went out at once with pistols and blazed away at each other, taking four shots each before Balmain received a flesh wound in the thigh. Phillip, who had been summoned, put a stop to the business by telling both men he would rather they drew blood with their scalpels saving life, than took it with their pistols. It was good advice and Balmain was later to save Phillip's life after he had been speared at Manly Cove during his meeting with Bennelong.

When Phillip left the colony in 1792, White also began to think about going home and sent a letter requesting his recall on the Dutch ship *Waaksamheyd.* Given the distances involved, it was hardly surprising that it wasn't until December 1794 that White actually set sail. He took with him his infant son by a convict mistress, Rachel Turner. She later married a settler, Thomas Moore, who became one of the richest entrepreneurs in the young town of Sydney. White's son Andrew was brought up by his relations whilst his father was serving at sea and, when White married in 1799, became an accepted part of the new household.

In 1795, after seeing his book on the colony through the press – and denying rumours that the detailed appendices on the natural history of New South Wales were actually the work of others – he was appointed chief surgeon of a Royal Navy hospital ship. Though he had received a number of grants of land in New South Wales, he never returned to the colony, serving out his time in various capacities aboard ship and later, ashore. He sold his land in Sydney through Thomas Moore, his old mistress's husband. His son Andrew became a soldier, served at the Battle of Waterloo and settled in Sydney in 1823, where he saw his mother Judith for the first time since 1792. Mother and son became close and he gave her his Waterloo Medal, which he always regarded as his most valuable possession.

On retirement, Dr John White was not, as was usual in the navy, reduced to a half-pay pension but kept his full salary as a tribute to his achievements and the high regard his long career as a medical man had earned him amongst his superiors. He died in Worthing, Sussex, at the age of 75 in 1832.

Bennelong

When the colonists first arrived at Sydney Cove, it must have seemed to Aboriginal Australians like Bennelong and his friend Colby, that one system of life, the convict settlement, could be placed over or against their traditional way of life without really impinging on it. However, it soon became clear that whilst Bennelong and his people lived and thought in what was, essentially, the timeless world of the dreaming, the newcomers were not only slaves to the clock but regarded everything not as it was but as it would one day become, when they'd cut it down, filled it in or changed its course and built around it.

The newcomers, at least those who thought about the Aborigines and their culture, saw them in the mould of unspoilt or savage man but without the beauty of the Polynesians. Though Governor Phillip was constant in his policy of protecting them from the worst excesses of the convicts and marines, there was nothing he could do to save them from the very attitude that he and every other European carried in their genes. It was, as Alan Morehead says, a fatal impact of cultures. If Australia had been annexed and colonised by anthropologists, the story might have been different, but with a shipload of thieves and a marine corps on the make, the fragile system was soon going to bend out of shape.

Phillip did his best to create an atmosphere of trust, or perhaps wary caution, between settlers and Aborigines and was the most active of the newcomers – apart, perhaps, from Will Bryant – in making attempts to get to know the original inhabitants. Capturing Arabanoo and keeping him in chains for the first few weeks of his captivity wasn't really conducive to a free exchange of views but was, as far as Phillip could see, the only way of inducing him to spend time inside the settlement and get used to its ways. The experiment worked in so far as Arabanoo eventually settled and, after the chains were removed and he was allowed to come and go as he wished, forgave his captors (Phillip felt considerable disquiet about his own actions) and was able to provide them with a certain amount of information about his way of life and language. However, the smallpox epidemic that ravaged the colony in 1789 and decimated the local tribes also struck him down and the colony was without an ambassador from inland.

In November 1789 an expedition captured two more Aborigines, Bennelong and Colby. Colby escaped almost at once but Bennelong was held for six months, until he too found an opportunity to get away. Phillip reflected that 'nothing will make these people amends for the loss of their liberty'.

A year later, news reached the colony that Bennelong and Colby were part of a large group of 'natives' gathered around the body of a beached whale at Manly Cove (so named by Phillip because of the manly bearing of some Aborigines he had seen there). Taking his cutter, the Governor hurried to the site, where, in spite of Bennelong's attempts to calm the situation, he was speared by one of the party. The wound was sufficiently serious for Phillip to dictate his will on the voyage back to Sydney Cove but he recovered and when, a few weeks later, Bennelong offered to meet again, Phillip jumped at the chance.

The meeting went well and shortly after, Bennelong and some friends came into the settlement. Collins describes the event: 'The welcome reception they met with from everyone who saw them, inspired the strangers with such confidence in us, that the visit was soon repeated; and at length Bennelong solicited the Governor to build him a hut at the extremity of the eastern point of the cove.'

Bennelong became something of a fixture in the settlement – though some amongst his own people began to find his attitude patronising and stuck-up: he was, obviously, a highly adaptable man and had the sort of personality that enabled him to mix easily and without suspicion. His friendship with Will Bryant – and possible collusion in the escape – is one aspect of this; another is his easy manner with the governor, who became, as far as we can tell, a real friend. This also reflects Phillip's nature: a reserved and private man, he was forced by his official position to avoid any appearance of favouritism amongst the officers, and it's surely no accident that Philip Gidley King, a young man for whom Phillip had both respect and great liking, was posted away from Sydney at Norfolk Island. With Bennelong, another young man of evident charm and ability, who had nothing whatever to do with the official life of the settlement, he was able to relax and pursue his inclination towards the study of the country he was colonising.

When Phillip's thoughts began to turn towards home he asked Bennelong and a friend, the sixteen-year-old Yemmerrawannie, if they would like to come with him. He'd earlier written to Sir Joseph Banks that much might be accomplished in the way of mutual understanding between the two peoples if Bennelong could be educated in the ways of England, an accomplishment that would be little trouble for him since he was 'very intelligent'.

So it was that when the governor embarked on the *Atlantic*, in 1792, the two Aborigines were with him; he assured them that they could come back whenever they wanted, though whether they really understood the times and distances involved is unlikely. The voyage to England was largely uneventful, though the appearance of 'Neptune' as they crossed the equator, and two shots fired by a French privateer as they approached England gave rise to puzzlement and some excitement.

Phillip's appearance in London, in May 1793, with kangaroos and 'two natives from New Holland,' occasioned a small stir of interest in the press; the general opinion was that these Australians were not really capable of civilisation, a judgement that must been made with closed eyes, since both men were – like all their people – brilliant mimics and could more than live up to the appearances that were commonly expected in drawing room and street. Their clothing was of the best quality; Phillip ordered and paid for complete outfits for each: coats, one green, one of pepper and salt pattern; waistcoats, blue and buff; corduroy breeches in a slate colour with silk stockings; an under-waistcoat, a spotted quilting waistcoat; silk and cotton hosiery, shirts, cravats, hats and razors. They were, in fact, as fully fitted out as any young gentlemen in London and at the end of May they were presented to King George.

Shortly after this they moved to lodgings in Grosvenor Square where they were given lessons in reading and writing and received visitors; they were taken out on the town to observe various aspects of English life and culture, and made visits to the Tower of London, St Paul's Cathedral and Sadler's Wells Theatre. In his study of Bennelong and Yemmerrawannie in England, Jack Brook gives the programme that night: it opened with acrobats who were followed by a series of tableaux illustrating great military campaigns, including the Siege of Valenciennes; next came tightrope walkers and the entertainment concluded with a pantomime, *Pandora's Box or the Plagues of Mankind*. Brook writes that though there are no reports of the Aborigines' impressions, they would, surely, have been delighted by all the theatrics.

During the summer and into the autumn the excursions and entertainments continued with visits to museums and trips out into the country to observe how the peasantry lived but as the weather got colder, it became clear that Yemmerrawannie's constitution was not up to coping with the English climate. Bennelong did not escape without the snuffles and sneezes, but he was able to throw off the infections in a way his young friend could not. Doctors were called, medicines prescribed, flannel drawers brought and a change of address advised to get the two away from the smoke and smog of London. They moved to Eltham, at that time a village in Kent, where they stayed for six weeks. Visiting, Arthur Phillip could see that the cold, wet weather was doing them no good at all; he ordered up yet more warm underwear, greatcoats and night caps but though Bennelong responded to the treatment, Yemmerrawannie did not. Balsams, quinine, draughts of every kind were prescribed, even bleeding and blistering was tried, but nothing appeared able to stop the general decline in the young man's health.

During December, Bennelong was often away at the theatre or on visits to Sydney Cove friends who were in town. He was seldom accompanied by Yemmerrawannie, who spent most of his time alone in his room, trying to keep warm. Jack Brook points out that by now the youth was surely beginning to feel severely homesick for his own people. Bennelong had spent far more time with the colonists and had always been something of an explorer himself, and besides, he was constantly being diverted with new sights, sounds and, above all, acquaintances. He was not, as Brook says, treated as an object of curiosity but as a guest with interesting things to teach as well as learn; and though it may have been extremely chilly for much of the time, Bennelong's visit was never anything short of stimulating. Yemmerrawannie, on the other hand, was still a boy and feeling far below his best, and he must often have been overwhelmed by the constant barrage of novelty and noise and have wished only for the peace and silence of his native woods and hills.

During February 1794, he recovered enough to join Bennelong on a few more theatre trips, although it was noticed by their companions that Yemmerrawannie's ankles and legs were swelling alarmingly. More medicines were prescribed, though, as Brook says, most of them were such as to debilitate rather than build up the young's man's constitution.

With summer at last on the horizon, Yemmerrawannie rallied and new suits were ordered for both men; their spirits were further lifted by the likelihood of being able to get back to Sydney in the near future. Captain John Hunter was going out to take over the governorship from Major Francis Grose, who was filling-in after Phillip's departure, and he was more than happy to offer a passage to the two men, both of whom he had known back in Sydney.

As it was, only Bennelong made the trip. Yemmerrawannie died of pneumonia on 18th May 1794 at the lodgings in Eltham. A Christian funeral was held at the local church, though Bennelong ensured that his young friend was named, on his gravestone, as an initiated member of his tribe. This was a matter of great importance, not only in the spiritual scheme of things but because back in Sydney Yemmerrawannie had been inordinately proud of the manly way in which he had gone through the painful and wearing rituals of maturity.

Bennelong joined Captain Hunter at Plymouth in January 1795 – the ships comprising Hunter's flotilla should have left months earlier but were being held up by bureaucracy; the future governor wrote constantly to the Admiralty, on occasion mentioning Bennelong's desire to go home and the advisability of removing him from the English winter which had 'laid upon him an apprehension that his lungs are affected'.

They eventually sailed in February, Bennelong aboard the *Reliance*, where the surgeon was George Bass, later – with Matthew Flinders – to be an explorer himself. He was also a good doctor and a good friend to his patient and by the time Bennelong landed at Sydney Cove, he was back in perfect health; he repaid Bass for his attentions by teaching him as much of the local languages as the surgeon could take in and note down, a circumstance that was late to stand Bass in good stead during his voyages of exploration.

Bennelong's return home was not to be as happy or successful as he'd hoped. At first he was welcomed back by his own people and his friends amongst the colonists and it must have seemed to him that, with his new skills, he would be able to balance old and new, settler and settled, successfully against one another.

He took care to appear to each as was expected: with his own people, he went naked (shrewdly setting aside the 'eight gowns and bonnets for the Native women of New South Wales' that had been packed by missionaries) With the colonists, he dressed as smartly – in many cases far more smartly and fashionably – than they. He hunted with the spear, he sat down at the linen-covered dinner table; he ate meat cooked over a fire in the open, he drank wine from crystal glasses; he fought his fellows over women, he gracefully flattered the colony wives; he settled quarrels and spoke up for his people with the English, he tried to explain them to the Aborigines. Gradually, however, the strain began to tell; stretching himself across two worlds, he was living in neither. His own people began to complain once more of his arrogance and the colonists started to become wary when too many glasses of wine had been drunk. Neither side can have been aware of the kind of pressure he was under as he tried to reconcile two cultures without betraying his own nature.

There was more drink, there were more quarrels and violence; he realised that he had to choose one or the other or he would be split in two. He chose his own people, his own culture but it was not, it could never be a totally happy choice; he had been on a journey of far greater length than any of the colonists who had come to his country, he had seen sights stranger than any of his own kind and in his mind he had crossed thousands of years and two cultures that were at opposite ends of the earth. He could never really come back home, never be content again.

He died at Sydney on 3rd January 1813.

Philip Gidley King

Philip Gidley King succeeded Captain John Hunter as the third governor in 1799. Arthur Phillip, who had long admired King's abilities, was both pleased and supportive but had no illusions about the task ahead of the new man. Neither did King.

In the years since the arrival of the New South Wales Corps with the second fleet, the colony had become awash with rum, as all spirituous liquors were now known, which the officers of the corps were selling to enrich themselves. King's first task was to stop the flow and put some kind of decency and continuity back into public life so genuine settlers could see the possibility of making a living out of honest, rather than dishonest, labour. His most implacable opponent was John MacArthur, who had come out with the corps as a lieutenant but had devoted most of his considerable energy to husbandry and was, by 1800, Australia's first sheep baron with over 4000 acres and 2500 animals. MacArthur supported a sort of aristocratic, capitalist free-for-all (despite the fact that his father was, so gossip had it, a stay maker) whilst King, the son of a tradesman, was always inclined towards a mixed economy.

The tension between governor and farmer became so great that King had MacArthur arrested and confined to his land; MacArthur, in the tradition of the corps, demanded a court martial to clear himself; King used the opportunity to have MacArthur sent back to England to answer the charges there.

However, solving one problem only opened the gates for another, and King found himself facing a full-scale revolt by the Irish prisoners at Sydney. Many of them, indeed most, had been transported for what were, in effect, political crimes and it was hardly surprising if there was both a profound sense of grievance and a burning desire for freedom amongst them. King was sympathetic – he had secured a pardon for the transported priest Father James Dixon, and paid him a government salary 'to perform his office for the benefit of all Catholics in the colony' – however, he could not allow sedition and at the first murmurings of political discontent he came down upon the Irish with maximum severity. It was the only possible move but it was also (as so often in Irish affairs) the wrong one and on 4th March 1804, convicts from Castle Hill seized weapons from the corps and marched on Sydney.

George Johnstone, who had come out with the First Fleet as a lieutenant and was now a major, met the rebels face to face. His troops were ready to fire, the Irish were ready to respond; a bloodbath was in the offing.

'I rode forward, attended by a trooper and Mr Dixon, the Roman Catholic priest, calling them halt, that I wished to speak to them. They desired I would come into the middle of them, as their captains were there. I refused, observing that I was in pistol shot and that it was in their power to kill me, and that their captains must have very little spirit if they would not come forward to speak to me. Upon which two advanced upon me. I called upon them to surrender. One of them replied that they would have death or liberty. I clapped my pistol to his head and they were both driven, their swords in their hands, to the Quartermaster. The detachment formed into a line and commenced a well-directed fire, which was but weakly returned. The rebel line being soon broken, they ran in all directions. One of their chiefs, presumed dead on the field, was brought up alive and I immediately ordered him to be hung up.'[11]

The revolt was over, bar the obligatory hangings and floggings. John MacArthur returned from England, having had all proceedings against him set aside. However, peace was now in his commercial interest and he and King made up and the colony moved into one of the more serene periods of its infancy, soon to be shattered by a terrible flood along the Hawksbury river which wiped out a year's harvest. King worked day and night to improve the situation but got little thanks for his efforts; the colonists tended to blame their governors for natural disasters. He retired, exhausted, from his office in 1806. He was succeeded by William Bligh, who wasted no time in quarrelling with everyone and generating the usual upsets, which resulted in the usual mutiny.

Whilst on Norfolk Island during the 1780s, King had taken a convict mistress, Ann Innet, with whom he had two children, Norfolk and Sydney. He later married Ann Coombs, a Devon woman, and started a dynasty which is still distinguished in Australia today. He died in September 1808, shortly after visiting his old friend Arthur Phillip in Bath.

Finding Boswell

After James Boswell's death his papers found themselves in a sort of limbo, moving between the Great Biographer's three executors: his lifetime correspondent, the earnest Reverend Temple in Cornwall; his collaborator, the scholarly Malone (without whom there would, probably, have been no *LIFE*) in London and the Scottish banker, the respectable Alistair Forbes, in Edinburgh. All three of them were busy men – Temple was facing death and trying to get his affairs and his family in order, Forbes was banking and Malone was working on his proposed complete edition of Shakespeare's works. The papers themselves, thousands upon thousands of sheets of letters, journals and notes, were spread across any number of different locations and were, more often than not, disorganised and unsorted. Moreover, they contained, whenever anyone did look closely at them, material that was not considered proper for publication or perusal by anyone other than men of the world – who were, by the nature of things, too busy with the world to do much perusing, considering that to be an effeminate kind of occupation. The papers thus passed between the executors, travelling the roads and turnpikes of England and Scotland and within a few years had become more or less invisible.

Someone had them somewhere – probably.

Temple was dead within the year; Malone was everlastingly busy but did what he could, working with Boswell's younger son, James, a serious young man who was, in his turn, to complete Malone's Shakespeare edition after the scholar's death. Forbes was less than comfortable with the subject matter and consigned (it was thought) the packets he received to the Boswell family. They, in the person of Alexander 'Sandy' Boswell, were not happy. Like his father, Sandy was a proud and touchy man, ever careful of the honour of the Boswells. As a boy he had suffered under the reports of his father acting like a buffoon, standing on chairs at public occasions, crooning Swedish love songs and making up to young girls at bibulous dinners. Certainly, Sandy loved his father (all the children did, Boswell was an immensely lovable and, in his way, innocent man – he'd never have got away with half the stuff he did if he hadn't been) but he simply could not consider him, try as he might, a respectable man and Sandy wanted a respectable family above all things. Even the Reynolds portrait of the Great Biographer was shuffled from one wall to another of the family home, eventually ending up in a shady corner, virtually unseen. The papers were consigned either to the fire (Malone made a note which might have meant they'd been burnt) or to some damp attic.

Sandy himself died in 1822 as the result of a bungled duel. He'd inherited his father's habit of penning articles attacking local politicians and others in power – but though he did have the sense to write anonymously, he did not have the guile to make sure his victims never found out who was mauling them in the public prints. One, an Edinburgh lawyer, James Stuart, did so and since Sandy had named him a coward in his lampoon, saying he'd draw bills, will and petitions, in fact anything but a trigger, Stuart was more or less obliged to issue a challenge. The two men met early one morning in the country. Sandy had first shot and, as a deadly marksman and a man of honour, was obliged to fire into the air. Stuart, who had never pulled a trigger in his life, shut his eyes, stuck out his arm and fired – hitting Sandy in the throat. He died two days later. Stuart was arrested and charged with murder but, when his defence offered pages from Boswell's *Life of Johnson* in which both the Biographer and the Great Cham supported the practice of duelling, the jury acquitted him.

The Boswell papers then vanished from history. The supposition was that they had been cleared out or lost or used for kindling or had turned to damp, soggy lumps in some attic. Boswell himself was seen as a great biographer but also as a great buffoon; the Victorians, on the whole, did not find his kind of character at all sympathetic and tended to regard him as a sort of idiot savant or naive chronicler who had achieved his effects by scrupulously copying down what he heard and saw. They'd read his book with pleasure but had he arrived for a visit, the butler would have sent him round to the kitchen door, where the dogs would have seen him off the property. Boswell the man was of no possible interest.

Then, in 1840, an Englishman on the continent, an ex-East India Company nabob named Stone, found himself buying butter in Boulogne and noticed it was wrapped in old manuscript paper. On looking closer, he read the name Boswell. He enquired of the shopkeeper as to where she got her wrappings and after buying every sheet in the shop, found the paper-peddler and bought all he had left. He found himself with the majority of a lifetime's worth of letters from James Boswell to his country friend Temple. Letters that were full of brilliant descriptions, deep moral dilemmas and amorous adventures, since the friendship between Boswell and Temple, after their time together at university, had been almost totally epistolary and Boswell, on paper at least, was rarely less than painfully, delightfully honest.

How the letters ended up wrapping groceries in Boulogne was a mystery but literary detectives suggest that after Temple's death his son-in-law, something of a con-man and spendthrift, left the country (a few steps ahead of his creditors) and stole the letters in case they might prove of value. They didn't, at least to him, but the general reading public was more fortunate – they were published in full, to general critical approbation – only eighty years later in 1924. There had been earlier editions but careful editors had removed all sensitive matter, which didn't leave much. The 1924 edition excited a renewed interest in Boswell the man, as opposed to his biography, and was edited by Professor C.B. Tinker, an American academic and one of the first Boswellians.

In 1920, whilst working on what Boswell papers were extant, for a proposed biography, Tinker advertised in the *Times Literary Supplement* for any Boswelliana which might be in private hands. He received a mysterious postcard with a scrawled signature (still unidentified) with the gnomic message: 'Try Malahide Castle.'

First he had to find out where the place was – a few miles from Dublin – and then decide whether the card was a hoax or not. Checking in a handy *Burke's Peerage*, he discovered that an Emily Boswell had, in 1873, married into the Talbot family who resided at Malahide Castle, which was currently the home of one Lord James Boswell Talbot. It seemed worth taking a chance and he wrote a letter to his lordship. The reply was not encouraging and Tinker let the matter drop for the time being and went back to his teaching.

The next year a university friend of Tinker's found himself posted to the US Embassy in Dublin and the professor, through his obviously respectable friend, tried again. This time he received an invitation to visit Lord and Lady Talbot at the castle. Lady Talbot was, it appeared, a recent acquisition; the secretive, shy peer had married late and his wife was a young woman of great charm, spirit and culture and it was she who served tea to the questing Professor and, over the cucumber sandwiches, told him there were indeed various Boswell papers in the castle and that the family had made tentative attempts to publish them over the years but no one, for a variety of reasons – but mainly due to their risqué nature – had been interested.

She showed Talbot a large desk stuffed full of papers – Boswell papers. He felt, he later said, 'like Sinbad in the valley of rubies'. However, he was not allowed to touch or examine any of the rubies and returned to Dublin, where he was staying, empty-handed and in a quandary as to what he should do.

It was clear that anything written about Boswell up to that point was based on partial evidence; what was in the desk at Malahide might change everything. But how to get access? The Talbots, certainly Lord Talbot, were firmly following the Boswell family tradition of acknowledging the biographer whilst brushing the rake under the hedge.

He shared his dilemma with an antiquarian friend, Edward Newton, back in the States: 'Everything here and nothing to be touched!' Newton could offer no suggestions but, later in the year, whilst crossing the Atlantic, he bumped into a fellow collector, Colonel Ralph Isham, a man of action, a man of culture and, Newton said, a devilishly fascinating fellow. He told Isham about the papers and about the family's reluctance to part with them. To the dashing Colonel it was an adventure like stalking big game and, over the course of the next year, he subtly insinuated himself into the Talbot's world, never mentioning the Boswell papers, not even hinting at his interest but rather playing on his personality and the general admiration of his 1914–18 war record (an American, he had joined the British army as a private on the first day of hostilities and had risen to rank of lieutenant colonel by the end).

Finally, he was invited to the castle for cucumber sandwiches and shown the desk. He didn't pick up a ruby that first day but over the next couple of years he gained Lady Talbot's trust and was able to buy a letter or two and then, after spending time going through and organising the papers (there were a number of journals as well as letters) with the Talbots, he was able to purchase larger and larger selections until at last he owned the entire collection.

Unfortunately, Lady Talbot, still with the family reputation in mind, took to blacking out what she considered to be 'unrespectable' passages before sending the papers off. Fortunately Isham and his researchers and editors were able to read the censored sections by holding the paper up to the light but it was a tiresome business and the Colonel had to exert all his charm to persuade Lady Talbot to put down her black pencil and agree that the letters and journals should be published as they were. And Isham needed to publish: he had spent something like £40,000 on the collection and had to recoup his expenses.

Deals were struck with publishers on both sides of the Atlantic and under the editorship of the British scholar Geoffrey Scott and then the American Frederick Pottle, the edition was painstakingly prepared for the press. In the meantime, the Great Depression had struck, businesses and businessmen fell at an alarming rate and so did Colonel Isham's bank balance – just at the time news came from Malahide Castle of another cache of Boswell papers found stuffed in a games box. Isham managed to raise the money to buy them and they were added to his collection.

By 1936 Pottle had finished his task and the Malahide papers were in print. At which point more news crossed the ocean: an academic researching an obscure eighteenth-century Scottish poet who had been a friend of the banker Alexander Forbes was going through the Forbes papers at the family home, Fettercairn House, near Aberdeen, when he came across a Boswell journal – then a packet of loose papers headed 'Concerning Ladies' – and finally a sack full of letters. In all, there was almost half as much again as Isham had bought – which put him and Pottle in the same situation that Tinker had been in with his newly published *Letters* at the time of the first finds.

In fact the papers had been discovered five years earlier but the news had been kept secret due to labyrinthine litigation over copyright. On top of this, Isham discovered yet more pages of Boswelliana on a visit to Malahide Castle which the Talbots generously allowed him to have for nothing. He did not, however, have the Fettercairn papers – there was, it appeared, an endless stream of Boswell descendents who thought that they were the heirs to the collection and, presumably, to the cash that would come from selling it. Isham was unable even to bid for the collection whilst the matter was before the courts and had to console his collector's instinct with the somewhat dissatisfying knowledge that he owned 'almost all' of the Boswell papers.

Then – it's a story full of 'thens' – came more news from Malahide. In an outbuilding which the local authorities had hired for storage, two large cases were discovered containing even more papers and the manuscript of *The Life of Johnson.* The Talbots decided to put these on the market – Isham was deeply hurt; he felt they owed him something at least and he wrote angrily about the matter to Lady Talbot. Relations were at a low ebb for a while but it was, by now, wartime again and not the time for personal quarrels. Isham was able to raise a loan and the Talbots sold the remaining papers to him. He was also able to buy the Fettercairn papers from the disputants in the case and, at last, in 1948, after the papers had crossed the Atlantic, Colonel Isham was able to consider his collection complete.

Obviously he was in no position – he wasn't getting any younger and his health was far from good – to administer the vast archive and he negotiated a sale to Yale University, where the papers were housed in 1949.

In 1950, Lady Talbot uncovered another five hundred letters and Isham expostulated: 'My God, is there no end to the Boswell sage?' So far, there hasn't been – odd papers have been turning up throughout the years; there are still whole series of letters and portions of the journals missing as are the intriguing two sheets of notes which James Boswell made from Mary Bryant's dictation whilst she was packing her box for the journey back to Fowey.

James Martin's Memorandums

James Martin, Being Convicted at they City of Exeter in they County of Devonshire Being found guilty of Stealing $16\frac{1}{4}$ lb of old Lead and $4\frac{1}{2}$ lb of old Iron property of Lord Courney powdrum cacle nere Exeter. Received sentence for to be Transported to Botany Bay for 7 years – Returned from thy Bar to Exeter Gaol and there remaind 2 months – from thence sent on board they *Dunkirk* there remained 10 months from thence put on Bord they *Charlotte* Transport Then Bound to Botany Bay.

March 12 1787 saild round to Spithead there remained to they 13 of May – then Sail in Company with 10 sail for Botany Bay under Commandand of Govonor Philips. Make they Peek of Tenereef 5 Day of June there remaind 7 Days, then sail for they island of Reiodegenira, being 8 weeks on our passage – there remaind 1 Month then saild for they Cape of good hope – Being Eight weeks and three Days on our passage – then Saild for Botany Bay Being 10 weeks on our passage.

Come to an anchor in port Jackson Send on Shore in 2 Days – they Convicts Being Sent on Shore So Began to work on governments account on being landed we were Encamped and formed in squads of six in a tent – after We Being Encamped We Some were to Clear They ground Others sent to build huts – I remaind on the island from January 1788 unto March 1791– .

On the 28 Day of March Made My Escape in Compy. With 7 men more and me with one woman and two Childn. – in an open six oar Boat – being of provisions on Bd. One hundred wt. Of flower and one hundd. wt. of Rice 14 lb of pork and about Eight gallons of water – having a Compass Quadrant and Chart.

After 2 Days sail reach a little Creek about 2 Degrees to they Northward of Port Jackson there found a quantity of fine Burng. Coal there remained 2 nights and one Day and found a Varse Quantity of Cabbage tree which we Cut Down and procured they Cabbage.

Then they Natives Came Down to which we gave some Cloathes and other articles and they went away very much satisfied. They appearance of they land appears more better here than at Sydney Cove here we got avarse Quantity of fish which of great refresment to us – After out stay of 2 nights and 1 Day we preceeded our Voyage to they Northward after 2 days sail we made a very fine harbour Seeming to run up they Country for many Miles and Quite Commodius for they Anchorage of Shipping –

Here we found aplenty of fresh water – hawld our Boat ashore her Bottom being very leaky they Better to pay her Bottom with some Beeswax and Rosin which we had a small Quantity Thereof – But on they Same night was drove off By they natives – which meant to Destroy us – we launched our Boat and Raod off in they stream Quite out of Reach of them – that being Sunday Morng. We Attempted to land when we found a place Convenient for to Repair our Boat we accordg. We put Some of our things – part being ashore there Came they natives in Vast Numbers With Speers and Shields etc we formed in parts one party of us Made towards them they better by signs to pacify them But they not taking they least notice accordingly we fired a musket thinking to afright them But they took not they least notice Thereof –

On Percieving them Rush more forward we were forced to take to out Boat and to get out of their reach as far as we Could – and what to Do we Could not tell But on Consulting with each other it was Determined for to row up they harbour which accordingly we rowed up they harbour 9 or 10 miles till we made a little white sandy isld. In they Middle of they harbour – which land. Upon and hawld up our Boat and repair her Bottom with what little materials we had.

Whilst our Stay of 2 Days we had no Interpon from they Natives – then we rowed off they main where we took in fresh water and a few cabbage trees – and then put out to sea – they natives her is quite naked of a Copper Colour – shock hair – they have Canoos made of bark then we proceedd. They Northard, having a leadg. Breez from they S:W – But that night they wind Changed and Drove us Quite out of sight of Land – which we hawld our wind having a set of Sails in they Boat.

Accordingly they next Day we Made Close into they land But they Surf rung. So very hard we Cd. Not attempt to land but kept along shore but Making no harbour or Creek for some three weeks we were much distress.d for water and wood – accordingly perceiving they Surf to abate two of our men swam on ashore thinking to get some water But being afraid of they natives which they see in numbers they return.d without any But a little wood which they Threw into the water which we took up.

We put over on the other side of the Bay expecting to meet with a Convenient Harbour we found a little River which with great difficulty we got up our Boat being very leaky at that Time that it was with great Difficulty that we could keep her above Water – were we Landed and hawld her up putting some soap in the Seams which Answered very well – at this Place we cou'd get no Shell Fish or Fish in any kind in this Bay.

Here we stopped two days and two Nights – then we left this Place and went down the Bay above 20 Miles expecting to meet with a Harbour and get some refreshments – but cou'd see none nor the End of the Bay the Wind being favourable we tack'd about and put to sea the Land here seem'd to be much the same as at Botany bay – accordingly we up grappling so stood to they Northward but our Boat being very Deep we were Obliged to trow all our Cloathing over Board they Better to lighten our Boat as they Sea Breaking over us Quite rapid –

That Night we ran into an Open Bay and Could see no Place to land at the Surf running that we were afraid of Staving our Boat to

Pieces – we came to a grappling in that Bay the same Night at 2 o Clock in the Morn.g our Grapling Broke and we were drove in the Middle of the Surf Expecting every Moment that our Boat wou'd be Staved to Pieces and every Soul Perish but as God wou'd have we Got our Boat save on Shore without any Loss or damage excepting one Oar we Hauld our Boat up and there remain two days and a Night.

There we kindled a Fire with great difficulty everything we had being very Wet – we Got Plenty of Shell Fish and Fresh Water the Natives Came down in great Numbers we discharged a Musquet over their Heads and they dispersed immediately and we saw no more of them.

We put out things in the Boat and with great difficulty we Got out to Sea for 2 or 3 days we had very Bad Wether our Boat Shipping many heavy Seas, so that One Man was always Employed in Balling out the Water to Keep her up – the next Place we made was White Bay being in Lattd. 27d. 00 we ran down that Bay 2 or 3 Leagues befor we cou'd see a convenient Place to Land the Surf running very High.

We saw 2 Women and 2 Children with a Fire Brand in their Hands at this Place we Landed the two Women being Frightened ran away but we made Signs that we wanted a Light which they Gave us Crying at the same Time in their Way we took our things out of the Boat and put them in two Huts which was there –

The next Morng. About 11 o Clock a great Number of Natives Came towards us – as soon as we saw we went to meet them and Fired a Musquet over their Heads as soon as they Heard they report they ran into the Woods and we saw no more of them the Natives there is Quite Naked – here we stopped two days and two Nights.

The Surf running so very high that we were in great danger of Staving ye. Boat that Night we drove out to Sea by a heavy Gale of Wind and Current expecting every Moment to go to the Bottom next Morn.g saw no land the Sea running Mountains high we were Under a Close reeft Mainsail and kept so until Night and then came too under a droge all the Night with her Head to the Sea thinking every Moment to be the last the sea Coming in so heavy upon us every now and then that two Hands were Obliged to keep bailing out and it raind very hard all that Night.

The next Morng. We took our droge in but could see no Land but hawling towards the Land to make it as soon as possible the gale of Wind still Continuing we kept under a Close reeft Main sail but cou'd make no Land at all that day – I will Leave you to Consider what distress we must be in the Woman and two little babies were in a bad condition everything being so Wet that we Cou'd by no Means light a Fire we had nothing to Eat except a little raw rice.

As Night we Come to under a droge as we did the Night before the next Morng. We took in our droge and kept to the Northwd. On purpose to make the land about 8 o Clock we made the Land which proved to be a little Island about 30 Leagues from the Main the Surf running so very High we were rather fearful of going in for fear of Staving our Boat but we Concluded amongst Ourselves that we might as well Venture in there as to keep out to Sea seeing no Probability that if we kept out to Sea that we shou'd every Soul Perish –

All round this island there was nothing but reefs but a little sandy Beach which we got in safe without much damage and haul'd our Boat up out of the way of the Surf we got all our things out of the Boat and then we Went to get a Fire which with great difficulty we got a Fire which being almost Starving we got a little Rice for to cook when we went to this island we had but one gallon of fresh Water for there was not a drop of fresh Water to be had on this island.

The island was about one mile in Cercumference after the Tide fell we went to Look for some Shell Fish but found a great Quantity of very fine Large Turtles which was left upon the reef which we turned five of them and hawld them upon the Beach this reef runs about a Mile and a half out in the Sea and Intirely dry when low Water.

We took and killed One of the Turtles and had a Noble Meal this Night it rain'd very hard when we spread our Mainsail and filled our two Breakers full of Water – we stayed on this island six days during that Time we killed 12 Turtles and some of it we Took and dry'd over the Fire to take to sea with us.

It seemed to us there had never been any Natives on this Island there is a kind of fruit that grows like unto a Bellpepper which seems to Taste very well there was a great Quantity of Fowls that stayed at

Night in Holes in the ground we Could not think of taking any live Turtles with us because our Boat would not admit of it.

We Paid the Seams of our Boat all over with Soap before we got to Sea at 8 o Clock in the Morng. And steered to the Northward: this Island was in Lat 26d. 27m. we made the main Land in the Evening and we passed a great Number of Small Islands which we put into a great many of them expecting to find some Turtle but never found any but found plenty of Fresh Water but nothing We could find fit to eat.

When we Came to the Gulf of Cerpentara which is Latt. 10d 11m. we ran down the Gulf 9 or 10 miles we saw several small Islands on which we saw several of the Natives in two Canoes landing on one of the small Islands we steered down towards them as soon as they saw us they sent their two Canoes round to the Back of the Island with one Man in each of them when we Came down to them they seemed to strand in a posture of defence against us we fired a Musquet over them and Immediately they began firing their Bows and arrows at us.

We immediately hoisted up our Sails and rowed away from them but as God wou'd have it none of their Arrows came into the Boat but dropped along side we could not get Hold of any of them but they seemed to be about Eighteen inches long the Natives seemed to be very stout and fat and Blacker than they were in other Parts we seen before there was One which we took to be the Chief with some shells Around his shoulders.

We down a little further down the Gulf and landed upon the Main for to get us some Water we found plenty of fresh Water we saw a small Town of Huts about 20 of them just by were some Fresh Water was there was none of the Inhabitants in their Huts or about them that we Could see their Huts was large enough for six or seven of them to Stand upright in they were made of bark and Covered Over with Grass we filled our 2 Breakers with fresh Water and Came on Board of our Boat again for we were Afraid of Staying on Shore for fear of the Natives we went three or four Miles from the Shore and dropt our Killock and there Stopped all Night.

The next morning we were determined to go the same Place to recruit our Water but as we were making to the shore we saw two very large Canoes coming towards us and we did not know what to do for we were Afraid to meet them there seemed to us to be 30 or 40 Men in each Canoe they had Sails in their Canoes seemed to be made of matting one of their Canoes was a Head of the others a little Way Stopt until the other Came up and then she Hoisted her Sail and made after us as soon as we saw that we Tack'd about with what Water we had —

Determined to Cross the Gulf which was about Five Hundred miles Across which as God wou'd have it we Out ran them they followed us until we Lost sight of them we having but little fresh Water and no Wood to make a Fire with but in four days and a half we made the other side of the Gulf we put on Shore to look for some fresh Water but cou'd find none at that Place but we kept along Shore until the Eveng. We saw a small river which we made to and got plenty of fresh Water.

We put to Sea the same Night we saw no more Land until we Came into the Lattitude of North End of the Island we hawled up to make the land but saw no Land but a heavy Swell running which was like to have Swallowed us up then we Concluded as the best Way to shape our Course for the Island of Timor with what little Water we had which made it in 36 Hours after we [text missing] Which we ran along the island of Timor until we came to the Dutch Settlements which we went on shore to the Governors house where he behaved extremely well to us.

Filled our Bellies and Cloathed Double with every [text missing] that was wore on the Island which we remd. Very happy at our work for 2 Months till Wm. Bryant had words with his wife went and informed against himself Wife and Children and all of us which was immediately taken Prisoners and was put into the Castle.

We were strictly Examined after being Examined we were allowed to Go out of the Castle 2 at a time for one Day 2 more and so we continued until Captain Edwards who had been on search of the Bounty Pirates which had taken some of the Pirates at Otaheiti which he lost the *Pandora* frigate betwixt New Guinea and New Holland which he made Island of Timor in the Pinnace Two yawls and his Longboat and 120 hands which was saved which Captain Edwards came to us to know which we were which we told him we was Convicts and had made our escape from Botany Bay which he told us we were his prisoners and put us on board *Rambang* Dutch Company Ship and put us Both Legs in Irons Called the bilboes which we were conveyed to bretavia which we were taken out the *Rambang* and put on a Dutch Guardship in Irons again.

There we lost the Child 6 Days after the father of the Child was taken Bad and Died which was both buried in bretavis 6 weeks after we was put on three different Ships bound to the Cape of Good Hope which we was 3 months before we reached the Cape which we came there the *Gorgon* man or war which brought the marines from Botany Bay which we was Put on board the *Gorgon* which we was known well by all the marine officers which was all Glad we had not perished at sea.

Was brought home to England in the *Gorgon* we was Brought ashore at Purfleet and from there Conveyed by the Constables to Bow st office London and was taken before Justice Bond and was fully committed to Newgate.

Wm. Moatton Navigator of the Boat Died James Cox Died Saml. Bird died A little girl 3 Yrs and a Quarter old died the mother of the 2 children Mary Bryant alive James Martin alive Wm. Allen alias John Brown alive Nathl. Lilly alive.

James Martin's *Memorandums* is part of the Bentham Papers, held in the special collection at the University of London Library.

Terra Australis

Nowhere on earth is quite like Australia. The island continent was once compared, by the French scientist Couvier, to a fragment of another planet that has dropped onto our own world, but that other planet is, in fact, our own distant past and it is still possible to see in Australia some of the earliest and most vital examples of life on earth: the stromatalites, simple blue-green algae which created the atmosphere which we all breath today.

The land we know as Australia began life about 140 million years ago, after the single world continent had broken apart and the great land masses were creeping across the face of the globe. A southern super-continent found itself being pulled northwards. Under un-imaginable pressures and over millions of years, it began to break apart; the land masses that were to become South America, Africa and India made new links with the northern super-continent whilst Antarctica and Australia, still joined, migrated south and, eventually split apart, one sliding down to the regions of ice and cold, the other carrying its cargo of life into the warmth of the Pacific.

Sea-pens and segmented worms from the Precambrian oceans can still be found fossilised in Australian rock over 600 million years old. The very nature of the Australian landscape, its comparative flatness, demonstrates the passage of millions of years of erosion by wind, ice and water. Over the ages, the shapes and contours have constantly changed as land and sea have battled, great mountain ranges have risen up and fallen to become desert. Huge inland seas have existed and shrunk to tiny lakes and then been engulfed by the advance of an ocean which, only 100 million years ago, covered most of the continent as we know it today.

It was during this period, the Cretaceous, which extended from 130 to 60 million years ago, that the dinosaurs were at their peak. The insects too were there, enjoying what was, for them, a perfect environment. Over the millennia, they were to evolve into more than 40,000 species with over 2000 different types of fly and, since nature loves a challenge, 1000 species of spider to prey upon them.

The flowering plants and grasses were beginning to spread across the landscape by the end of the Cretaceous and as the seas fell back and the lands rose, there was more space for them to grow and provide food for the birds and mammals which were to supplant the dinosaurs. And just as Australia can boast some of the earliest rocks and most basic of plants, so it can also show us the earliest mammals, the monotremes, animals so strange that when European naturalists first examined them in the mid-nineteenth century, they were convinced they were the victims of an elaborate hoax. These living fossils, the echidna and platypus, appeared to inhabit a hinterland between mammal and reptile, where the basic functions of life had become blurred and uncertain.

At first the scientists simply refused to believe that the platypus laid eggs. They must have been placed, cuckoo-like, in the nest by some other animal or stolen by the platypus for food. It was not until a female was shot (and the early explorers tended to shoot rather than capture) with an egg inside her body that the experts were forced to face the impossible: an egg-laying mammal that suckled its newly hatched young not from a nipple but with milk fat that exuded like sweat through the skin.

The monotremes survived in only a couple of species but their more sophisticated cousins, the marsupials, were to do far better in the new land and by the beginning of the Pliocene age, 8 million years ago, they were the dominant species.

The land too was beginning to settle into its final form, or, at least, the form in which we know it today: the western plateau, forming two-thirds of the country, and including most of its deserts; the low-lying central basin, with its riverine plains, and the eastern uplands with their mountain systems, once forested and now rich in coal, were all more or less stable by 2 million years ago.

The marsupials were the kings of this world and some of them were regal indeed. The diprotodon, a grass eater, weighed in at two tonnes and resembled our present day rhinoceros; genyornis, a flightless bird, was the height of an emu but weighed four times as much. The great kangaroo was able to browse on leaves three metres above the ground; there was a giant wombat more than a metre high and a marsupial lion, which may have been carnivorous, and the thylocene, the Tasmanian tiger, which definitely was. These and their smaller brothers, the reptiles and birds, the insects and spiders were, for thousands of years, the inheritors of the land – but then, things changed.

In the nineteenth and early twentieth centuries the general view was that the first Australians had migrated to the island continent some 10–15,000 years ago, but modern archaeological studies have pushed that date steadily back to somewhere between 60,000 or even 100,000 years. They probably came from South-East Asia at a time when sea levels were considerably lower than they are now and island hopping by canoe was a feasible method of travel. They may have crossed from New Guinea to the continent by a land bridge or they may have arrived from the tip of Indonesia – or Australia itself (or adjacent lands now sunk) may have been one of the places that humanisation and hominisation actually occurred.

Aboriginal commentators have said that 'though the antiquity of the human species is not here in our land of the dreaming, it does contain the oldest known relics of modern human beings. People in other parts of the world believe that we came here across the seas, but still they cannot show us our tracks anywhere but here. They can find nobody older than us anywhere else on earth. Whatever puzzle the origin of human beings might hold, we became human here.'

What is certain is that the continent provides good evidence of a continuity of human culture over many thousands of years; as Dr Eric Wilmott, the aboriginal educationalist and inventor, says, the Australians were amongst the first, possibly the first human beings to contemplate their own nature and construct systems of religious thought. Cave paintings of great antiquity reflect, in their use of symbolism, an attempt to grapple with the duality of the spiritual and temporal world in which their creators lived.

From the start, these newcomers in an old land moved in small groups, establishing tribes and territories; there was more than enough land for all and though conflict wasn't absent, it was probably rare until the arrival of European settlers, who began to disrupt tribal boundaries, creating a ripple effect, squashing and distorting borders which had existed unchanged for thousands of years:

'We managed the land in our own way. This meant that in our own place we had to move constantly. This land of ours showed us how to survive and we listened to her. We hunted, we tracked our prey. With clicks of the tongue we could call the crabs from their holes in the mango swamps or stop the goanna with the cry of a hawk or drive the prey from a hollow log with a hiss like a snake. We learnt to find water where there was none to be seen, in roots that stretched far underground from the malee scrub. If the stream was baked dry, we would stamp our feet like rain on the riverbed and deep under the ground the toads bloated with their own water would think the wet had come and croak and give themselves away.

'We wandered many places. Deserts and mountains, forests, shores and swamps. Where there was fish, we trapped it with baskets or lines and nets and bone hooks. We knew about the plants, which to eat, which made us better, which killed. And we learned to use fire. To warm us, to drive prey from cover, to make smoke or drive away insects, to give light if we were fishing in the dark, from small fires in our canoes. We lived in a burning land, we carried a glowing stick with us always, we were a people of fire and would often burn for the joy of it – and to clear the undergrowth and give new life room to grow.'[12]

Eric Wilmott points out that these early men and women, as they travelled across country, were amongst the first human beings to move from maintenance to extractor tools by taking stone and bone implements and fixing them to wood. They also used stones to grind flour and create colours for their cave paintings. They met and traded with other tribes, for there were many differences among them. There must have been hundreds, perhaps thousands of tribes and as many separate languages and dialects. The first Europeans found that the tribes on either side of Sydney Cove spoke quite different languages.

For each tribe, its language and, most of all, the land it moved across, comprised the whole world, physical and spiritual. They believed absolutely that the Sky Heroes, the Great Rainbow Snake, the Ancestors, the Gods created the land in every particular: each hill, each gully or river, every stone or mountain path, every swamp or desert was an indivisible part of the whole, just as they were and just as their stories, their rituals and beliefs were too. It was no wonder they took care of the land – they would no more rip up a tree carelessly than they would rip their own arm off. They believed that this world had always been there and always would be there and they lived with it in harmony:

'*First there is the spirit which is called from its home by the magic of the father, and finds within the body of the mother the substance that will clothe it. As soon as it is born, the child is part of its people, with it's own totem. There is also a strong and wide-ranging system of kinship and everyone the child encounters will be related to it in some way and have certain obligations towards it.*

'*As they grow the children are taught by all, by the games they play, by the world around them. From his first moments the child will have known the songs and the dances of his people but, at the age of four or five, he will begin to learn these more seriously. Life is still play at this age, there are few responsibilities. These will come later.*

'*A girl is closer to the sacred by nature. At puberty she will often be decorated with red and white feathers and go through certain ceremonies to mark her passage. In parts of the country, at the climax of these ceremonies, all the women of the group will gather together at a stream or pool and swim together.*

'For a boy his initiation into the responsibilities of adulthood is often a harder and more demanding process. Firstly the Elders must consider he is worthy of undergoing the ceremonies and then he must learn obedience and to overcome fear and pain. In some places the youth is consumed by an ancestral spirit who vomits him out a new being. In others he returns to the great mother and is reborn through her.

'Unlike women, young men show no ordinary sign that they have reached maturity and so they are marked on their bodies. In some places these ceremonies include circumcision, the extraction of a front tooth and marks on the chest.

'All this is only a beginning to his life as a man. Throughout his life a man will learn more of the sacred rituals, depending on his ability and desire to know. His initiation is only a step across a line which marks the beginning of his journey. He may be old indeed before he reaches an end.'[13]

It is easy to be sentimental and forget the many hardships and brutalities of their lives, but on the whole, the Australian of the seventeenth or eighteenth century had, as Geoffrey Blainey has pointed out, a far higher standard of living than the great majority of Europeans. They did not work for the sake of it, they did not labour for the profit of others; they spent, it has been estimated, an average of five hours a day working to supply their material needs and the rest of the time was given to enjoyment and spirituality. They didn't maximise their technology, rather, they trimmed it back to the point of greatest efficiency, where they used it rather than the other way round. In an unchanging land, where their lives followed an equally unchanging seasonal pattern, this made a good deal of common sense.

They had all they wanted materially, artistically and, of far greater importance, spiritually and all of these were tied to the land. Most human beings have a loyalty or love of their own place but for the Aborigines, the place was as much a part of them as their nervous system or backbone – there was no border between the man or woman and the landscape over which they moved during the changing seasons. To alter or destroy the place or the path would be to alter or destroy them. It was a truly elegant system which worked beautifully and had done so for thousands of years but in some ways it was also terribly brittle and once a foreign element was introduced, once someone else set foot on the shore and established settlements, a process began which would, in the end, all but destroy the dreaming.

The west had speculated on the nature of the unknown south from the moment they first began to be curious about the world beyond their own doorstep. If, certain Greeks and Romans felt, the world really was round then surely the great mass of land on one side – the known world – must, according to all the laws of physics, be balanced by an equal weight on the other side, the *terra australis incognita*, the unknown southern land.

Theopompous wrote of 'certain islands named Europis, Asia and Libia, which the ocean sea circumscribes and compasses round about; and without this world there a continent or parcel of dry land which in greatness is infinite and unmeasurable and has green meadows and pasture plots and big and mighty beasts and men who exceed our stature by twice.'

This was pure speculation, as was St Augustine's remark that there could be nothing more absurd than the idea that there might be inhabitants in the regions of the earth opposite to ours, and Friar Roger Bacon's 'place beyond Capricorn which is of best habitation, seeing it is in the higher part of the world and the more noble; and hence the opinion of some that paradise is there.'

Not until the 1450s did European explorers begin to set sail beyond the sunset and discover what might be there. Prince Henry of Navarre often spent the whole night rooted to the spot, studying the movement of the stars and it was his men, navigating down the side of Africa, always keeping the shore in sight, expecting to be boiled alive as they rounded the next cape, who opened up the possibility of discovery beyond imagination and wealth beyond avarice – though, as it was to turn out, European avarice stretched an awfully long way and has never been satisfied yet.

Within a hundred years of those first, hesitant voyages, the Portuguese had reached Indonesia. Here, they built forts to protect traders and missionaries and though there is no record of them going on to discover the southern continent, some of their seamen must have glimpsed or even landed on the coast of Australia.

The first recorded sighting by a European – it is possible that the Chinese visited the northern coasts in the early fifteenth century – came in 1606. The Dutchman Wilhelm Jansen, sailing down through the Malay archipelago, touched on the north coast in the region of Arnhemland. He mapped part of the coastline, under the impression it was New Guinea, but after landing to fill up his water casks and having a man killed, he sailed back home.

It was later in the same year that a Spanish expedition led by Luis Torres discovered and passed through the straights that now bear his name between Cape York and Papua New Guinea. He wrote: 'We found islands towards the north, and among them one bigger than the rest; and as night fell we anchored in five fathoms at half a league from the island. At midnight the ship began to touch bottom, which, had it not been of clay, would have holed us. We lightened the deck and lowered more cable and God was pleased that we should find more water, and the wind being strong went out at the north.'

It was the Dutch rather than the Spanish who were really interested in this part of the world. They saw in it the opportunity of good profit for little cost and had, in the Dutch East India Company and its ships, the perfect tool for finding and holding a commercial empire.

In 1616 Captain Dirk Hartog landed on the west coast, leaving behind a pewter plate inscribed with his name. After this, the company included in its sailing orders specific instructions to its captains to 'land at different spots and examine the country and observe the inhabitants, their religion, politics and wars, and what sort of vessels they have. And you must pay particular attention to any gold, silver, lead, copper or precious stones you may find there.'

1636 saw the arrival of a new governor in Batavia by the name of Anthony Van Diemen. He was an intelligent, well-read man who had taken the trouble to inform himself about the Spanish and Portuguese voyages and ambitions in the area. He was also unusual in that he was more interested in discovery than in gold, though he was canny enough, when selling the idea of further voyages to his company backers, to lay out the material advantages: 'The expense and trouble that must be bestowed in the eventual discovery (of new lands) will be rewarded with certain fruits of material profit.'

Van Diemen was no sailor, but the man he chose to lead the voyages of exploration, Abel Tasman, was both competent and farsighted. He was also avid for some of those fruits of material profit, though he was to find neither gold nor silver; what he did discover, on 24th November 1642, was an island he named Van Diemen's land, 'in honour of our great governor'. It was later renamed after Tasman, though he never returned to its shores.

When he got back to Batavia, he was upbraided by the syndics of the company: where was the gold, the silver, the new trade routes? Van Diemen defended Tasman and persuaded the company to stump up for another voyage, this time mapping the north coast of what was being called New Holland and becoming separated, in the general mind, from the *terra australis incognita*, which was presumed to lie further south.

By the end of his second voyage, Tasman had created a reasonably good outline of most of the north coast, an astounding achievement of navigation and chart-making which received a predictable response from the money men back in Batavia. 'We cannot anticipate any great results,' they wrote, witheringly, 'from the continuation of such discoveries which may entail more expenditure by the company.' With this, the Dutch shut up shop as far as any further exploration of New Holland was concerned.

The next visitor to the unknown shores was an Englishman who was also interested in gold – he'd started out as a pirate – but who had an insatiable curiosity about the natural world and an understanding of the sea and sailing which amounted to genius. His name was William Dampier, a farmer's son from Devon who went to sea at the comparatively late age of eighteen, in 1670. After a few years knocking about he ended up in Jamaica where, more to indulge his curiosity than to get wealth, he joined the buccaneers.

He took part in the siege and sacking of Portobello and joined a number of piratical cruises, during one of which he was nearly eaten by the starving crew, even though he pointed out that he was a lean and stingy man whilst the captain was 'lusty and fleshy'. He resolved to climb the ladder of promotion within the buccaneering brotherhood as fast as possible, so that next time he could choose the meal.

His first contact with New Holland came when a privateering venture in the Pacific went wrong and his ship, crippled by storms, made landfall on the north coast. After a series of adventures including shipwreck and escape from a Dutch prison, he arrived back in Britain and wrote a colourful account of his voyage that was to prove highly popular. On the strength of this, he was asked by the government (who believed every word he'd written) to take a new ship, the *Roebuck*, on a voyage of discovery through the south seas.

On 31st August 1699 Dampier stepped ashore on the north coast of New Holland near what is now known as Roebuck Bay. 'We went armed with cutlasses and muskets for our defence, expecting to see people there; and carried also shovel and pickaxes to dig wells. While we were at work there came nine or ten of the natives to a small hill and stood there threatening us and making a great noise. I went out to meet one and came within fifty yards of him, making all the signs of peace and friendship I could, but he ran away, neither would any of them allow us to come nigh, though we tried two or three times.'

Dampier was able to map much of the coast but the poor condition of his ship forced him to set out for home after only five weeks. The *Roebuck* was in worse condition than any of its crew realised; she sank off Ascension Island and Dampier lost a 'great part of my books and papers'.

However, he saved enough to write another bestseller on his return home in which, amongst other things, he included his poor opinion of the Aborigines he had encountered. 'They all of them have the most unpleasant looks and the worst features of any people that ever I saw.'

What the Aborigines made of Dampier is unrecorded, though they were making contacts of their own along the north coast with Indonesian fishermen who were visiting every summer to fish for trepang, a sea-slug eaten by the Chinese. Trade sprung up between the two peoples and some young Aborigines signed aboard the Indonesian vessels and adopted fashionable beards, which the fishermen had copied from the Dutch.

However, it wasn't the Chinese or the Indonesians who were to take the next steps, but the British, spurred on by Dampier's narratives and an explosion of curiosity and colonialism.

On 19th April 1770 a young British scientist stood on the deck of a converted collier, bracing himself against a heavy swell. He wrote in his journal: 'With the first day light this morn the land was seen. It rose in gentle sloping hills which had the appearance of the highest fertility. Every hill seemed clothed with trees of no mean size. At noon, a smoke was seen a little way inland.'

The scientist was Joseph Banks, a rich amateur who had inveigled himself and his retinue onto an official voyage of discovery. Beside him on the deck that day stood the ship's captain, a middle-aged Yorkshireman, James Cook. His notes were more technical, as befitted his position and responsibilities. 'Thursday 19th. In the p.m. had fresh gales at SSW, and cloudy squally weather with a large southerly sea. At 5 set the topsails close reef'd and at 6 saw land extending from NE to West at the distance of 5 or 6 leagues, having 60 fathom water, a fine sandy bottom.'

The ship was the *Endeavour*, its mission two-fold: to observe the transit of Venus from the Island of Tahiti and secondly, and secretly, to search for that old hope, the counterweight continent, *terra australis*, that should, apparently, lie astride the south pole.

The readings had been taken, the continent remained *incognita* and after a year and a half at sea the *Endeavour* was heading home. Cook's instructions made no mention of New Holland but he decided to follow its east coast and make for Batavia, where the *Endeavour* could be laid up and careened before the long haul back to Britain. It was a hazardous undertaking for there were no charts or maps, but both

Cook and Banks were men of deep curiosity and it was hardly likely they would miss the chance to explore an unknown coastline. As they proceeded, Banks noted in his journal:

'Large fires were lighted this morn at about 10 o'clock. We supposed the gentlemen ashore had a plentiful breakfast to prepare. The country, tho' in general well enough clothed, appeared in some places bare; it resembled the back of a lean cow, covered in general with long hair, but where her scraggy hip bones have stuck out further than they ought, accidental rubs and knocks have entirely bared them of their share of covering.

'The land this morning appeared cliffy and barren, without wood. An opening appearing like a harbour was seen and we stood directly in for it. A small smoke directed our glances its way and we saw about ten people who on our approach left the fore and retired to a little prominence where they could conveniently see the ship.

'At night many moving lights were seen in different parts of the bay. These people seemed totally engaged in what they were about; the ship passed within a quarter of a mile of them yet they scarce lifted their eyes from their employment.'

Captain Cook wrote in his own journal of finding an anchorage: 'At daylight we discovered a bay which seemed to be tolerably well sheltered from all winds, into which I resolved to go with the ship.' He named it Botany Bay but the *Endeavour* only stayed three or four days, enough for a few short trips ashore, before they sailed on. It was to be almost four months later, after a hazardous trip along the east coast, that Cook applied to New Holland the instructions he'd been given about *terra australis*.

On a small and deserted island just off Cape York, Cook, 'having satisfied myself of the great probability of a passage, which I intended going with the ship, and therefore may land no more upon this eastern coast of New Holland, and confidant that this place was never seen or visited by any European before us … I now hoisted English colours and took possession of the whole eastern coast by the name of New South Wales. After which we fired three volleys of small arms, which were answered by a like number from the ship.'

Eighteenth-century Slang

A

Abbess – a woman who is a brothel keeper

Abraham-sham – a feigned illness

Academician – a whore

Academy – brothel

Adam and Eve it – sexual intercourse

Adam tiler – pickpocket's lookout

Admiral of the Narrow Seas – a drunk who vomits into a neighbour's lap

Adrift – discharged

Adzooks! – an expletive

Air and exercise – a flogging at the cart's tail

Akerman's hotel – Newgate prison

All nations – a mixture of drinks from unfinished bottles

Altitudes – to be drunk

Amen-curler – a parish clerk

Amidships – the belly

Anatomy – a very skinny person

Angler – a thief who uses a line with a hook to snag goods

Anne's fan – thumbing one's nose

Apple-dumpling shop – a woman's bosom

Arse upward – in good luck

Ask bogy – an evasive reply

Avast! – Stop!

B

B, as in 'not to know B from a bull's foot' – to be ignorant

Bacon-faced – full-faced

Bacon-fed – fat and greasy

Bag, empty the – to tell everything

Baggage – woman

Baggage, heavy – women and children

Bagpipe – a long-winded talker

Bailed man – a man who has bribed the press gang for immunity

Baked – exhausted

Banbury story – nonsense

Bark at the moon – to agitate uselessly

Barnacles – spectacles

Barrel fever – ill health caused by excessive drinking

Bear – a very gruff person

Beard splitter – penis

Beau-Nasty – finely dressed but dirty

Beef-head – idiot

Beer-garden jaw – rough or vulgar language

Beggar-maker – a publican

Belly-gut – greedy, lazy person

Belly ruffian – penis

Bender – a sixpence

Bingo – brandy

Bird-spit – a small sword

Bit – purse

Bit of red – a soldier

Black arse – a kettle

Black cattle – a parson

Black dog – depression

Black eye, give a bottle a – empty a bottle

Blashy – rainy weather

Bleed – lose money

Blood and 'ounds! – an exclamation

Blouzalinda – whore

Blow the widd – give the game away

Blowes – whore

Blue as a razor – extremely blue

Blue pigeon flyer – thief of lead from roofs

Blue stocking – a learned woman

Blue tape – gin

Blue-veined piccolo – penis

Blunt – cash

Boarding school – Bridewell prison

Bob – gin

Bob, to shift one's – to move or go away

Bog orange – a potato

Bollocks – testicles

Bollocks, Mister – Priest

Boots, to marry old – to marry another man's mistress

Bosom friend – a body louse

Botany Bay – vagina

Bottom – courage

Bowman – safe

Bowse – drink

Bowser – drinker

Brains, to have some guts in one's – to be knowledgeable

Brandy-face – a drunkard

Brattery – a nursery

Bread, bad, to be in – a disagreeable situation

Break-teeth words – words hard to pronounce

Bridge, gold – an easy and attractive means of escape

Bridgeport dagger, to be stabbed with a – to be hanged

Bring one's ass to an anchor – sit down

Bring to one's bearings – cause to see reason

Broganeer – one with a strong Irish accent

Brown cow – a barrel of beer

Brown George – ship's biscuit

Buck fitch – an old lecher

Bull beef – big and grim

Bull calf – a big clumsy fellow

Bull's eye – a crown piece (five shillings)

Bung one's eye – drink heartily

Bung upwards – on his face

Bunter – whore

Butter-bag – a Dutchman

Buttock-ball – a dance attended by prostitutes

C

Cackle – inform

Calfskin fiddle – a drum

Cant – slang

Canting crew – criminals

Capabarre – the looting of naval stores

Caper – to be hanged

Captain Copperthorn's crew – all officers

Captain Grand – a haughty, blustering man

Captain Standish – penis

Captain Tom – leader of a mob

Case – house or shop

Cast up one's accounts – to vomit

Cat-sticks – thin legs

Caterpillar – a soldier

Caulker – a dram

Chalk – to strike someone's face

Chatter-broth – tea

Christened by a baker – freckled

Cinder-garbler – a female servant

Cite stage – the gallows

Civil reception, house of – a brothel

Clapper-claw – to thrash someone soundly

Click – snatch

Clicker – one who shares out the booty

Cloak – watch case

Closh – Dutch sailors

Coach wheel – a crown piece

Cock and pie! – a mild oath

Coffee-house – a water-closet

Cold cook – an undertaker

Cole – money

Comb-brush – a lady's maid

Comb one's head – to scold

Commons, house of – a privy

Condiddle – to steal

Conveyancer – a thief

Cool crape – a shroud

Corinth – a brothel

Corporal and four – masturbation

Corporation – a large belly

Cotswold lion – a sheep

Country-put – a silly rube

Cove – fellow

Covent Garden ague – venereal disease

Crab lanthorn – a peevish fellow

Crap – money

Crinkums – venereal disease

Croak cockles – hanged

Crown-office – the head

Cucumber – a tailor

Cully – fellow

Cut throat – a dark lantern

Cutter, swear like a – swear violently

D

DV – God willing

Daffy – gin

Dam of that was a whisker – a great lie

Dancers – stairs

Dangle in the sheriff's picture-frame – to be hanged

Darbies – irons, also fists

Dasher – showy harlot

Deadly nevergreen – the gallows

Devil among the tailors – a row or disturbance

Devil-drawer – a bad artist

Devil may dance in his pocket – he is penniless

Diddle – gin

Diet of Worms, gone to the – be dead and buried

Dilly – a coach

Dim mort – pretty girl

Dip – pickpocket

Dog booby – an awkward lout

Dog laugh, enough to make a – very funny

Dog-vane – a cockade

Dog's portion – a lick and a smell

Dog's soup – water

Dot and carry – a person with a wooden leg

Double Cape Horn – be cuckolded

Douglas with one eye and a stinking breath, Roby – the breech

Draggle-tail – a nasty, dirty slut

Draws straws – to feel sleepy

Dr Johnson – penis

Drunk as Davy's sow – very drunk

Drury Lane vestal – a whore

Duke of limbs – a tall awkward fellow

Dull-swift – a stupid fellow

Dun – debt

Dunghill, die – die cowardly

Dustman – a dead man

Dutch concert – everyone plays or sings a different tune

Dutch feast – the host gets drunk before the guests do

E

Earwig – a malicious flatterer

Engine – penis

Ensign-bearer – a drunkard

Eternity box – a coffin

Eternity, step into – hanged

Expended – killed

Eye, to have fallen down and trodden upon one's – to have a black eye

F

Face making – to beget children

Facer – a glass full to the brim

Faggot – a man hired to appear on a muster-roll

Fallen away from a horse load to a cart load – to become fat

Fantastically dressed – very shabby

Fegary – a prank

Fence – receiver of stolen goods

Fiddler's money – all small change

Fiddlestick's end – nothing

Finger-post – a clergyman

Fire a gun – introduce a subject unskillfully

Fire shovel, to have been fed with a – to have a big mouth

Fish-broth – salt water

Flag of defiance – a drunken roisterer

Flag of distress – the cockade of a half-pay officer

Flap with a fox tail – a rude dismissal

Flapdragon – venereal disease

Flash the gentleman – pretend to be a gentleman

Flash it away – show off

Flash mob – fashionable criminals

Flat – a fool

Flats and sharps – weapons

Flawed – drunk

Flay the fox – vomit

Flump – an abrupt or heavy fall

Fly in a tar box – nervously excited

Footpad – thief on foot, mugger

Foreman of the jury – one who monopolises a conversation

Fork – pick a pocket

Foul a plate – dine with someone

Frenchified – infected with venereal disease

Frig – sexual intercourse
Frig-pig – a fussy trifler
Froglander – a Dutchman
Full as a goat – very drunk
Fumble cunt – impotent
Fumbler's hall – vagina
Fustilugs – a dirty slattern

G
Gallied – hurried, vexed or over-fatigued
Gallows – enormous
Game – plucky
Game pullet – a young whore
Gammon – nonsense
Gardy-loo – Look out!
Gaskins – wide breaches
Gentleman in red – a soldier
Gentleman's companion – a louse
George – half a crown (coin)
Gib cat, melancholy as a – dispirited
Give one's head for washing – to submit to be imposed upon
Glass-eyes – person wearing glasses
Glaziers – eyes
Glim – lantern
Glorious – ecstatically drunk
Glue-pot – a parson
God permit – a stage coach
Golden grease – a bribe
Gomorrhan – homosexual
Goose, to find fault with a fat – grumble without cause
Gooseberry – simple
Gooseberry, to play old – play the devil
Gospel-shop – a church
Gotch-gutted – pot-bellied
Grapple-the-rails – whisky

Green-bag – a lawyer

Green goose – young whore

Greenwich goose – a Greenwich Hospital pensioner

Groggified – tipsy

Grub, to ride – ill-tempered

Guinea-gold – dependable

Gun, to be in the – tipsy

Gundiguts – a fat, portly fellow

Gut-foundered – extremely hungry

H

Half an ounce – a half crown

Half seas over – half drunk

Hand like a foot – clumsy handwriting

Hang-gallows look – a villainous appearance

Hanktelo – a fool

Hare, to swallow a – to get exceedingly drunk

Hatches, to be under – dead

Heaver – chest

Hempen bridle – a ship's rigging

Hen-frigate – a ship ruled by the captain's wife

Herring-gutted – tall and very thin

High Toby – a highwayman or woman

Hock, to be drinking old – drinking stale beer

Hog in armour – a finely dressed lout

Hogs to market, to drive one's – to snore

Holiday – a spot left unpainted

Honey or all turd with them, it's all – either friends or bitter enemies

Honker – penis

Hooks, off the – peevish

Hopper-arsed – large bottomed

Horne – erection

Horse ladder, send for a – send on a fool's errand

Horse's meal – food without drink

Houghmagandie – sexual intercourse

I

Illfuar'd – mad
Irish apricot – a potato
Irrigate – take a drink
Itchland – Scotland

J

Jack Adams – a fool
Jack in office – an imperious petty official
Jack Ketch – a hangman
Jack of legs – an unusually tall person
Jack Weight – a fat man
Jacob – ladder
Jade – wild girl
Jakes – a privy
Jaw-me-down – a very talkative fellow
Jean Crapau – Frenchman
Jenkin's hen, to die like – die unmarried
Jericho, been to – be tipsy
Jerk the jelly – masturbate
Jerrymumble – to shake
Jerusalem, going to – to be drunk
Jimmy Round – a Frenchman
Job's dock, to be laid up in – be treated in hospital for venereal disease
Jordan – chamber pot
Josephus Rex – joking
Juan Dago – a Spaniard

K

Kate – pick-lock
Ken – house
Kicksees – breeches
Kidder – confidence man
Kill-devil – rum

King's Head Inn – Newgate

King John's man – a small fellow

King's English, to clip – to be drunk

Knob – an officer

Knock-down – strong liquor

L

Laced mutton – a whore

Lappy – drunk

Lay – good prospect for theft

Lay one's legs upon one's neck – run away

Lazy as the tinker who laid down his budget to fart – very lazy

Leg, to cut one's – become drunk

Lie with a latchet – tell a great lie

Lift – shoplifting

Light-timbered – weak

Line of the old author – a dram of brandy

Link boy – lantern carrier

Little house – a privy

Live lumber – passengers in a ship

Live stock – body vermin

Looking glass – a chamber pot

Lotman – a pirate

Louse-land – Scotland

Lumping pennyworth – a great bargain

M

Mab – to dress carelessly

Mag – chatter

Make – steal

Make mice-feet of – destroy utterly

Maltoot – a sailor

Man-a-hanging – a person in difficulties

Married to Brown Bess – enlisted in the army

Mauled – exceedingly drunk

Maulies – fists

Member mug – chamber pot

Milk the pigeon – attempt the impossible

Mischief – a wife

Miss Laycock – vagina

Moll – girl

Moll – homosexual

Molly – homosexual

Monkey's allowance – more rough treatment than money

Moon-curser – a link boy who leads pedestrians into the clutches of footpads

Mopus – a dull, stupid person

Morris – to decamp

Mourning shirt – a dirty shirt

Muffles – boxing gloves

Munge – dark

N

Nails, to eat one's – do something foolish

Navel-tied – to be inseparable

Ned – a guinea

Newgate steps, born on – of criminal extraction

Nim – steal

Nip-cheese – a purser

Nit, dead as – quite dead

Nose, make a bridge of someone's – pass the bottle past someone

Number the waves – to waste time

O

Oaken towel – a cudgel

Oatmeal, to give – to punish

Off the hooks – crazy

Ogles – eyes

Old Robin – an experienced person

Open lower-deckers – to use foul language

Overshoes, over boots – completely
Owl, take the – become angry

P

Paddy-whack – an Irishman
Painter, cut the – send a person away
Palette – a hand
Paper-skull – a fool
Parleyvoo – the French language
Parson Palmer – one who slows passing the bottle by talking
Peach – betray
Pease-kill, make – to squander lavishly
Pego – penis
Penny lattice-house – a low alehouse
Peter-gunner – a bad shot
Peter Lug – one who drinks slowly
Pintle-merchant – a whore
Piper's wife – a whore
Pipes, tune the – cry
Piss more than he drinks – said of a braggart
Pitt's picture – a bricked up window
Plump – false witness
Plump currant – in good health
Pontius Pilate – a pawnbroker
Popper – a pistol
Prancer – horse
Prattle-broth – tea
Prig – thief
Princod – a plump, round person (Scottish)
Property, alter the – disguise
Prow – a bumpkin
Public ledger – a whore
Pudding-bellied – very fat
Pump ship – urinate
Punch-house – a brothel

Q
Queer – a rogue

R
Rabbit hunting with a dead ferret – a pointless undertaking
Rag-water – bad booze
Rammaged – tipsy
Rapping – perjury
Rattler – coach
Ready – money
Red-letter man – a Catholic
Remedy-critch – chamber pot
Repository – a jail
Resurrection man – a grave robber
Rhino – money
Rib-roast – to thrash
Ride as if fetching the midwife – to go in haste
Ride the forehorse – to be early
Roast meat, to cry – boast of good fortune
Roast-meat clothes – holiday clothes
Rocked in a stone kitchen – a little weak-minded
Rogue in spirit – a distiller
Rowie – a salty, leavened breakfast pastry (Scottish)
Royal image – a coin
Rum – good, sound
Rum – any hard liquor
Rum gagger – one who tells false sea stories of hardship
Rump, loose – wanton
Rusty guts – a blunt, surly fellow

S
Sack, buy the – tipsy
Saddle the wrong horse – lay blame on the wrong person
Saddle one's nose – wear glasses
Salamugundy – a cook

Salt eel – a thrashing with a rope's end

Sandy – a Scotsman

Sauce – venereal disease

Sawney – a Scotsman

Sawny – to whine

Scald – infect with venereal disease

Scandal-broth – tea

Scarlet horse – a hired horse

School of Venus – a brothel

Scotch casement – a pillory

Scragged – hanged

Sea-crab – a sailor

Settler – a parting drink

Shab-rag – very worn

Shake a cloth in the wind – be hanged

Shapes – a name given an ill-made man

Sheep by moonlight, to keep – hang in chains

Sheep's head – a very talkative person

Shifting ballast – soldiers aboard ship

Shiners – money

Shreds – a tailor

Shut-up house – land headquarters of a press gang

Sick of the idles – a very lazy person

Silver-cooped – deserting for the merchant service

Silver darling – herring or other silvery fish

Sink for a nosegay – be very gullible

Sky-blue – gin

Smart as a carrot – very smartly dressed

Snabbled – killed in battle

Snack – share of a robbery

Snail's gallop – move very slowly

Soldier's bottle – a large bottle

Solo player – a very bad musician

Sot-weed – tobacco

Sovereign's parade – the quarterdeck of a man-of-war

Spanish trumpeter – a braying donkey

Spoil pudding – a long-winded preacher

Squeak – betray

Squire of the placket – a pimp

Steven – money

Stiff-rump – a haughty person

Stepney baby – child born at sea

Stoupe – to give up

Strip-me-naked – gin

Sunburnt – having many children

Surly boots – a grumpy person

Surveyor of the highway – a reeling drunk

Swag – shop

Swipes, the purser's – small beer

Swizzle – liquor

T

Tail – sword

Tallow-breeched – having a large bottom

Tears of tankard – drink-stains on a waistcoat

Tea-voider – a chamberpot

Thornback – an old maid

Three skips of a louse – worth little or nothing

Tickle-pitcher – a drinking buddy

Tiff – thin or inferior liquor

Tilly-tally – nonsense

Tilter – a small sword

Tinker, swill like a – drink immoderately

Tol-lol – pretty good

Tommy – lesbian

Tongue enough for two sets of teeth – a very talkative person

Topping man – a rich man

Topsail, pay one's debts with – run off to sea leaving unpaid debts

Toss off – masturbate

Tripes and trillabubs – a fat man

Trunkmaker-like – more noise than work
Two stone wanting – castrated

U
Untwisted – ruined
Urinal of the Planets, the – Ireland

V
Vaulting school – a brothel
Velvet – tongue
Venus' girdle – noose

W
Waltham's calf, wise as – very foolish
Wamble – an uneasiness in the stomach
Wap – intercourse
War-caperer – a privateer
Water bewitched – weak beer
Water in one's shoes – a source of annoyance
Whigland – Scotland
Whisk – an impertinent fellow
Whister-clister – a cuff on the ear
Whither-go-ye – a wife
Wife in watercolours – a mistress
Wind up the clock – sexual intercourse
Windy – conceited
Wipe – handkerchief
Wrapt in warm flannel – drunk

X
X or cross – throwing a fight

Y
Yea-and-nay man – a Quaker
Yellow boys – guineas

Z
Znees – frost

This list is based mainly on a list created by Leon Bienkowski, drawn from Eric Partridge's *Dictionary of Historical Slang*, for the Revlist– Webpage for the study of the Revolutionary War – www.liming.org/ revlist – with additions from *Slang Down the Ages* by Jonathon Green and *The New Canting Dictionary* of 1725 and various contemporary works of fiction

Sources and Acknowledgements

For Mary Bryant, the primary sources were Judith Cook's biography *To Brave Every Danger*, which presents an unrivalled picture of life in Cornwall in the eighteenth century and gives the reader a sympathetic and well researched portrait of her subject and her times. *The Transportation, Escape and Pardoning of Mary Bryant* by C.H. Currey presents a clear and elegant appraisal of the story and the evidence. James Martin's *Memorandums* evokes the time, the place and the journey and was indispensable. Frederick Pottle's *Boswell and the Girl from Botany Bay* gave the story its first telling, and though Pottle did not know of James Martin's *Memorandums*, he presents the tale in a manner that brings Mary to life for the reader. *Fowey, a Brief History* by Kerdroya (I.D. Spreadbury), is a concise but well documented history of Fowey town and its society; *The Church of St Fimbarrus, Fowey*, also by Spreadbury, gives the history of the church Mary would have attended as a child. Quiller-Couch's Troy Town stories are based upon the nineteenth-century town of Fowey where the author lived for many years. Mary's stroll down Oxford Street is based upon a contemporary account by Sophie V De La Roche quoted in *London 1800* by Mary Cathcart Borer.

James Boswell is a dab hand at telling his own story and the Yale Edition of the *Journals* for the years 1762–63 (ed. Pottle), 1769–74 (ed. Wimsatt & Pottle), 1774–76 (ed. Ryskamp & Pottle), 1784–89 (ed. Lustig & Pottle) and 1789–95 (ed. Danziger & Brady) were invaluable and hugely entertaining. Boswell's *Hypochondriack Columns* from the *London Magazine*, 1777–83, often reveal more than their writer intended. *James*

Boswell: The Earlier Years by Pottle and *James Boswell: The Later Years* by Brady present the man in full. Adam Sissman's *Boswell's Presumptuous Task* is a justly celebrated portrait of the biographer and his struggles. Conversations with Marcy Kahan illuminated Boswell; Stu McNeil gave sage advice on the vernacular and Jean McNeil conjured up the finest rowies in Aberdeen. Roy Porter, in *Flesh and The Age of Reason*, has many fascinating things to say about Boswell and his world.

Arthur Phillip, His Voyaging by Alan Frost supersedes all other biographies and has utterly changed our view of the man and his early career. Anyone writing of Phillip must acknowledge a huge debt to Frost's scholarship and his lively retelling of a fascinating life. Earlier biographies: *Phillip of Australia* by M. Barnard Eldershaw and *Admiral Arthur Phillip* by George Mackaness are still fascinating mines of information and Sir Frederick Chapman's *Governor Phillip in Retirement* presents a brief picture of the old admiral. In the 70s I worked with the filmmaker Bill Leimbach on the scenario for a proposed film, which later became a thirteen-part television series, on the first four years at Sydney Cove and the relationship between Arthur Phillip and Bennelong. The research we did at the time and conversations we had over three months proved exceptionally valuable in bringing Phillip to life. The series was never produced but became the genesis for my own thirteen-part series on the history of Australia for BBC Radio 4, celebrating the nation's bicentenary. Once again I benefited from conversations with the producer, Shaun Maclaughlin, and from the performance of Michael Pennington as Arthur Phillip which, for good or bad, has influenced my point of view ever since.

The voyage to Botany Bay and the settlement at Sydney Cove are covered by a number of vivid contemporary accounts: *Sydney's First Four Years* by Watkin Tench; *An Account of the English Colony in New South Wales* by David Collins; *The Journal of Ralph Clark*; Arthur Phillips' own account (actually ghostwritten), *Voyage to Botany Bay*; and *Journal of a Voyage to New South Wales* by James White. All give lively and accurate accounts of events. Neither Clark's nor Arthur Bowes Smyth's journals were published at the time and are quoted with the kind permission of the Mitchell Library, Sydney NSW, where the originals reside. Any enquiries as to their use should be addressed to the Intellectual Property Librarian. John Cobley's brilliant series of day-by-day reports of life at Sydney Cove from 1778 through to 1795 enable the reader to experience the pace of life and how the many crises must have felt to the convicts and keepers alike. Professors Manning Clarke, Geoffrey Blainey, Dr Eric Wilmott, Dame Professor Leoni Kramer and Dr Ross Fitzgerald all took part in the Radio 4 series *Australia* and their many points of view have percolated through into this book. The Aboriginal viewpoint is harder to come at, since the spread of settlement wiped out the local tribes and their oral history. Conversations with Bill Leimbach (his was the idea of a silent Sydney Cove disturbed by the sounds of oars squeaking against metal rowlocks) and the thoughts of the Aboriginal actors, poets and activists Charles Perkins, Eve Fesle Jnr, Kath Walker (as she was at the time) Pat Dodson, Robert Brofoe, Shortie O'Niel, Marcia Langton and Yami Lester, who contributed to the Aboriginal sections of the Radio 4 series *Australia*, helped to evoke some of the dilemmas and the richness of a culture that was under threat – but I am sensible that I have not even scratched the surface of a subject that is as vast and enigmatic as Uluru. *Australian Dreaming* edited by Jennifer Isaacs presents many dreamtime myths in the words of their tribal tellers and I have drawn on this material for the story of the great serpent who lived in the pool on the top of a mountain. Jack Brook, in his deeply researched article *The Forlorn Hope: Bennelong and Yemmerrawannie go to England* in *Australian Aboriginal Studies (1)* opens up a hitherto hidden area and I have drawn upon his work in the historical note on Bennelong.

Select Bibliography

Ackroyd, Peter. *London, The Biography*, London 2000

Alexander, Caroline. *The Bounty*, London 2003

Annals of Newgate, London 1776

Bate, Jonathan. *John Clare*, London 2003

Bateson, Charles. *The Convict Ships*, Sydney 1974

Bindman, David. *Hogarth and his Times*, London 1997

Blainey, Geoffrey. *The Tyranny of Distance*, London 1975

Blainey, Geoffrey. *Triumph of the Nomads*, London 1976

Bond, Bob. *The Handbook of Sailing*, London 1996

Borer, Mary Cathcart. *London 1800*, London 1988

Boswell, James, *The Life of Samuel Johnson*, London 1791

Boswell, James. Hypochondriack Columns from the *London Magazine*, London 1777

Boswell, James. *Boswell's London Journal 1762 63*, Frederick A Pottle (ed.) New York and London 1950

Boswell, James. *Boswell for the Defence 1769– 74*, William K Wimsattt & Frederick A Pottle (eds.) New York and London 1959

Boswell, James. *Boswell: The Ominous Years* 1774–76, Charles Ryskamp & Frederick A Pottle (eds.) New York and London 1963

Boswell, James. *Boswell: The English Experiment 1785– 89*, Irma S Lustig & Frederick A Pottle (eds.) New York and London 1980

Boswell, James. *Boswell: The Great Biographer 1789– 95* Marlies K Danziger & Frank Brady (eds.) New York and London 1989

Bradley, Robert. *The Country Housewife and Lady's Director*, London 1732

Bradley, William. *A Voyage to New South Wales*, Sydney 1969

Brady, Frank. *James Boswell, The Later Years 1769– 95*, London 1984

Brewer, John. *Sentimental Murder*, London 2004

Brook, Jack. The Forlorn Hope: Bennelong and Yemmerrawannie go to England, *Australian Aboriginal Studies*, (1), 1998

Chapman, Frederick. *Governor Phillip in Retirement*, Sydney, 1962

Clarke, C.M.H. *Select Documents in Australian History*, Vol 1, Sydney 1950

Clark, Ralph. *Letters and Journals 1787–91* (ed. Fidlon & Ryan) Sydney 1982

Chesterfield, Philip Stanhope, Earl. *Letters to his Son*, London 1774

Cleland, John. *Fanny Hill, Memoirs of a Woman of Pleasure*, London 1749

Cobley, John. *Sydney Cove 1788*, Sydney 1961

Cobley, John. *Sydney Cove 1789–90*, Sydney 1963

Cobley, John. *Sydney Cove 1791–92*, Sydney 1965

Collins, Captain David. *An Account of the English Colony in New South Wales*, London 1796

Donald, Diana. *Followers of Fashion: Graphic Satires from the Georgian Period*, London 2002

Donald, Diana. *The Age of Caricature*, New Haven and London 1996

Eighteenth-century Women Poets (ed. Roger Lonsdale), Oxford 1989

Fletcher, Loraine. *Charlotte Smith*, London 1998

Gay, John. *The Beggar's Opera*, London 1729

George, M.Dorothy. *London Life in the Eighteenth Century*, London 1923

Glass, Hannah. *The Art of Cookery Made Plain*, London 1747

Godfrey, Richard. *James Gillray*, London 2001

Green, Jonathon. *Slang Down the Ages*, London 1993

Harris's Young Ladies of Covent Garden, London 1792

Hammond, J.L & Hammond, B. *The Village Labourer*, London 1911

Hayes, John. *Rowlandson: Watercolours and Drawings*, London 1975

Henderson, Tony. *Disorderly Women in Eighteenth-century London*, London and New York 1999

Historical Records of New South Wales, 1898

Hitchcock, Tim. *English Sexualities, 1700–1800*, London 1997

Hollander, Anne. *Fabric of Vision*, London 2002

Hughes, Robert. *The Fatal Shore*, London 1987

Hunter, John. *An Historical Journal 1787–92*, London 1793

Ingleton, Geoffrey C. *True Patriots All*, Sydney 1952

Isaacs, Jennifer, *Australian Dreaming*, Sydney 1980

Johnson, Barbara, *A Lady of Fashion, Barbara Johnson's Album of Styles and Fabrics*, London 2000

Kemp, Peter & Ormond, Richard. *The Great Age of Sail*, London 1992

Kidson, Alex. *George Romney 1734–1802*, London 2002

King, Philip Gidley. *Journals 1778–90*, (eds. Fidlon & Ryan) Sydney 1980

Knapp & Baldwin. *The Newgate Calendar*, 1826

Landstrom, Bjorn. *The Ship*, London 1961

Linnane, Fergus. *London's Underworld*, London 2003

Martin, Joanna. *Wives and Daughters, Wives and Children in the Georgian Country House*, London & New York 2004

MacArthur, Ellen. *Taking on the World*, London 2001

McCormick, E.H. *Omai, Pacific Envoy*, Auckland 1977

Moore, Lucy. *Con Men and Cut Purses, Scenes from the Hogarthian Underworld*, London 2000

Murray, Bill. *Crisis, Conflict and Consensus*, Sydney 1984

Nicol, John. *Life and Adventures*, London 1822

Nivelon, Francis. *The Rudiments of Genteel Behavior*, London 1737

O'Connell, Sheila. *London 1753*, London 2003

Oxford Book of Eighteenth-century Verse (ed. David Smith) Oxford 1926

Peakman, Julie. *Laviscious Bodies*, London 2004

Perouse, JF de la. *A Voyage Around the World Performed in the Years 1785, 1786, 1787 and 1788 by the* Bousole *and the* Astrolabe, 1799

Phillip, Arthur. *Voyage to Botany Bay*. London 1789

Picard, Lisa. *Dr Johnson's London: Life in London, 1710–70*, London 2000

Pointon, Marcia. *Hanging the Head*, New Haven and London 1993

Pope, Alexander. *Essay on Man*, London 1733–34

Porter, Roy. *English Society in the Eighteenth Century*, London 1982

Porter, Roy. *Flesh in the Age of Reason*, London 2003

Pottle, Frederick A. *James Boswell, The Earlier Years 1740–69*, New York and London 1966

Rawson, Geoffrey. *The Strange Case of Mary Bryant*, Sydney 1938

Rees Sian. *The Floating Brothel*, London 2001

Reynolds, Henry. *The Other Side of the Frontier: Aboriginal Resistance to the European Invasion of Australia*, Sydney 1982

Rowlandson, Thomas. *Amorous Illustrations*, London 1983

Rudé, Geroge. *Protest and Punishment*, Oxford 1978

Salmond, Anne. *The Trial of the Cannibal Dog*, London 2003

Sawyer, Tom. *Noble Art*, London 1989

Shesgreen, Sean. *Engravings by Hogarth*, New York 1973

Sissman, Adam. *Boswell's Presumptuous Task*, London 2000

Smollet, Tobias. *The Adventures of Roderick Random*, London 1748

Smollet, Tobias. *The Expedition of Humphrey Clinker*, London 1771

Smyth, Arthur Bowes. *Journals 1787–89* (ed.Fidlon & Ryan) Sydney 1979

Spraggs, Gillian. *Outlaws and Highwaymen*, London 2001

Spreadbury, I.D. *Fowey*, Cornwall (no date)

Spreadbury, I.D. *The Church of St Fimbarrus, Fowey*, Cornwall (no date)

Sterne, Lawrence. *Tristram Shandy*, London 1759

Tench, Watkin. *Narrative of the Expedition to Botany Bay*, London, 1789

Tench, Watkin. *Complete Account of the Settlement at Port Jackson in New South Wales*. London 1793

Treherne, John. *The Canning Enigma*, London 1989

Vulliamy, C.E. *Ursa Major: Doctor Johnson and his Friends*, London 1946

Walker, Mike. *Australia, a History*, London 1987

Walpole, Robert. *Letters*, London 1961

Wark, Robert R. *Drawings by Thomas Rowlandson in the Huntingdon Collection*, California 1975

White, Surgeon-General James. *Journal of a Voyage to New South Wales*, London 1793

Wilkes, John. *Essay on Women*, London 1764

Websites

Byrnes, Dan. *The Blackheath Connection*, available at www.danbyrnes.com/blackheath/index.html

Notes

1   From the *Newgate Calendar*
2   Hannah Glass, *The Art of Cookery Made Plain*
3   Goldsmith, *The Deserted Village*; *Oxford Book of Eighteenth-century Verse*
4   *Journal of the House of Commons*
5   Goal Book for the Western Assizes, 1786
6   Boswell, *Journals*
7   La Perouse, *Voyage*
8   *Historical Records of New South Wales*
9   Tench, *Complete Account*
10 Home Department Papers
11 *Historical Records of New South Wales*
12 Walker, *Australia*
13 Walker, *Australia*

Index of Names

Index of Vessels